Women and Heroin Addiction in China's Changing Society

Routledge Advances in Criminology

1 **Family Life and Youth Offending**
Home is Where the Hurt Is
Raymond Arthur

2 **China's Death Penalty**
History, Law, and Contemporary Practices
Hong Lu and Terance D. Miethe

3 **The Politics of Antisocial Behaviour**
Amoral Panics
Stuart Waiton

4 **Hooked**
Drug War Films in Britain, Canada, and the United States
Susan C. Boyd

5 **The Violence of Incarceration**
Edited by Phil Scraton and Jude McCulloch

6 **Violence, Prejudice and Sexuality**
Stephen Tomsen

7 **Biology and Criminology**
The Biosocial Synthesis
Anthony Walsh

8 **Global Gambling**
Cultural Perspectives on Gambling Organizations
Edited by Sytze F. Kingma

9 **Social Class and Crime**
A Biosocial Approach
Anthony Walsh

10 **Security and Everyday Life**
Edited by Vida Bajc and Willem de Lint

11 **Women and Heroin Addiction in China's Changing Society**
Huan Gao

Women and Heroin Addiction in China's Changing Society

Huan Gao

Routledge
Taylor & Francis Group
NEW YORK LONDON

First published 2011
by Routledge
711 Third Avenue, New York, NY 10017

Simultaneously published in the UK
by Routledge
2 Park Square, Milton Park, Abingdon, Oxon OX14 4RN

Routledge is an imprint of the Taylor & Francis Group, an informa business

First issued in paperback 2013

Typeset in Sabon by IBT Global.

Library of Congress Cataloging-in-Publication Data

Gao, Huan.
Women and heroin addiction in China's changing society / by Huan Gao.
p. cm. — (Routledge advances in criminology ; 11)
Includes bibliographical references and index.
1. Women drug addicts—China. 2. Women—Drug use—China. 3. Heroin abuse—China. I. Title.
HV5840.C6G36 2011
362.29'30820951—dc22
2011006084

ISBN13: 978-0-415-89318-3 (hbk)
ISBN13: 978-0-415-85214-2 (pbk)

To Ko-lin Chin
Whose work inspired this undertaking,
And whose guidance and support sustained it.

Ruili Port, under the Dehong Autonomous Prefecture, is located on the southwest border of Yunnan Province, adjacent to the port city of Muse in Myanmar. The distance between Ruili and Yunnan's capital city, Kunming, is about 495 kilometers. It is the largest first-class land border port in Yunnan between China and Myanmar. Illicit drug trafficking in the area has been very intense since the beginning of China's new drug epidemic in the 1980s. Heroin abuse in China originated here around 1986. (All photos in the book were taken by the author.)

Wanding, a small town with a population of only about 10,000, is a subdivision of Ruili, and is one of the three largest first-class land border ports in Yunnan. The famous Wanding Bridge (pictured) forms the boundary between Wanding (China) and Jiugu (Myanmar). In the right corner of the picture is a casino complex on the Myanmar side of the border.

A Border Marker between China and Myanmar in a village in Ruili. Villagers on the two sides can visit each other quite easily, just by crossing the road. The border check-point station in Myanmar is visible in the picture; the Chinese check-point is about 30 meters away.

Kunming, the capital city of Yunnan Province has a long history and splendid culture. The famous Yunnan Military Academy in Modern China's history was founded a century ago and is open to tourists.

Kunming's Green Lake Park is located in the center of the city. One of my interviews was conducted here.

Downtown Kunming —the largest commercial area in Kunming shows the modern look of the city.

The Northern Train Station area (NST area) in Kunming is a cluster of settlements (referred to as "*cheng zhong cun*"), which are occupied by many low-income migrants from the rural areas. Local drug trafficking hot spots are mostly located in this area.

Another picture of the Northern Train Station (NST) area. A few of Kunming's notorious downscale *momo* dance halls (*momo* = "intimate touching") are located in this area.

Kunming is a city in transition: many settlements in the city have been replaced by new, modern skyscrapers.

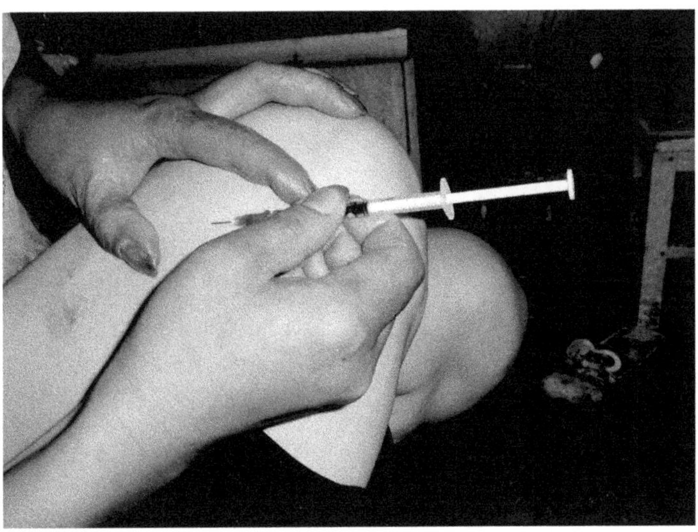

A home visit: the moment of heroin injection. This picture was taken in a woman heroin user's home in the NST area. Drug injection is very painful for heroin users, especially those who have a long injection history — they can hardly locate the vein. It took over an hour to get the shot right.

International Day against Drugs, June 26, 2008. A public performance in a city park presented by male drug abusers (mainly heroin users) who are serving time in the compulsory drug rehabilitation center in Kunming.

International Day against Drugs, June 26, 2008. Here, the performers are female drug users (mainly heroin users) from the compulsory drug rehabilitation center in Kunming, wearing costumes representing ethnic minorities.

Contents

Figures

Tables

Preface

In the spring of 2005, as I finished all required courses for my graduate studies, I was also thinking about possible areas of research for my dissertation. My previous legal education and practice in China had always motivated me toward thinking about carrying out research in China, where issues related to drugs had already drawn my attention. It is generally well known that there is a long tradition of opium use in China. However, during the thirty-year period following the establishment of the People's Republic of China, Chinese society was drug free. Although some old folks still indulged their habits of opium use, they were only to be found in remote border areas, in particular in the southwestern region of China. In the wake of China's economic reform and open-door policy in 1978, illicit drugs—mainly heroin, emerged in the late 1980s, and developed into a serious social problem. In this new drug epidemic, women, who have always played very traditional roles in Chinese society, became particularly vulnerable. Women heroin users, engaging in income-generating activities to support these drug habits, especially by participating in the sex trade, also became the predominant transmitters of HIV to the general population in China.

While the number of female heroin users has greatly increased in the country, little is known about women's heroin use in the context of a rapidly changing society. Are there any significant sociological and individual factors in women's lives that render them prone to involvement with the heroin culture? My curiosity with respect to this initial research question motivated me to conduct research on women and drug related issues, and carried me through the past five years. Since the publication of Rosenbaum's influential book "*Women on Heroin*" in 1981, only a few books on women and drug related issues have become available, including Taylor's "*Women Drug Users: An Ethnography of a Female Injecting Community*" (1993) and Maher's "*Sexed Work: Gender, Race, and Resistance in a Brooklyn Drug Market*" (1997). However, these books were all published at least ten years ago. With increasing global concern about women's abuse of illicit drugs, this study has important policy implications for China as well as for international society.

A review of the literature indicates that feminist scholars tended to focus on gender-specific factors to explain women's drug use, which differentiated their research from that focusing on the general drug use population; a qualitative research methodology was the primary research strategy employed by these scholars, allowing them to provide vivid life histories of women drug users. My research goal was to study women's heroin use in China, against the backdrop of the dramatic social changes that have transformed Chinese society since the country's economic reform in 1978. I was curious as to how the changing social context in China connected with women's heroin use. A gender-specific theory alone appeared to be limited in its ability to reach this goal. The career concepts proposed by Goffman (1959) in the field of sociology, and their application by Becker (1963) to the study of deviant careers, eventually helped me to lay out the study's theoretical framework, and this guided my initial data collection. By adopting a career perspective, the study explores women heroin users' drug use careers from initiation into heroin, through continuation and cessation of drug use, and the connections of these phases to income-generating illegal activities.

Due to the exploratory nature of the study, qualitative research methods, frequently adopted by feminist scholars, were employed for data collection and analysis. Kunming, the capital city of Yunnan Province, was chosen as the research site for two primary reasons: firstly, the heroin epidemic in China originated in Yunnan Province and secondly, the province has the largest heroin user population in the country. Though I had never been to Kunming prior to my fieldwork, my social connections with local people helped me locate initial key informants and women subjects. By using snowball sampling and theoretical sampling strategies, women heroin users (N=90) were interviewed in the summer of 2005 in Kunming, and participant observation was conducted on the research site as well. The follow-up study was made in the summer of 2008 three years after the original fieldwork. In addition to re-interviewing women heroin users (N=25) who previously participated in this research, I also interviewed more women heroin users who were primarily engaged in drug dealing (N=25) or prostitution (N=16) in order to improve my understanding of women heroin users' involvement in these illegal activities. During the follow-up study, I went to Ruili—one of the most important heroin trafficking sites on the border between China and Myanmar; I made multiple trips to local drug selling hot spots, nightclubs and dance halls; I also visited women heroin users' homes on several occasions. The intensive fieldwork allowed me to get closer to the real lives of the women, and understand their drug use in the context of the local culture.

While in the field, talking to the women, listening to their stories and observing their daily activities, I was astonished by the remarkable changes that took place in their lives due to their addiction to heroin, and the many tragedies that occurred among these women. I also understood that, even as they were struggling with heroin use, they all expected to make changes in their lives. Since many of the women in the study initiated their heroin use at the beginning of China's heroin epidemic, this study is uniquely positioned to examine patterns and developments of women's drug use careers over the past two decades. The evidence suggests that the drug use careers of women were characterized by both social and individual factors. Women's drug use careers involved a socialization process with evolving phases, which were dynamic in nature, and magnified by changing legal and social policies on narcotics control in China. The research also suggests that there are considerable similarities as well as differences between women's drug use careers in China and those of women in Western countries.

Due to its unique features, this volume—the first ever on women's heroin use in China—will appeal to scholars and students from diverse disciplines, including criminal justice, sociology, women's studies and public health among others, as well as to a more general audience with interest in Chinese studies, within and beyond the United States and China. The book is based on real life experiences of actual women heroin users. Direct quotes from my interviews with women are frequently cited in the book. Thus, although it is a scholarly publication, the book will, nevertheless, also appeal to people generally interested in the topic, yet lacking specialized knowledge.

Acknowledgments

This study is the result of five years of research and writing. The debts incurred in the production of this ethnographic work are numerous. Accomplishing this task would have been impossible without the support, encouragement and assistance of many people.

First and foremost, I would like to express my sincere gratitude to my mentor, Dr. Ko-lin Chin of the School of Criminal Justice at Rutgers University, for his guidance, gentle pressure and sustained encouragement. There is no question that this study would not have been accomplished without his incredible patience and support. When I was working on my dissertation, Dr. Chin read my entire manuscript several times and provided me with his insights, even when he was traveling in Asia on his own projects. After I graduated from Rutgers University, Dr. Chin continuously guided me in this research and encouraged me to publish this work in book form. Much respect and appreciation also goes to my dissertation committee members, Dr. Mercer Sullivan, Dr. Bonita Veysey and Dr. Eloise E. Dunlap for the expertise and suggestions they provided to strengthen this study. In particular, the qualitative research methods that have guided this study are a direct benefit I gleaned from taking Dr. Sullivan's class on the subject. His enthusiasm for qualitative research has been a great encouragement to me. Dr. Veysey provided me not only with thoughtful suggestions on gender-related issues since the inception of the study, but also with sustained emotional support ever since I joined the graduate program at Rutgers University. The opportunity to participate in one of her research projects on women, albeit for a short period, provided me with very practical research skills. Dr. Dunlap, from the National Development and Research Institutes, extended her expertise in the field of inner-city New York substance abuse to my study in China, and offered me precious comments and suggestions from a cross-cultural standpoint.

A debt of gratitude is owed to Ms. Yu Feng at Yunnan Daytop Center who offered me very generous support since the first day of my fieldwork in Kunming and continuously provided me with invaluable help over a three-year span. I owe thanks to Ms. Libo Song from the same center for help in gaining quick access to the local social and heroin use culture. I also wish to thank my key informants in Kunming. They helped me locate the women who comprised the initial subjects in my study. Several other key informants also made every effort to help me locate my women subjects during the follow-up study. My special thanks to the women who were willing to participate in this research project and to those who also referred their drug-using peers to me. They entrusted me with their life histories, even sharing very sensitive information, thus providing me with the opportunity to explore women heroin users' drug use careers in great depth.

I want to thank my parents, who passed away in an accident three months before my doctorate graduation ceremony, for all the love they gave me throughout my life. I also want to thank my husband Yaling Huang, in particular, for his emotional and financial support during my graduate studies. Special thanks to my only son, Ziming Huang, who, little as he was, walked through all the difficult times with me over the past seven years. He has brought me so much joy and has uncomplainingly endured the hardship when I was too busy with my work and research to give him the attention he deserved. I also want to thank my mother-in-law and father-in-law for all the love and support they have given me. I am grateful to my uncle Xinyan Zhou, for his love, friendship and support since the time I was a little girl in middle school. Thanks to my aunt Guizhen Li, my parents' lifelong friend, who treated me as her own daughter and always backed me up after my parents passed away. I would also like to recognize other family members and friends for their invaluable support.

Thanks are due to Dr. Madhuri Mukherjee of the William Paterson University of New Jersey, whose support and excellent editorial help have made this writing more precise. In particular, Dr. Mukherjee's friendship and constant encouragement over the past three years transformed the tedium of writing into a pleasant journey, not to mention the many insights she shared with me. I would like to thank the School of Criminal Justice, Rutgers University for the Dean's Research Grant that helped me embark on this research, the Graduate School (Newark) of Rutgers University for a Dissertation Fellowship that supported me while I was finalizing the dissertation, and the Research, Scholarship and Creativity Activity Committee and the founding Dean, Dr. Carolyn Stefanco of the College of Humanities and Social Sciences at the California State University, Stanislaus, for research funding for the follow-up study. All this support made this project possible. I would also like to thank Dr. Phyllis Gerstenfeld at the Department of Criminal Justice, California State University, Stanislaus, whose support helped me better manage my time between this research and my teaching responsibilities. Thanks to Mr. Cameron Pallotta who developed a map of China for this book. Special thanks to my editor at Routledge, Max Novick, for his enthusiasm and interest in this research, and to senior editorial assistant Jennifer E. Morrow for her excellent editorial support—they have made this endeavor a pleasant task.

1 Social Changes and Illicit Drug Use in China

One of the most important events in all of China's history was the establishment of the People's Republic of China (PRC) in 1949.[1] Led by the Communist Party of China (CPC), China, a country recognized for its long history of opium abuse, had not only eradicated illicit drug use, gambling and prostitution within only a few years after 1949, but also continued as a drug free society for several decades (Zhou 2000).[2] However, after China launched its economic reform and an open-door policy to modernize its economy in 1978, the nation was no longer immune to illicit drug abuse.

China's economic reform has led to increasing economic gains for its people, accompanied by changes in the social, cultural and political spheres of their lives. Crime rates in all categories have escalated tremendously, particularly, illicit drug trafficking since the early 1980s. With the emergence of a soaring drug trafficking trade, illicit drug use made its appearance in the border areas between China and the Golden Triangle, and quickly spread, first among the southwest provinces, and then to other provinces in the country. The dominant illicit drug consumed in China in this new drug epidemic is heroin. In the past two decades, rapidly increasing heroin abuse has caused unprecedented social problems in the country.

While, in the beginning, heroin users were predominately males, as the drug-using population in the country has been growing, the number of female drug users nationwide has also been rising rapidly. Heroin use by women, in particular by injection, and related income-generating activity—specifically prostitution—has not only caused individual lives to take a down turn, but also brought great harm to Chinese society. The most significant social consequence of this new epidemic is a rapidly growing HIV infection rate in the country. Unfortunately, while heroin use and related social problems are increasing in China, the study of women heroin users has remained largely unaddressed. In an effort to advance the understanding of heroin use by women in China, this study begins its discussion about women's drug-use careers with an overview of the changing social context in China in the reform era.

SOCIAL CHANGES IN THE REFORM ERA

After the PRC was founded in 1949, all aspects of Chinese society, including politics, the economy, culture and ideology gradually came under the strict control of Mao Zedong. Developing the nation's economy was not a priority in Mao's regime; instead, the concept of "politics to take command" was not only a political slogan, but also a primary concern of national policies.[3] China launched several politically-oriented mass mobilizations, in particular, the Cultural Revolution (1966–1976), with disastrous consequences for Chinese society. Thirty years after liberation, the Chinese people as a whole were still living in poverty. The supreme concentration of power personified in Mao ended with his death in 1976, an event that propelled China into both an economic crisis as well as a crisis of faith. Meanwhile, China was virtually isolated and had almost no normal economic, political or cultural contacts with countries in the West. By the end of the Cultural Revolution, the country's economy was on the verge of collapse.[4,5] After Mao's death in 1976, Deng Xiaoping regained his political power in the CPC and began economic reform, launching the open-door policy in 1978. Since then, advancing the nation's economic prosperity became the number one priority of the Party-State. One of the most important aspects of urban economic reform was to transform the country's economic structure, laying the foundations, beginning in 1993, for the building of a market economy.

After the events of 1949, the country's privately-run economy was virtually wiped out and replaced by state-owned enterprises and collective sectors. The central government controlled the nation's economy through a highly centralized and controlled economic system. As a downside, the central government had to assume responsibility for losses incurred in the state-owned enterprises. People were not strongly motivated to be industrious, and therefore productivity was very low. After Mao's death, in order to encourage a variety of domestic sectors to participate in developing the country's economy, private ownership was endorsed by the central government;[6] this striking change in policy was exemplified by Deng Xiaoping's metaphor "It does not matter whether it is a black cat or white cat. As long as they can catch rats, they are all good cats."[7] With the development of multiple economic sectors in the marketplace, the CPC seemed to wholeheartedly approve the transformation of China's economic structure from the planned economy of the past to a socialist market economy from 1993 onward. These changes were written into the revised Constitution in that same year. To provide a fertile environment for investment, the central government decided to open Shenzhen, Shantou, Zhuhai and Xiamen as Special Economic Zones in 1980.[8] When Hainan Province was established in 1988, it became China's largest Special Economic Zone. These Special Economic Zones have been viewed as "windows" of the economic reform and open-door policy, and have played a critical role in stimulating economic development in other inland areas.

While the so-called "socialist market economy system with Chinese characteristics" is still evolving, China's remarkable economic development has been widely recognized by international society.[9] At the same time, the economic reform and open-door policy have not only developed China's domestic economy, but also brought about dramatic social changes in the country. In a short period of time, China has evolved from a closed agricultural country into an open, industrialized one, and has witnessed rapid urbanization. Most importantly, the Chinese people have experienced two radical transformations since the economic reform: in economic status and in social values.

In 1949, with the establishment of the new China, an affluent social class, typically capitalists in the cities, and landlords in the rural areas, was completely eradicated. An individual's place in society was primarily determined by his/her political status (social class of the family). Since then, egalitarianism, rather than wealth, was instilled in the social/political culture of the time (Deng and Cordilia 1999). In the reform era, however, the social constraints prevailing during Mao's regime gradually gave way to more social and political support for the pursuit of financial gain. As a result of Deng Xiaoping's economic initiatives—aimed at achieving a common prosperity for all—new social and economic groups reemerged in Chinese society. In the early 1980s *wan yuan hu* (a household with 10,000 yuan) was indicative of people who were rich. At the present time, billionaires who own large corporations have become the most important social and political players in the country. China is now returning to a society with economic stratification and a new social hierarchy (Wang 2004).

According to Inglehart (1997), economic, cultural and political changes are mutually supportive within a country's modernization process. The core process of modernization manifests at both the societal and individual levels: "economic growth becomes the dominant societal goal and achievement motivation becomes the dominant individual-level goal" (Inglehart 1997, 5). While advancing economic growth had been laid out as a governing goal at the societal level, social values, in particular, the spread of materialism together with individualism gradually superseded collective social values. Along with China's rapid increase in economic growth, people are highly motivated by individual success in the modernization process. In Mao's era, communitarian values based on Marxism-Leninism-Mao Zedong Thought were institutionalized, and served as social norms. To a certain degree, the communist ideology was endowed with "a functional equivalent to religion" in constraining the behavior of individuals (Inglehart 1997, 38). Although in Deng Xiaoping's ideological legacy, Marxism and Mao Zedong Thought were still viewed as the foundation and assurance of a socialist political system (Kang 2004), his symbolic speech—to "get rich is glorious" and "let some people get rich first"—acted as precursors to promote individuals' materialism and individualism (Deng and Cordilia 1999). Eventually, extreme materialism and individualism led to a significant breakdown in social norms; mutually shared social norms, which had sustained Chinese society for decades, largely disappeared (Fisac 2003). As demonstrated by the results from the third (2003), the fourth (2004) and the fifth (2005) National Survey on Concerned Social Issues, the erosion of social convention (*she hui feng qi*) was reported as one of the most serious social problems the public was concerned with over three consecutive years (Wang 2005; Liu 2006).

The Party has constantly emphasized the importance of both spiritual, as well as material civilization in an effort to restore its control of social norms in the reform era, but it no longer has the power to spread the socialist ideology in all spheres of social life as before. The unique informal social control mechanisms, which played an important role in Chinese society, gradually lost their influence on individuals' beliefs and social behaviors due to frequent population migration. In particular, the increasing influence of Western culture also became more intense after the economic reform. Younger generations were more likely to be driven by individualistic goals than by collective values. A study conducted in Shanghai (and its suburbs) in the late 1980s concludes that the stronger the Western influence, the stronger the endorsement of individualism (Chu and Ju 1993). The experiences of other socialist countries (the former Soviet Union and East European countries) illustrated that the state has largely lost the power to "accommodate individualism and pluralism when simultaneously confronted with the fragmenting forces of globalization, modernization, capitalism and commercialism" (Ogden 2002, 240). The weakening of collective social values coincided with increasing materialism and individualism in Chinese society. Wealth was no longer merely gratifying in itself; it also represented prestige and reputation. Extreme individualism, where the interests of the individual take precedence over those of society, has produced unprecedented social harm.

DRUG TRAFFICKING IN THE REFORM ERA

The reform era has seen crime in China increase at an alarming rate. The relationship between modernization and an increasing crime rate was first formulated by Durkheim. In his anomie theory, Durkheim (1893/1965) linked the high crime rates with the state of anomie in a society undergoing rapid social change accompanied by modernization.[10] Durkheim viewed the breakdown of social norms as the key to understanding an increasing crime rate in the modernization process (Vold, Bernard and Snipes 1998). Differing from Durkheim, some scholars explained increasing crime rates in the modernization era by economic factors. Shelley's (1981) modernization theory concludes that it is the economic gap between rich and poor that has fostered the sense of deprivation. Neuman and Berger (1988) argue that social inequality was the reason for rising crime rates rather than the breakdown of collective values caused by modernization. In spite of disagreements as to how modernization is connected with crime, it is evident that modernization itself is a fundamental factor in explaining changing crime rates across different societies (Vold et al. 1998).

In studying crime trends in China, the most challenging part is to gather crime data, in particular, crime data before the economic reform. Although studies on crime trends in China have repeatedly reported that China had long maintained a very low crime rate before economic reform, these conclusions are largely based on estimates rather than on annually published official data. Except for crime rates reported in 1950—93.02 per 100,000 population (Bakken 1993; Zhang 2002) studies on crime rates between 1951 and 1977 generally do not show consistency. According to the information posted by the Ministry of the Public Security of China (2006), the total number of criminal cases (from 1950–late 1970s) was estimated to be between 160,000 and 600,000. Given the population in the country during the same period, crime rates were calculated at being at approximately 30 to 60 per 100,000 members of the population. The figures were quite con-

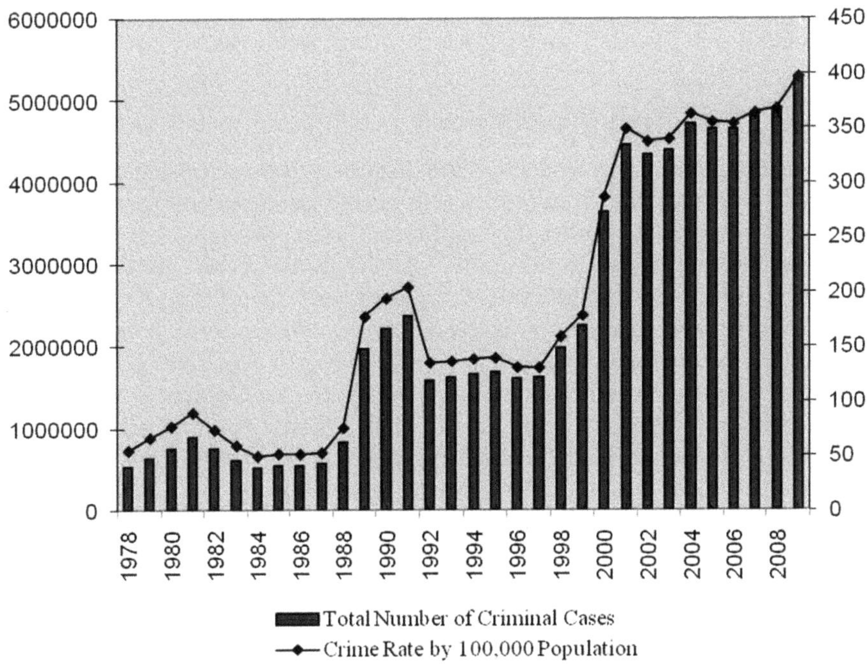

Figure 1.1 Criminal cases filed by law enforcement in China, 1978–2009.
Data sources: crime data from 1978–1980 drawn from Zhang (2002), also from Bakken (1993) as reference; crime data from 1981–2009 drawn from Law Yearbook of China (1981–2008); crime data in 2009 taken from Chinese Academy of Social Sciences (2010); the annual population data drawn from National Bureau of Statistics of China (1978–2009).

sistent with other available studies, which confirmed the low crime rates before the reform era (ibid).

Since economic reform, crime rates in China have been rising at a disturbing rate (see Figure 1.1). There has been a significant increase in crime rates between 1978 and 2009: in fact, three significant waves were identified. The first one started in 1978 and ended by 1981. The change in the crime rate was from 55 per 100,000 to 89 per 100,000. The second wave, seven years after the first wave ended, occurred in 1988, beginning with a rate of 76 per 100,000. Like the first wave, the second wave lasted only three years, but crime rates increased substantially by 1991, with a rate of 204 per 100,000 of the population. After another seven years of steadiness, the third wave started in 1998 and reached a historical peak in 2009, with an increase to 397 per 100,000 of the population. The lower crime rates between these waves of crime were partially attributed to major crackdowns on serious crimes in 1983, 1991 and 1996 (Feng 2001; Liu and Messner 2001). On the whole, in the past three decades, three crime waves have set crime rates in China at a significantly high level. Each crime wave set up the conditions for a further expansion in criminal activity. Observing the similarity of offenses, and acknowledging Shelley's (1981) modernization theory, Liu and Messner (2001, 18) proposed that "China is in the early stages of modernization process."

Emerging Drug Trafficking Business

Afghanistan, Myanmar, and Lao PDR are the top three opium-producing countries in the world; Vietnam has also played an important role in opium production (UNODC 2006). The Golden Triangle overlaps the mountains of these four countries. Traditionally, illicit drugs from the Golden Triangle were first trafficked to Thailand, Singapore, and then Hong Kong. Using Hong Kong as a transit center, illicit drugs would eventually be shipped to destination countries in Southeast Asia and North America. In the early 1980s, due to the presence of military forces in the Golden Triangle and harsh strikes on drug trafficking by Thailand, Myanmar and other Southeast Asian countries, drug trafficking organizations began seeking new drug trafficking routes (Cui 1999; Ma Mina 1999).

Historically, the southwestern region of China, especially Yunnan Province and the Guangxi Zhuang Autonomous Region had been gateways to the Southeast Asian countries.[11] While Guangxi is adjacent to Vietnam, Yunnan Province by itself shares a 4,000 kilometer border with Myanmar (formerly Burma), Lao PDR and Vietnam. The southwestern flank of the Xingjiang Autonomous Region in the northwest of China borders Afghanistan. As we have seen, following the establishment of the PRC in 1949, opium production, trafficking and consumption had been eradicated from Chinese society. In the early 1980s, however, the ongoing open-door policy created numerous open ports and channels of trade between southwestern provinces on the border and neighboring countries. The long borders between China and countries with drug sources, the increase in the number of open ports, and the harsh strikes on drug trafficking by Southeast Asian countries were factors that together created new opportunities for drug trafficking organizations beyond China's borders.

As crime rates rose in the country, the nature of crime itself changed, from individual crime to group-oriented crime. After 1949, criminal gangs and criminal organizations—the major perpetrators of serious crime—had been quickly uprooted from Chinese society. By the 1980s, however, criminal groups had quickly reemerged in the country. Between 1986 and 1990, the total number of criminal groups burgeoned from 30,476 to over one million (He 2001). Criminal groups, as the prototypes for organized crime,

Figure 1.2 Map of the People's Republic of China.
Data Source: http://www.esri.wm
ESRI®Date & Maps Series. Published by ESRI on April 1, 2008.

provided the basis for large-scale drug trafficking networks in China. Documented drug trafficking cases indicate that large-scale drug trafficking businesses were mainly operated by well-organized criminal gangs both inside the country and beyond its borders (Ma Minai 1999). Loosely knit criminal groups began playing more important roles in the drug trafficking trade in the recent years (NNCC 2006).[12]

Due to its geographical proximity to the Golden Triangle, illicit drug trafficking in China occurs predominantly in the country's southwest region.[13] Illicit drug trafficking across the border between Yunnan and Myanmar was still occurring on a small scale in the early 1980s, but by the mid-1980s, drug trafficking in the area had increased in frequency and intensity (Cui 1999).[14] Before the drug consumption market developed within China, the country was only considered a place of transit between the Golden Triangle, Hong Kong and other foreign destinations. Within a few years, three major drug trafficking routes, known as the "China Passage," were developed inside China. These routes all used Yunnan Province as a gateway, and its capital city, Kunming, as a distribution center. Illegal drugs were eventually trafficked to other inland provinces and coastal provinces, mainly Guangdong and Fujian, either as destinations or transit centers to Hong Kong or other countries (Ma Hongbo 1999; Liao and Li 2003). Gradually, several large-scale local distribution centers were also identified in the northwest provinces, including Shaanxi, Gansu and Ningxia (Huang 1995; Chu 2001). Nowadays, drug trafficking activities are still most frequent and most severe in the southwest, southeast and northwest of China.

Precise official statistics of drug trafficking were, unfortunately, not generally available until 1991, when the publication of the *Law Yearbook of China* made statistics available for analysis. The number of apprehended drug-related cases was only 8,395 in 1991.[15] This figure kept growing during the early 1990s, until it reached a historic peak of 184,000 in 1998. In 1999, a sharp reduction occurred (64,000), and in the following years, a generally stable pattern emerged (around 100,000 cases annually) (*Law Yearbook of China*, 1991–2004). In 2005 there was another sudden decrease in apprehended drug-related cases by about 50 percent. From 2006 to 2009, the number steadily increased every year from 45,400 to 77,000 (NNCC 2006–2010). Still, the degree to which this police data reflects actual drug trafficking, or other factors, still remains uncertain.

Illicit Drugs Trafficked in China

In the past two decades, the traffic of illicit drugs in China reveals a changing pattern. As mentioned earlier, officially published statistics were not available before 1991. As shown in Figure 1.3, before 1989, opiates were the dominant illicit drug trafficked in China, and involved relatively small amounts. The total quantity of confiscated opiates and heroin was below 0.5 ton in 1987 and 1988. In 1989, heroin trafficking began to surpass opiate trafficking: two times more heroin than opiates was confiscated that year. Since then, the amount of heroin confiscated annually began to surpass the amount of confiscated opiates, except in 1991, when both amounts were almost the same. From 1991 to 2000, the total quantity of heroin confiscated in China amounted to around 5 tons annually. This number suddenly soared to 13.2 tons in 2001—a record high. Afterwards, the amount basically stayed at about 10 tons per year until a sharp reduction to 6.9 tons in 2005. In 2008, the total amount of confiscated heroin dropped even further to 4.33 tons. The increase in seized heroin might be attributed to increased cooperation between China and other countries in the Southeast since 1995, and the setting up of a police task force—the Narcotics Control Bureau—in 1998, which fought against drug-related crime at both the national and provincial levels (NNCC 1998). Meanwhile, shortly after the police task force was set up, several large-scale drug distribution centers in the country, including Weishan (Yunnan Province), Puning (Guangdong Province) and Linquan (Anhui Province) were closed down (Yang 2005).

Figure 1.3 also indicates that crystal methamphetamine (crystal meth or "ice") emerged in China's illegal drug market in the early 1990s. The amount of crystal meth confiscated in China sharply increased from 1.6 tons in 1998 to 20.2 tons in 2000.[16] The emergence of crystal meth in the illegal drug market did not immediately shrink the heroin market. However, beginning with 2006, the amounts of crystal meth confiscated began to exceed those of heroin. Due to inadequate data from official sources, it is impossible to draw conclusions regarding a developing trend. Nevertheless, it is evident that in recent years, these drugs have gained much popularity among the youth in China.

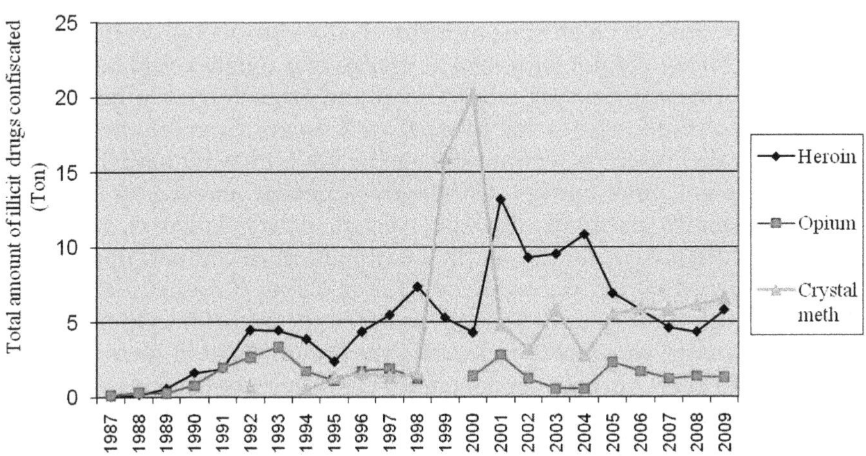

Figure 1.3 Illicit drugs confiscated by law enforcement authorities in China, 1987–2009.
Data Source: Data in 1991–1998 from *Law Yearbook of China* (1991–1998); data in 1987–1990 and1999–2009 from NNCC (1999–2010).

In addition, major illicit drugs mentioned in the government's official reports, also include Ecstasy (MDMA), ketamine (or K powder), and cannabis. The *Law Yearbook of China* began, albeit unsystematically, to report confiscated cannabis in 1992. While the total confiscated amount was generally below 2.0 tons each year, it reached its peak point—8.7 tons in 2009 (*Law Yearbook of China* 1992–1997; NNCC 2009). In 2000, the National Narcotics Control Committee also began to compile data on confiscated ecstasy (no data, however, is available for 2007 and 2008). While its report indicates that the total amount confiscated reached a record high of 3 million tablets in 2004, the number began to decrease since then, but still remained at 1.06 million in 2009. In addition, confiscated ketamine was recorded at 2.6 tons in 2005. From 2007 to 2009, this amount stayed steady between 5.3–6 tons annually (NNCC 2000–2010). The amount of prohibited chemical substances (raw materials or chemical agents for manufacturing illicit drugs) confiscated by law enforcement also increased over the past decade. While the total amount was only 58.8 tons in 1992 (*Law Yearbook of China* 1992), the amount reached 1,113 tons in 2008(NNCC 2009).

ILLICIT DRUG USE IN CHINA

It is well known that China has a long history in the use of opiates. It has been documented that opium was brought into China in the eighth century by Arab traders. For several centuries (until the 500s) the Chinese were interested in opium for its medicinal use (Brown 2002). Since the Song Dynasty (960–1279) medical books have recorded opium's effectiveness in treating such chronic ailments as diarrhea, cough and stomach pain. The Chinese did not gain the knowledge that opium could be smoked until the seventeenth century when Dutch and English traders introduced the method of smoking—lacing tobacco with opium from Southeast Asia. Opium was then used for entertainment (Brook and Wakabayashi 2000). Although opium smoking was at first only a prestige enjoyed by the noble class, it gradually spread through all levels of society (Dikőtter, Laamann and Zhou 2002). And, finally, by the early eighteenth century, opium consumption turned into a serious social issue in China (Brown 2002). In the mid-nineteenth century, following its defeat in the notorious Opium Wars, the Qing Dynasty was forced to legalize the opium trade in its treaty with Britain and other European countries. After that, opium-related social problems intensified.

Around 1909, of the 450 million people in China, 25 million were opium users (5.56 percent; UNODC 2006). When the Qing Dynasty, the last feudal dynasty in Chinese history, was overturned and replaced by the Republic of China (1911–1949), China did not solve its existing drug-related problems.

Moreover, due to numerous conflicts among warlords, and the Japanese invasion, opiate production and trafficking became more severe than ever. New illicit drugs, including heroin, morphine and cocaine, also became available to drug users, even though they did not gain the same popularity enjoyed by opium in China (Baumler 2002).

With liberation in 1949, among a total population of 400 million in the country, there were approximately 300,000 drug manufacturers and traffickers and 20 million drug addicts (5 percent of the total population; NNCC 1998). Right after the new government was established, the State Council promulgated *The General Order for Prohibition of Drugs* in 1950 to control illicit drugs. As a result, opium dens all over the country were prohibited; illicit drug producers and traffickers were arrested. Those who committed more serious drug crimes were sentenced to death (Guo 1997). After nearly three years of the anti-drug campaign, illicit drug use (mainly opiate use) was ultimately eradicated in China (*Law Yearbook of China* 1992). After that, even among high-prevalence areas of drug use there were no more new cases identified between 1950 and 1980 (Hao et al. 2002). However, illicit drug use in the border areas, such as Yunnan Province, was never completely eradicated (Liang and Lu 2000).

Because the resurgence of illicit drug use in the reform era was largely provoked by drug trafficking from the Golden Triangle, drug consumption patterns were closely linked to drug trafficking routes, and to the types of drugs trafficked. It is recognized that the resurgence of illicit drug use in China was due to the use of opiates by peasants in the border areas of Yunnan Province (with Myanmar in particular) in the mid-1980s (Cui 1999). The long tradition of opiate use in the area, a permissive local culture, together with easy access to drug sources all opened the way for new epidemics of drug use. With increased heroin trafficking, heroin use soon gained popularity. A study of six high-prevalence drug sites in six provinces, from the mid to late 1980s, shows that illicit drug use began to spread from the border areas to other areas (Hao et al. 2002). In particular, the cities and towns on the drug trafficking routes that were close to major public transportation networks became the first targets (Yang and Cui 1999). Until 1989, illicit drug use (mainly heroin) had extended to twenty-seven provinces. By 1995, without exception, all provinces in China had identified illicit drug use (Huang 1995).

Since the resurgence of illicit drug use in the reform era is linked with drug trafficking from the Golden Triangle, the prevalence of illicit drug use among different regions varies. Provinces along drug trafficking routes have relatively higher rates of use. Given the fact that most drug distribution centers are located in the western region and eastern coastal regions, provinces in those areas, including the southwest, northwest and southeast, suffer more severe drug-related problems (Guo 1997; Yang and Cui 1999). In 1999, among the top six provinces affected by illicit drug use in the country, five were from the western region, including Yunnan, Guangxi, Guizhou, Sichuan and Gansu (Li 2004). Identified drug users in the western provinces amounted to 360,930 in 1998 (596,000 in the country), which accounted for 61 percent of all registered drug users nationwide, although the total population in the western region only represents 23 percent of the entire country (Liu, Li and Shi 2003). In eastern China, Guangdong and Fujian Provinces were not only on the major drug trafficking routes, but also became the country's largest synthetic drug manufacturing sites. Hence, illicit drug use populations in these provinces are larger than in other eastern provinces.

The Chinese government was criticized for its reluctance to publicize information about the use of illicit drugs at the beginning of the epidemic (Zhou 2000). After the *Law Yearbook of China* was released in 1991, the China National Narcotics Control Commission (NNCC) started publishing an annual report, beginning in 1998. Although there are some major methodological concerns regarding this annual report, basic information on drug related issues from official sources became accessible in a more systematic manner. The number of registered drug users in the country was first documented by the *Law Yearbook of China* (1992) at 148,000 (based upon data in 1991). Since then, that number has increased steadily each year. In 2009, registered drug users numbered 1.34 million (NNCC 2010). As to the many drug users beyond official control, the actual number is believed to be much greater.

The prevalence of illicit drug use in the reform era underwent two major changes. First, heroin replaced opiates and, by the end of the 1980s, became the dominant illicit drug in the country. Second, with the increased trafficking of chemically synthesized artificial hallucinogens and stimulants since the early 1990s, drugs of choice in the country began to show a more diverse pattern. In recent years, "new types of drugs" a fuzzy term frequently used in official reports and by the media, refers to a variety of chemical entities: crystal meth, MDMA (ecstacy), ketamine, cannabis, etc. These synthetic drugs became prevalent in bars, dance halls, karaoke lounges and other entertainment venues among the urban youth. While synthetic drugs have also become an increasing concern in China in the recent years, according to the official report for 2009, registered heroin users in China still consisted of 73.2 percent of the entire drug-use population (known to officials) with 97,300 new heroin users identified that year (NNCC 2010).

ILLICIT DRUG USE BY WOMEN IN CHINA

As discussed previously, with the shifting social and cultural norms, and increase in crime brought about by the economic reform, there has been a resurgence of illicit drug use in Chinese society. The increasing use of illicit drugs by females, too, is essentially linked to China's changing society in the reform era, and the resultant changing role of women in society. In addition to the surging sex business throughout China, illicit drug use by women has become another widely distributed example of deviant behavior by women.

The Role of Women in China's Changing Society

In Chinese history, Confucianism has been the dominant social philosophy, governing all aspects of social life since the Han Dynasty (AD 25–220). As a cultural tradition, patrilineal, patrilocal and patriarchal mores were overwhelmingly emphasized in Chinese society (Gallagher 2001; Ebrey 2002). Women did not have roles either in social or in family life. The Three Obediences derived from Confucianism made clear that throughout a woman's entire life she was subordinate to men.[17] Foot-binding, a mark of gender identification that was widespread since the Song Dynasty (960–1279), is a typical example of the patriarchal oppression of women in China's long history (Ping 2000).[18] Meanwhile, women were not authorized to have property rights, and were not allowed to receive education from any social institution regardless of the social class they belonged to (Ebrey 2002). Even early reformers such as Zheng Guanying (1842–1923) and Liang Qichao (1873–1929), who advocated women's education in the early 1900s, did so in the belief that educated women would assist their husbands and correctly raise their sons at home by being "virtuous women, virtuous wives and virtuous mothers" (Bailey 2001, 321).

The twentieth century witnessed groundbreaking changes in Chinese society and women's roles in society began shifting as well. In the first decades of the century, the education system began to accept girls both at the primary and secondary school levels. In 1919, for the first time in Chinese history a small number of women were able to enter institutions of higher education that had been founded by the government (Bailey 2001). The breakdown of the feudal imperial system in 1911, the increasing influence of the West, and, several decades later, the establishment of the new China, are three vital events that have shaped women's roles in Chinese society (Gallagher 2001). After 1949, women's roles in society were protected by the Chinese Constitution, and in spite of changes in the Constitution, the right of women to equality with men in political, economic, cultural, social and family life has been maintained.[19] In particular, women's fundamental rights, including equal education, equal work, equal pay and freedom of marriage are specified by the Constitution. The Marriage Law enacted in 1950 was revised twice in the reform era to protect women's personal and property rights in greater detail.

With the resumption of the National College Entrance Exam in 1978, the number of women in higher education institutions is increasing year by year.[20] In 2004, women made up 45.7 percent of students enrolled in institutions of higher education—a significant increase compared with 17.8 percent in 1947 and 32.6 percent in 1975. Accordingly, women working in skilled professions comprised 43.6 percent of the country's total working population in 2004 (SCPRC 2005). In Mao's era, men and women in urban areas worked largely for state-owned industries, whereas people in rural areas were members of communes. With economic reform, the private economy began to be strongly encouraged by the Party-State. Women started to open small businesses, such as grocery stores, beauty salons, barbershops, fashion boutiques and so on. Many of these early pioneers later became owners of large enterprises. In 2004, women comprised 20 percent of all entrepreneurs in the country (SCPRC 2005).[21] However, with the increase in failing state-owned enterprises, and a corresponding high unemployment rate, women workers in urban areas are more vulnerable to lay-offs. The number of female employees in cities dropped from 58.89 million in 1995 to 44.11 million in 2000, a reduction that was primarily due to the layoff of women workers from state-owned sectors during those years (Zheng 2003).

Regardless of women's changing roles in Chinese society, conventional values, especially in rural areas, are more favorable to boys than to girls. With the One Child Policy instituted in 1979, China witnessed a significant change in the sex ratio at birth. From 1982 to 2004, the number of boys born per 100 girls increased from 108.5 to 121.2 (Fang, Zheng and Yang 2005).[22] Because of the growing cost of education, parents in rural areas were often reluctant to spend money on their daughters' education (Gallagher 2001). With increasing opportunities in the eastern coastal and metropolitan areas, girls who quit their studies during their teenage years, particularly those from rural areas, were more likely to migrate to these developed areas looking for job opportunities (Jacka 2005).

With greater opportunity in the market economy and changes in economic status and social values, Chinese women have generally achieved a more open-minded attitude toward life in general, and toward sexuality and marriage in particular. In contrast, in Mao's era, the social culture under stringent political pressure supported the perceptions that "overt signs of femininity in dress were considered the reflection of individualistic and bourgeois interests," and therefore, "fancy clothes were a metaphor for moral degeneration and ideological impurity" (Evans 1997, 134–135). Women were afraid of showing their femininity and were expected to wear the same homogenized, dark-colored clothes as men.

In Mao's era, a woman's freedom to marry was largely constrained by her social contacts and by political factors. Most women entered into marriages based on arrangements by family members, work mates, or intimate friends. A woman's parents had considerable power over when and whom their daughter would marry (Evans 1997). A woman's expectations of love were further restrained by political considerations on account of the importance accorded to the political status of individuals in society. For instance, marrying a man whose family had a problematic political orientation would block a woman's potential career development. Thus, pressures from parents and society interfered with a woman's autonomy in marriage. Narrowing options eventually determined that once a woman married, it was inevitable that her husband and family became her entire life and she "had no role of her own beyond the family" (Chu and Ju 1993, 80).

The reform era, however, brought changes to women's economic and social status. Nowadays, women are more encouraged to show their sexuality. Cosmetics, sexy clothes, fancy shoes and stylish accessories, both manufactured domestically and imported, are now available in the market. Young, beautiful female movie stars, singers, TV hosts, and so on, with their elegant photos and quick success stories are featured dramatically in magazines, newspapers, and advertisements. Modern women can find a variety of social activities in the urban areas, hanging out at parties, chatting and making friends on the internet, drinking and smoking with friends in bars, dancing in dance halls, singing in karaoke lounges and so on. Young Chinese women have more opportunities to enjoy multicolored lives, and to find dating partners and mates for themselves.

With increasing materialism in society, women's attitudes toward the meaning of marriage, too, have changed radically. In 1997, the "Surveys of Social Values among Women in Contemporary China (1997)" indicated that the financial status of a man was not an important factor in a woman's decision about marriage (Chen 2003). But in recent years, this has changed dramatically. After the changes introduced by economic reform, a young woman who became involved in the sex industry, or acted as the lover of a rich married man for a luxurious lifestyle or financial gains was an old story. "*Marrying a rich man is better than working hard*"—while once a cliché in society, has gradually become common wisdom among many female college students (Xia 2005; Zhang 2006). The extreme pursuit of materialism among female college students further suggests that there has been a widespread change in social values among young Chinese women.

The economic independence of women, along with the changing social values which affected women's attitudes toward marriage, has also altered their attitudes towards divorce. Between the 1950s and 1970s, a woman's sense of self largely gave way to her primary role in the family as mother and caretaker. In the early 1980s, women who committed suicide or threatened to commit suicide when their husbands chose to divorce them were often reported in the media. By the end of the 1980s, however, women's attitudes toward failed marriages changed dramatically. Women were more likely to be in favor of ending an unhappy marriage. The divorce rate in China has shown a rising trend since the economic reform in 1978. While the divorce rate was only 0.35 per 1,000 of the population in 1978, it reached to 1.85 per 1,000 of the population in 2009 (MCAPRC 2005; MCAPRC 2009). These figures suggest that the modern Chinese attitude toward marriage and divorce tends to be more liberal than in the past decades. It is hard to see how such a change in attitude could have occurred without women's economic independence, and their new status in the culture. Thus, the economic independence of women, along with changing social values has affected many aspects of women's lives in contemporary China.

Women and Substance Abuse in China

Although illicit drug use (mainly opium) was quite prevalent in Chinese history, drug users were mostly men. Under the regime of the Republic of China, the majority of opium users were middle aged or elderly men; very few drug users were females. Those females who did use opium were mainly from the wealthy families of government officials, landlords or businessmen (Qin 1998). Before liberation, it was also widely recognized that drug use was quite prevalent among prostitutes. After a crackdown on prostitution in Beijing in 1949, among the prostitutes sent to Rehabilitation and Working Centers for Women, many were identified as addicted to opium or heroin (Ren 1993).

When illicit drug use reemerged in the late 1980s, drug users were still mainly males. Female drug users only made up about 10 percent of the drug-using population at the national level (Shao 2002). After the 1990s, female drug use began to increase all over the country. In the year 1999, official sources reported that female drug users made up about 20 percent of the total population of drug users in the country (NNCC 2000). A longitudinal study based on six high-prevalence areas in six provinces reported that the percentage of female drug users increased from 10.1 percent to 17.1 percent and to 22.4 percent based on studies conducted in 1993, 1996 and 2000 respectively (Su et al. 2005). However, it was believed that in some regions, in particular the southwest and southeast, the percentage of female drug users was as high as 40 percent (Shao 2002).

At the present, there are no data or systematic studies on female drug use at the city (or county), provincial or national levels. Only a broad outline can be drawn from scattered studies. Based on a few studies of the general population of drug users, and of women users specifically, some demographic characteristics of female drug users emerged. Firstly, according to the national report, drug users were primarily young adults who were less than 35 years old (NNCC 2006). Studies conducted in compulsory rehabilitation centers in Kunming, Shenyang, and Wuhan, indicated that the ages of female drug users were consistent with this pattern—the majority of female drug users fell into the 20–40 age group (Zhou et al. 2001; Wang et al. 2001; Zhao 2001).[23] Secondly, in terms of education, studies in Shanxi Province (Yu 2002), Fujian Province (Zhu 2001), Hangzhou (Su and Guo 2004) and Dalian (Liu et al. 2004) consistently reported that illicit drug users were more likely to be those without education beyond the middle school level. This result was confirmed by studies on women drug users from different geographic regions (Chen et al. 1999b; Yang et al. 2002; Zhao et al. 2005).

Previous research also indicated that female drug users were more likely to be single (Su et al. 2005). As a whole, women drug users had a relatively high unmarried and divorced rate, and were more dissatisfied with marriage than those who were not drug users (Chen et al. 1999b; Cha et al. 2003; Yang et al. 2004; Wang 2004). A study also suggests that women drug users had a high likelihood (53 percent) of living with drug-using partners (Chen et al. 1999a). Last, as suggested by the official report (NNCC 2006) and previous studies, unemployment rates were extremely high among drug users (normally over 50 percent). High unemployment rates (range 50 to 72 percent) were also suggested in studies specific to women (Chen et al. 1999b; Zhou et al. 2001; Wang et al. 2001; Yang et al. 2002; Yang et al. 2004; Zhao et al. 2005). Aside from the high unemployment rates, owning a small business was likely to be the occupation for both genders (Yu 2002; Li 2004; Wang et al. 2001; Zhao et al. 2005).

Due to the high cost of illicit drugs, the way in which women drug users in China support their drug use has significant consequences for themselves and for society. Except for sporadic reports in the media on an individual female drug-user's illegal activities, there have been no systematic studies designed to examine the relationship between women's drug use and criminality. Official reports have only roughly stated that a high percentage of female drug users are involved in drug trafficking, stealing and prostitution in order to support their drug habit; these reports rarely show any empirical support for such conclusions. A few reports from international organizations also only suggested rough numbers with respect to illegal activity by females.

Another consequence of drug use by women is related to the prevalence of HIV/AIDS in the country. Illicit drug use, especially rising injection rates, has produced immediate social harm to Chinese society. The first HIV infection case linked to injection drug use (IDU) was identified in Yunnan in 1989 (Gorbach et al. 2002). A mere seven years later, the HIV/AIDS epidemic among IDUs was identified as being present in all provinces in China (Padmohoedojo 2004). The most critical geographic areas of HIV prevalence were those provinces with severe drug-use problems, including Yunnan, Xinjiang, Guangxi, Guandong and Jianggxi (UNODC 2004). By the end of 2007, it was estimated that about 700,000 people in China (71.3 percent male vs. 28.7 percent female) were either infected by HIV or were AIDS patients. The top risk factors linked with HIV infections in China were heterosexual transmission (40.6 percent), homosexual transmission (11 percent), injection drug use (38.1 percent), blood and plasma collection (9.3 percent) (State Council AIDS Working Committee Office/UN Theme Group 2007).

The prevalence of HIV/AIDS has proved to be very high among female IDUs. A study conducted in the southeastern region of Yunnan Province indicated that HIV prevalence among female IDUs was as high as 81.2 percent, which was significantly greater than that among males (68. 2 percent). Needle and syringe sharing are the most critical risk factors in the spread of HIV (Zhang et al. 2002). A study conducted in the Shenzhen

Drug Rehabilitation Center reported that female IDUs were more likely to have multiple sex partners than non-IDUs.[24] Among female IDUs, 60 percent engaged in prostitution, and nearly 40 percent of them failed to use condoms with commercial sex partners in a consistent manner (Lau et al. 2005). Because of syringe sharing and prostitution, the high-risk group of female IDUs has been established as a potential vehicle for the spread of HIV to the general population in China.

Another route by which females spread HIV/AIDS to the general population is through mother-to-child transmission (MTCT). In Yunnan, about 500 HIV-infected newborns were reported per year (U.S. Embassy 2000). The HIV infection rate through MTCT was 1.3 percent and 2.1 percent in 2004 in Guangdong and Gansu respectively (Li 2004; Liao et al. 2004). Although the overall MTCT rate in China is still low (1.2 percent), compared to transmission by injection drug use and through sexual contact (State Council AIDS Working Committee Office/UN Theme Group 2007), with the population of drug users increasing each year, this will be a rising challenge confronting China.

PERSPECTIVES ON WOMEN AND ILLICIT DRUG USE

Despite the increasing social consequences of drug use by women, few studies on this topic are available in the literature in China. Moreover, as a general practice, these studies are often based on subjective judgments rather than on empirical investigations. Due to these reasons, the current study has been developed based on drug-related research largely conducted in the United States. Specifically, a career perspective on drug addiction has been used as a general theory to guide this research.

Drug Addiction from a Career Perspective

As early as the 1940s, when Lindesmith (1947) proposed his sociological theory of opiate addiction, he indicated that drug addiction, by its very nature, involved a socialization process. He clarified that addiction arose not due "to a single event, but to a series of events, thus implying that addiction is established in a process" (Lindesmith 1947, 8). Although Lindesmith did not propose a career concept to frame his study, his view on drug addiction as a socialization process is essential to interpret drug addiction from a career perspective. In follow-up studies, among other scholars, Goffman (1959) was the first to take the career concept into the field of sociology, by applying it to the moral career of mental patients. Unlike conventional views of the career concept, he suggested that the career concept should be understood in a broader sense, regardless of whether the occupation concerned is respectable or not. To Goffman, a career concept reflects the natural history of an individual's life that changes over a life span, together with common features among individuals living in the particular social strata. Thus, taking Goffman's interpretation, the career concept is connected not only to an individual's path, it also represents changing perceptions toward certain social groups to which the individual belongs.

In a later study, Becker applied the career model to studies of deviant careers, in particular, drug addiction. Becker (1963, 24) indicated that the importance of the career conception lies in building up "sequential models of various kinds of deviant behavior." Accordingly, he identified three distinct and continuous stages during the drug-use career of a marijuana user: beginner, occasional user and regular user. According to Becker, the career model not only helps to study drug users whose paths follow a stage by stage career pattern, but also those who drop out of the careers at the early stages. He emphasized that factors that both contributed to, and prohibited, a deviant career are equally important because they are all good indications of the career's development. Since Becker's work (1963), studies on illicit drug use began to utilize a career model to construct their theoretical frameworks (Feldman and Aldrich 1990). A career perspective was credited as being a valuable tool for "understanding the developmental social dynamics of the addicts' lifestyle" (Coombs 1981, 73). Subsequent studies also identified a set of sequential patterns of drug-use careers. Based on a review of the drug related literature, Fagan and Chin (1991) indicated that a drug-use career has largely been analyzed in terms of four developmental phases: initiation, escalation, maintenance and discontinuation (sometimes renewal).

With respect to how drug users move up along the career path, Becker (1963) proposed two sets of important factors in his concept of "career contingency" —factors accounting for career mobility. To Becker (1963, 24), "career contingency" includes "both objective facts of social structure and changes in the perspectives, motivations, and desires of the individual." It implies that changes in a drug-user's behaviors are influenced by two sets of factors: social structural factors at the societal level and subjective factors at individual level. Thus, an individual drug-user's socialization process toward furthering his/her drug-use career is expected to show differences due to variations in social- and individual-related factors. Stated more specifically, Goffman (1961) linked transformations of deviant careers to changes in social values. He pointed out two essential social values related to careers: public image and self-identity. The following statement articulates the relationship between self-identity and public image: "The concept of career, then, allows one to move back and forth between the personal and the public, between the self and its significant society, without having to rely overtly for data upon what the person says he thinks he imagines himself to be" (Goffman 1961, 127).

This suggests not only that an individual's career experience shapes his/her thinking about the career, but that an individual's self-perception will also be greatly affected by the public's attitudes toward that particular career. Thus, it is not the career itself, but social meanings attached to the career–self-identity and public image that emphasize the significance of the career in individuals' lives. From Goffman's standpoint, how drug users organize their daily routines around drugs (getting off, coping and hustling) helps to build their self-identity and also contributes to subsequent public images about drug users as a whole. Subsequently, the public is more likely to form their concepts about drug users based on their understanding of the groups and will then apply these concepts to individual drug users regardless of significant individual differences. Naturally, a drug-use career, to an individual drug user, is a process in which he/she struggles between his/her self-identity and that of the public. A drug-use career may then be defined as "a series of meaningful related status, roles, and activities around which an individual organizes some aspect of his or her life" (Faupel 1991, 24).

The above analysis together with other studies suggests that the career perspective has been a valuable instrument in studies of deviance and illicit drug use in the past several decades.[25] Adopting the career concept to construct a theoretical framework will make a significant contribution to our understanding of illicit drug-use behaviors. First of all, it suggests that illicit drug use involves a socialization process characterized by evolving phases, which allows us to explore the developmental patterns of a drug-use career. Second, it permits us to examine how factors, both at the societal level and the individual level, affect individual drug-users' careers during each phase and throughout their entire careers. To a certain degree, factors at the individual level are diverse, while factors at the societal level are relatively stable during specific historic periods. Both sets of factors are important to improve our understanding of changes in drug-use careers within a changing society. Finally, it implies that drug-use careers are dynamic by nature and intertwined with significant self and social identity changes. It will further assist us in analyzing the social meanings of drug use, both from the individuals' own perceptions and the views of the public. Given these unique characteristics of the career perspective, it is expected that a study based on a career model will offer great potential for the exploration of heroin use by women in China.

Drug Use by Women from a Career Perspective

As in the case of studies on criminality, it has been a common practice that studies on illicit drug use also focus predominantly on males. Gender, as one of the strongest predictors of deviance and crime, has largely been ignored (Inciardi, Lockwood and Pottieger 1993; Belknap 2001; Warr 2002; Bloom, Owen and Covington 2003). Research on illicit drug use by women confronts the same difficulties as research on female criminality. Feminist scholars have suggested two possible strategies for research in the field of women and deviance studies: developing independent theories to explain female criminality, and re-testing theories (based on male samples) by using female samples (Bloom et al. 2003). In practice, however, studies on drug use by women have primarily chosen to develop their own theories, rather than re-testing previous theories drawn from studies on males.

Although drug-related research has been conducted for decades in the U.S., studies on drug use by women emerged largely only in the 1980s. Compared with research on male drug users, studies concerned with women drug users are relatively small in number. In general, most of these studies have attempted to develop their own theories on drug use by women, based on life histories, in-depth interviews and participant observation, a method that is consistent with studies on female criminality (Belknap 2000). The qualitative methods have provided a unique approach for these studies to explore life events linked with women's drug-use careers. Among the few precise studies on women and hard drugs, a career approach was utilized to construct overall theoretical frameworks (Rosenbaum 1981; Talyor 1991). Rosenbaum's (1981) pioneering study on women heroin users has offered a precise picture of women heroin users by looking at their socialization process: an initial stage; a becoming stage; a maintaining stage; an on again, off again stage and a conversion stage. As one of the most comprehensive research projects on drug use by women, Rosenbaum's (1981) study did not, however, attempt to give a thorough review of each stage of women's drug-use careers, specifically, what kinds of social- and individual-related factors influenced drug use by women for each evolving stage of their drug-use careers.

Given the "career contingency" proposed by Becker (1963), factors affecting drug use by women at the initial stage are certainly different from stages later in the drug-use career. In order to present a more systematic analysis of women's heroin use in China, the current study intends to investigate the most important social- and individual-related factors linked to each stage (initiation, escalation, maintenance and discontinuation) of drug use in women's careers. Given the fact that existing literature on illicit drug use is mainly based on studies in the United States, whether these studies from different social, cultural and political systems could be used to guide research in China remains to be determined.

As Becker (1967, 171) has indicated, an individual's subjective experiences with drugs varied "according to when they occur in the history of use of a given drug in a society." The study suggests that an individual's experience with drugs varied with the time, the place, the historic stage of drug use, and changing social contexts. Accordingly, it is expected that illicit drug use within different countries under different social, economic, political and cultural backgrounds will show some variations. In response to these challenges, the current study not only borrows from existing theories and previous research as major resources, but also draws on personal experience in China, as well as on thought research to construct its guiding theoretical framework.[26] This attempt will help avoid two pitfalls in qualitative research: either not relying enough on existing theories or over-relying on them (Maxwell 2005).

Based on the guidelines just described, the theoretical framework of the current study is mainly built upon the career perspective. The career perspective will assist the study in laying out four distinct phases in women's drug-use careers, namely, the phases of initiation, escalation, maintenance and discontinuation. A career perspective will provide great potential to explore factors related to drug use by women at both the individual as well as the societal level. China's dramatic social changes are expected to have considerable influence on women's drug-use careers in China. Meanwhile, due to the critical role of women's family relationships and intimate relationships, it is also expected that these will substantially affect their drug-use careers through each phase of the socialization process.

In the phase of women's initiation into heroin, demographic factors, family background, peer influences and social bonds with family and society will be fully analyzed. While studies of illicit drug use by adolescents reveal the considerable importance of peer influences, female-specific studies are more likely to emphasize the victimization of women and the importance of intimate relationships with men. Due to the significance of these variables in past research, the current study will give each factor equal attention, so as to determine how they affect the drug careers of women heroin users in China's social contexts.

In the phase of women's continuation (escalation/maintenance) of their drug-use careers, the purpose of the study is to look at how, and with whom, women heroin users continued their drug-use careers. In particular, the study will attempt to determine how women were able to obtain the necessary knowledge about drugs, along with the skills required for drug use, and for involvement in income-generating activity. Women's peer relations and social bonds with family and society are two major considerations to be taken into account to uncover any possible patterns. Due to increased drug use, and emerging illegal activity during this phase, women heroin users' contacts with law enforcement are also investigated.

As regards the last phase, namely, discontinuation, the main purpose is to identify factors related to women's cessation of drug use. While peer relations and social bonds have been reserved, two other factors, voluntary treatment and formal sanction, are retained to see whether they have any significant impacts on the decision by women addicts to discontinue their drug-use careers. Since these treatments with distinct Chinese characteristics, this study will, therefore, examine how these ongoing treatment programs affect women heroin users' drug careers in China, and assess potential policy implications. In sum, due to the paucity of pertinent research in China, the construction of the conceptual framework for this study is based on research carried out in western countries. The theoretical framework, thus constructed, is expected to reflect both relevant research as well as the specific social contexts of Chinese society.

CONCLUSION

As specified in this chapter, since the launching of the economic reform, China has embarked upon its journey to modernization. While China has successfully transformed its undeveloped economy into a socialist market economy, Chinese society is experiencing many dramatic challenges in several spheres of life. Among other factors, China's booming economy and its openness to international society are essential forces that have contributed to significant changes in the material lives of the Chinese people, as well as in their ideological lives, which now seem to be characterized by the pursuit of materialism and individualism. Within such a social context, with growing social and economic roles in society, women who endured more traditional social and moral constraints in Chinese society have shaken off the shackles of these conventions. Women have redefined their thinking about themselves (their self-values), and their traditional gender roles, both within the family and in society.

An increase in crime is one of the by-products of the intensified pursuit of materialism and individualism, both among the general population, and among women as well. The emergence of heroin use by women in China occurred, not solely under the influence of the general social contexts discussed above; it is also a direct result of increasing illicit drug trafficking from the Golden Triangle to China, which has provided women with more convenient access to heroin. Based on these findings, illicit drug use by women in the reform era is deeply rooted in China's changing social context. Heroin use by women was facilitated by a series of social, economic and cultural changes occurring in contemporary Chinese society, rather than by a single event. A full understanding of these tremendous changes and their impact on women in particular, is necessary in order to offer a thorough analysis of drug use by women.

2 Reaching Out to Women Subjects

Due to the illegal nature of drug use, it is recognized that drug users constitute the most typical hidden population. Studying the behavior of illicit drug users—a population largely hidden from the public and inaccessible by traditional survey methods—is a challenge to researchers.[1] This chapter introduces specific methodological issues encountered in the research process, including the rationale for qualitative methods, research site selection, sampling, data collection, analytical strategies and issues related to the study's validity and reliability. The strength of qualitative methods on the study of hidden populations has provided precious instruments for the exploration of women's own perceptions on heroin use in China.

ACCESSING HIDDEN POPULATION

In regard to the hidden population of illicit drug users, qualitative research, and specifically, ethnographic research, has made incomparable contributions to the literature. The values of qualitative research on studies of hidden populations were recognized as early as the nineteenth century. De Quincey's (1822/1985) work, *Confessions of an English Opium Eater* is viewed as the origin of qualitative research on illicit drug use in the modern era (Feldman and Aldrich 1990; Rhodes and Moore 2001). Throughout the twentieth century, ethnographic research has been considered a valuable instrument for drug-related research, in spite of shifts in agendas (Rhodes and Moore 2001). In particular, studies by Lindesmith (1947) and Becker (1953) have demonstrated the strength of this methodology on studies of illicit drug use. Based on interviews with opium addicts, Lindesmith (1947) proposed the first sociological theory of opiate addiction. Taking the same approach, Becker (1953) conducted his influential studies on marijuana users. These pioneer works, together with studies from the 1940s to the 1960s, have largely changed theoretical thinking about addiction (Feldman and Aldrich 1990). Moreover, from the 1980s onwards, with the increasing concerns about HIV and AIDS, qualitative methods have further demonstrated their great potential to uncover "drug-related risk behaviors and its social contexts" which are linked to hidden populations (Rhodes and Moore 2001, 283).

The contributions of qualitative research on hidden populations and illicit drug use have demonstrated the distinctiveness of this methodology for drug-related research. Qualitative methods were credited as "the only appropriate means available for gathering sensitive and valid data from otherwise elusive population of substance abuse" (Wiebel 1990, 5). Qualitative research not only offers an access to the hidden population, it also allows researchers to collect more precise data in a natural setting (Sifaneck and Neaigus 2001). Unlike quantitative studies, the analytical strategy utilized by qualitative methods is inductive by nature, which makes it possible to obtain the "live experience" based upon drug users' own perceptions (Rhodes and Moore 2001, 288). In particular, qualitative methods have made significant contributions to drug-related research in the "exploratory and descriptive stage" (Lambert and Wiebel 1990, 2).

Among a variety of qualitative inquiries, the grounded theory approach is viewed as the most prominent paradigm by researchers. Grounded theory, as interpreted by Strauss, is "not really a specific method or technique," but "a style of doing qualitative analysis" which includes some distinct features in sampling and data analyzing process (Strauss 1987, 5).[2] Its distinctive contributions to qualitative analysis are on account of its capability of developing theories from data, and therefore, "offering insight, enhancing understanding and providing a meaning guide" to the understanding of social phenomenon (Strauss and Corbin 1998, 12). Most importantly, the grounded theory approach has provided the study both a methodological and an analytical framework (Dunlap et al. 2002).

Due to the exploratory nature of the current study, grounded theory is well suited as a foundation of the study's methodology, guiding its data collection, sampling and analysis. The purpose of the current study is to develop an exploratory theoretical framework for heroin use by women so as to improve our understanding of this emerging social problem in China. As discussed in the previous chapter, guided by a career model conceptualized by Western scholars, the study explores the careers of women heroin users in China under changing social contexts in the reform era. More specifically, the study investigates the impacts of sociological and individual factors on women's heroin use in each developing stage of their drug-use careers; and how they moved up to the next stage. The study also examines the social consequences of women's heroin use, by looking at connections between women's heroin use and criminality, and the change in women's social relations after heroin use. Finally, the study analyzes the impact of current narcotics control policies on women's heroin use careers to ascertain the considerable impacts of these policies on women's drug-use behaviors.

RESEARCH SITE

Yunnan Province is located at the southwest region of China, with a population of 45.71 million (NBSC 2009). It shares more than 4,000 km borders with Myanmar, Laos and Vietnam, which provides the province with easy access to Southeast Asian countries, and to the Golden Triangle as well. As a province dominated by mountains and plateaus (covering 94 percent of its terrain), most of its population comprises rural residents. Adverse circumstances and the large rural population have hindered Yunnan's economic development. Among the 129 counties in the province, 73 (57 percent) are financially supported by the central government—the extent of poverty in Yunnan is the highest in the country (Yunnan Yearbook 2005). In 2006, the total number of people living in poverty in the rural areas in Yunnan was 5.4 million, which amounted to 12 percent of the province's population (NBSC 2009).

Known for its ethnic diversity, Yunnan has the second largest minority nationality populations in the country—twenty-five nationalities co-exist in the province, comprising 33.5 percent of the entire population (Yunnan Yearbook 2005).[3] Some minority nationalities reside on both sides of the border, speak the same languages, have the same cultural traditions, and are even related by ties of kinship. Intense poverty, and easy access to the Golden Triangle, produced many *beidu* villages at the borders, and many peasants acted as *mazai* regardless of the death penalty.[4] As introduced in the previous chapter, almost all major trafficking routes in China have taken Yunnan as a gateway.

The study was conducted in Kunming, the capital city of Yunnan Province. Kunming is the largest city in Yunnan, with a population of 6.24 million (KBS 2009). As shown in Figure 1.2, Kunming is located in the eastern part of the Yunnan Province. It is bordered by mountains to its north, west, and east; and by a large lake, Dianchi, to the south. Like most places in Yunnan, Kunming is distinguished by its ethnically diverse population. It is a city with a rich history, and has long been the economic, political and cultural center of Yunnan.[5] With the start of the economic reform, Kunming has undergone several expansions. Anning and Donchuan became subdivisions of Kunming in 1995 and 1998, respectively, based on State Council's Decisions.[6] Nowadays, there are five districts, one municipal city (Anning) and eight satellite counties under the administration of Kunming municipality. The city is centralized into four districts, namely, Wuhua, Panlong, Xishan and Guandu. Due to its distinct geographical location (proximity to the Golden Triangle and a hub of public transportation) Kunming has been playing a leading role in China's anti-drug trafficking regime since the late 1980s. As per the Ministry of the Public Security, all three drug trafficking routes identified in Yunnan (of the five major drug trafficking routes in China) involved Kunming as a transit and distribution center (Tian and Yang 2004). Except for drug trafficking, Kunming was one of the first of several Chinese cities identified as having heroin abuse problems since the late 1980s. Even today, it still has one of the largest heroin use populations in the country.

Indeed, Yunnan has a long history of opium cultivation and consumption. Opium cultivation in Yunnan had begun as early as during the Ming Dynasty (1368–1644). Opium produced in Yunnan was called *yuntu*, and was famous for its color, smell and taste (Xian 2005).[7] Opium cultivation in Yunnan was widespread in the early twentieth century (Yun 1993). Both the Qing Dynasty (1644–1911) and the Republic of China (1911–1949) had attempted to control opium production in Yunnan; however, opium prohibition was always interrupted by more lenient policies due to strong objections from provincial governments (Qin 1998). Until 1949, opium cultivation accounted for one fifth of all the farmland in the province (Liang and Lu 2000). No documentation pinpoints the exact date when opium began to be consumed for pleasure in Yunnan. Based on historical records, however, it could not have been later than the Wanli Era (1563–1620) in the Ming Dynasty (Zhu1999).

Opium consumption in Yunnan was widespread among officials, soldiers, businessmen and local residents by 1838. By the end of the Qing Dynasty the estimate of opium users in Yunnan was 360,000 (5 percent of the population). Until the new China was established in 1949, approximately 2 million (12.6 percent) of the approximately 15.9 million population of the province were drug addicts (predominantly opium addicts). In Kunming, there were 1,181 opium dens by then (Yun 1993). By the end of the 1950s opium consumption had been eliminated from most parts of the province, but a small number of elderly users in the border areas still maintained their opium habits (Liang and Lu 2000). Even before the heroin epidemic, local people had always used opium for traditional medicinal purposes.

As discussed in Chapter 1, heroin use was initiated in the border areas of Yunnan. As a general practice, both official reports and studies in China only roughly report registered drug users without specifying the types of drug they used. It is difficult to make an accurate evaluation of the extent of heroin abuse in Yunnan. Kunming was one of the first of several Chinese cities identified as having heroin abuse problems since the late 1980s. It is estimated that heroin use in Yunnan extended to only a very limited number of people in 1987 (YPOART 1999). But in 1988, the total number of drug users increased to 4,000 in the province. In 1989, it jumped to 10,000 (Yang and Cui 1999). By 1990, the total of registered drug users in Yunnan reached 57,000.[8] From 1993 to 2000, the number of registered drug users shifted back and forth around 40,000 (Yang 2003). In 2003, most of Yunnan province's counties and cities suffered serious drug-use problems (YNCB 2003). By the end of 2004, the number of registered drug users in Yunnan attained 68,172 (Sun 2005). However, with fast-growing drug use nationwide, Yunnan's share of the drug-use population against the national total is declining.

Kunming, as the largest city in Yunnan, exemplifies the seriousness of heroin abuse problems in the province. Nevertheless, only few sources have reported the extent of heroin use in Kunming. According to Chinese experts on illicit drug use, the first heroin use case was identified in Kunming in 1988 (Yang and Cui 1999). By 2005 identified drug users in the city numbered approximately 23,000 (Yang et al. 2005). The prevalence of heroin abuse and the high rates of IDUs make Kunming and Yunnan province more vulnerable to HIV/AIDS infections.

As addressed in the first chapter, the first HIV infection case linked with injection drug use was identified in Yunnan in 1989. In 2005, the province held the highest HIV infection rates in the country, which were closely linked with injection heroin (64.5 percent) (Wang and Gan 2005). At the end of 2008, a total of 11,811 HIV infections were identified in Kunming and the infection rate among IFUs reached 48.36 (percent) (Zhang 2008). Based upon the previous discussions, Kunming is no doubt, the ideal research site in China to study heroin use among women from the late 1980s to the present time.

DATA SOURCES AND SAMPLING

For reasons to be discussed, the primary methodological tool used to achieve the research objectives of the current study was the in-depth interview. Generally speaking, in the study of illicit drug use, three resources are of substantial significance to researchers: institutional and professional authorities, indigenous informants and secondary indicator data (Wiebel 1990). In the case of the present study, however, there was no officially published, uniform crime data on illicit drug use available in China. When the study was conducted in 2005, two modalities were in place for mandatory drug treatment: compulsory drug rehabilitation and re-education through labor. These were under the supervision of the Kunming Municipal Public Security Bureau and the Kunming Municipal Justice Bureau respectively. Interviews with women detainees in compulsory drug rehabilitation centers would certainly have posed substantial threats to the validity of the study. Moreover, if samples came exclusively from these compulsory drug rehabilitation programs, they would not reveal the true diversity of drug use by women. It would also have been difficult to gain access to conduct in-depth interviews with detainees in compulsory drug rehabilitation facilities because of the sensitive nature of issues involved in the study. Based on these considerations, the most meaningful approach for the study was to conduct in-depth interviews with women in local communities. Women heroin users (N= 90) from the local communities of Kunming were interviewed in 2005. Women heroin users, who were at least 18 years old, who resided in Kunming and who had a heroin addiction history of at least six months, were selected for interviews. Both chain-referral (snow-ball sampling) and theoretical sampling strategies were used to gain access to women heroin users in Kunming.

Along with the in-depth interviews, the study also conducted a two-month participant observation, and carried out informal conversational interviews in a community drop-in center for drug users in Kunming. The values of participant observation have been recognized by both the early pioneer work by De Quincey (1822/1985) and by the modern drug ethnography by Dai (1937/1970; Feldman and Aldrich 1990). Participant observation creates opportunities for ethnographers to observe lives of people in a natural setting. It also allows the ethnographers to actively participate in the daily routines of research subjects and have informal contacts with them. Informal conversational interviews with women subjects, their male partners and their drug-using peers in the natural setting further enriched my formal interviews. Importantly, participant observation and informal conversational interviews have helped the study by fostering the development of a rapport with women subjects, particularly in the early stages of the research, and thus, to gain a better understanding of their behaviors within their cultures (Hammersley and Atkinson 1995; Fetterman 1998).

To study hidden populations, chain-referral sampling is identified as one of the most valuable tools for qualitative research (Dunlap and Johnson 1999; Heckathorn 2002). In particular, chain-referral sampling is a more realistic approach for the current study due to its "economical, efficient and effective" features (Meter 1990, 37). In chain-referral sampling, informants are viewed as the most precious resource to reach the hidden population (Wiebel 1990). As a former legal practitioner from China, my familiarity with Chinese culture and connections with local sources helped me to locate initial informants and interviewees in Kunming. All of my female informants were either past or present heroin users (there were a few male heroin users as well). They not only acted as my initial research subjects, but also introduced me to more women subjects within their networks—mostly their closest drug-using friends. Although several key female informants referred more women drug users to me, recruiting informants was a continuous process until the end of the research, and was not limited only to the initial period of the research.

Whereas a chain-referral sampling strategy was the primary tool in locating women subjects, the current study also applies a theoretical sampling strategy to increase the heterogeneity of the samples. Theoretical sampling is viewed as one of the most important techniques for developing grounded theories. This strategy views sampling as a continuous, rather than predetermined process, and one that evolves during the ongoing research (Strauss and Corbin 1998). Although the nature of the current study—on a hidden population—has to a certain extent, limited the study's capacity to conduct a strict theoretical sampling, it still allows the study to maximize its opportunities by including samples with diverse characteristics, and enables the drawing of constant comparisons. For example, during the initial interviews, I found that the women heroin users' age, marital status, and experience with compulsory drug rehabilitation had considerable impact on their heroin use careers. In the subsequent sampling process the study maximized its chances to select women heroin users who revealed more diversity with respect to these characteristics. On the whole, theoretical purpose and relevance have been adopted as two of the most important criteria for conducting theoretical sampling during the interview process (Glaser and Strauss 1967).

DATA COLLECTION AND ANALYSIS

There are three well-known community drop-in centers for drug users in Kunming. They were all located in residential areas and two of them had easy access to the Northern Train Station—a drug dealing hot spot in the city. These centers were supported, but not affiliated with the local government. Rather, they were fully or partially funded by different organizations from Western countries. Regular visitors to these centers all had a heroin use history, and included ex-users, current users and drug users who were recently released from compulsory treatment programs. Many of them preferred to walk back and forth between these centers frequently. Therefore, individuals who appeared in one center were often regular visitors in another. For this reason, the interview and participant observation have only focused on one of these drop-in centers, where normally received more regular visitors. Because the center was located in a crowded neighborhood with more migrants living in rented apartments, visitors had no mental pressure while walking in and out of the center; and the neighbors were not concerned much about their visits. The drug dealing hot spots were within walking distance of the center. Therefore, these visitors could have easy access to the drugs if needed. Most women subjects were from the nearby communities; some others had to travel for a long distance from the other side of the city. The center consisted of a few offices and a conference room equipped with simple furniture, such as tables and chairs, and some basic entertainment equipment, including a TV, table tennis equipment and mahjong tables.

Workers at this center, including the supervisor, staff and volunteers, were all ex-heroin users. Most of the volunteers were recently released from compulsory drug rehabilitation centers. They would have a chance to be promoted to staff based upon good job performance. Both staff members and volunteers got paid, but staff members had better salaries than the volunteers. Still, newer volunteers were much more likely to use heroin occasionally, which was rare among the staff. The visitors were diverse in their current drug use status. Although they mostly had a desire to restrain their heroin use, there was no certainty about the results. Among these visitors, the number of males and females was quite similar, but heroin users who were over 30 years old were more likely to be frequent visitors.

Considering drug-users' daily routine, the center was open nine hours a day (12:00 PM to 9:00 PM). Daily recreational activities were available to the visitors, such as watching TV, playing mahjong or table tennis. Occasionally, the center held lectures by counselors who were also ex-heroin users from a well-known voluntary drug treatment center. Sometimes there were even foreign visitors to give lectures or to talk about their personal experience with drugs. Because all people who routinely visited the center had connections with heroin, either in the past or at the present time, they felt secure and relaxed during their stay at the center. Still, it seemed that the regular visitors were very alert to newcomers. Unless people got familiar with each other, they seldom chatted in a group or even had a direct conversation. To encourage more drug users to visit the center, the police were not allowed to conduct any form of investigation or to arrest drug users inside the center. However, on a few occasions the undercover police parked their unmarked car near the gate entrance to the center. During those times the number of visitors to the center was significantly reduced. After a few days everything went back to normal again. Such incidents occurred a few times during my fieldwork. Although daily or occasional drug users were scared about being taken into police custody for drug testing, most people simply did not want to be questioned at the local police station.

The In-depth Interview

I conducted face-to-face interviews with women heroin users (N=90) in the summer of 2005. As mentioned earlier, the interviews were conducted at a local community drop-in center. The rationale for choosing this site as my field office was based on several reasons: First, it was easy for me to recruit potential women subjects from among the visitors to the center; second, women subjects felt more comfortable about talking when they remained in a secure and familiar setting; third, though only one formal office was available at this site for the director, staff and volunteers of the center, a private room was always at my disposal whenever needed for interviews during the center's regular working hours. Each interview took about ninety minutes. Before each interview, the consent form in Chinese translation was given to the subject, and the purpose of the study was explained thoroughly, ensuring that the procedures for confidentiality were fully understood. A digital recorder was used to record the interviews while brief notes were also taken. Right after each interview, a profile of the woman heroin user was produced, including an initial impression of the interviewee and comments regarding the flow of the interview. A brief interview transcript was also made after each day's work for an immediate analysis of data to facilitate future interviews. All recorded interviews and transcriptions are labeled with a file number and corresponding pseudonym.

To study hidden populations, building up rapport is critical, and stipends for interviews and field expenses have great potential to increase the subjects' incentives for cooperation (Dunlap and Johnson 1999). For this reason, each interviewee was informed of the fee they would receive prior to them coming in for an interview. Due to limited funds of the study, women subjects were not paid much for their interviews, and this was a serious concern to me during the initial stage of my fieldwork.[9] I wondered whether women subjects would be willing to participate in my study and confide in me. As my interviews continued, there was no indication that the low payment was a major barrier to a successful interview because all women were referred to me by their drug-using friends. Plus, my age, gender and personality helped to increase the women's trust in me. Like many women in the study, I am married and the mother of an 11-year-old boy. Several women did not want to accept the stipends after the interviews because they appreciated the opportunity to share their experience with me—they told me that nobody really wanted to listen to their stories after they were on heroin for so many years, not even their family members. Knowing that I was a former attorney in China, several women intended to ask legal advice from me on matters of divorce and related property disputes.

Building a rapport with women interviewees was a continuous process throughout my fieldwork. It became extremely important during the early stage of my interviews. I learned that having a good understanding of women's culture was very critical. During my first several interviews, I observed that most women found it intolerable to sit through an hour-long interview without smoking. They often asked me whether smoking was allowed during the interviews. After two women kindly suggested that I should leave a packet of cigarettes on the table for the convenience of the interviewees, I quickly adopted the suggestion. Although it was not something I condoned, I began asking women whether they wanted a cigarette right after they sat down in front of me. To a certain degree, this invitation released the initial tension between the women and me: they were all very pleased with this invitation. But as a non-smoker, and a person who had barely smelled cigarette smoke in five years, I had to overcome my initial distaste for the situation.

The majority of women in the study had no previous interview experience. Only a few had been interviewed by the media, and a small number had participated in survey research by answering questionnaires.[10] Therefore, the women were very curious about my research project. An explicit explanation of the purposes of the study not only helped them to understand their contributions to this research, but also to dispel any misgivings they had. The interview questions also played an important role in releasing initial tensions. After explaining the study, I began to ask questions related to the women's background—about their family and school lives prior to heroin use. The women felt unperturbed in answering these questions. After this introductory conversation, women were more open to further questions. This initial strategy not only reduced opening tensions, but also gave me a sketch of the women's background, and therefore aided me in directing further individual-specific questions.

At the beginning, I conducted the interviews based on pre-prepared semi-structured questions. After I had interviewed several women, I realized that women always showed enthusiasm on certain topics and liked to talk more; they often followed their thoughts rather than my questions. If I rigidly followed my pre-prepared questions, I might lose the chance to listen to each woman's unique experience. Therefore, keeping the interview natural and flowing became my primary concern. As Hammersley and Atkinson indicated (1995, 152), interviews do not necessarily follow "a fixed sequence" and one may not be able to "ask each interviewee exactly the same questions." On the whole, I made efforts to keep my interviews smooth, and allowed women to express their unique experience and thoughts. Meanwhile, I had to direct the conversation back to the original topic if women kept talking about things that were irrelevant.

Another benefit of doing qualitative research reflects in its flexibility in the fieldwork. As the interviews continued, and new themes emerged from the conversations, I began to update my interview questions based upon these emerging thoughts. For instance, women repeatedly told me that they had either immediate family members or close friends who had died of heroin. In order to explore whether such an event had an impact on women's decisions regarding cessation of their drug habits, I raised this issue with other women in subsequent interviews, and made constant comparisons between different subjects.

Participant Observation

I began my fieldwork at the same time as my interviews with the women. Participant observation was made at the same community drop-in center where the interviews were conducted. During these observations, many casual and friendly conversations with women subjects, women's male partners (mostly boyfriends), staff members, volunteers and other visitors were conducted. These interactions not only helped me to collect more information about my women subjects, but also allowed me to understand the women in the context of their culture (Spradley 1979). My observations were recorded in the form of a memo at the end of each day, which included my informal conversations with the women subjects, notes on their associations with other peers, and on their activities in the group setting. Memos were then filed by dates and put together with audio-recorded interviews and transcripts—all were kept in a secure place.

While entering the field for participant observation, I was very cautious about managing the impression I would convey, about revealing my personality and about my role in the field (Hammersley and Atkinson 1995). During my first several days at the drop-in center, as the only person without drug-using experience, I felt tensions with respect to the other visitors, both males and females. To gain their trust, I carefully managed my impressions—wearing casual clothes, invisible make-up, and carrying a casual bag rather than a portfolio. I also used my actions to show that I am a person committed to my research—arriving at the center shortly after the door was open, and staying there until it closed late at night. After a short period of time, I was cordially invited to join them at lunch and have dinner with the staff and volunteers who worked in the late evening.[11]

It is most important, as suggested by ethnographic research, to develop a good rapport between researchers and human subjects during participant observation. A good relationship has the same value as the interview process. As suggested by Dunlap and Johnson, (1999), one of the key components in building a good rapport is to show respect for human subjects. My interest in the women's life histories, and concern about their everyday lives and my commitment to my field research revealed my respect for them as human beings. I participated in a donation organized by the center for a daughter whose drug-user mother was re-arrested for relapse. I gained a lot of respect from the women when they knew I donated money.[12]

Meanwhile, I was actively involved in seminars and activities organized by the center. I sat in at community meetings, listening to very different perspectives about heroin use from drug users, their family members, local police officers, and staff members from voluntary drug treatment centers. Once, I served as a translator for a guest speaker from the United States who was an ex-heroin addict. I also went out to drug-dealing hot spots, with the staff and volunteers working at the drop-in center, to advocate needle exchange programs.[13] With the passage of time, I gained more information about the women I had interviewed, as well as about other male and female drug users coming to the center. Thus, the participant observation allowed me to be close to the women subjects' everyday lives, have opportunities to talk to their male partners and peers, and most importantly, to understand their behavior within the context of their culture.

Women Subjects

The demographic characteristics of women subjects (N=90) is shown in Table 2.1. Although the study is mainly based on a chain-referral sampling strategy, it is able to reflect the diversity of the women heroin users in Kunming on major aspects because of the size of the sample. Among women in the samples, 18 percent belonged to minority nationalities, including Hui, Yi, Dai, Bai, Tujia, Mosuo, Miao and Mongolian. With respect to religion, most of the women were non-religious (84 percent). A small of portion of them (15 percent) were believers, Muslim, Buddhist or Christian.[14] Three women were migrants from places other than Kunming; two of these migrants, together with three others from counties under the administrative division of Kunming were rural residents. Without exception, all these women migrated to Kunming by themselves with a dream of better opportunities in life.

At the time of the interviews, thirty-eight women (42 percent) were over 35 years of age (mean=34.28). Still, women whose ages were between 30 and 34 years old represented the largest percentage in the samples. In contrast, women who were 25 years old or younger were disproportionately represented. Such an age distribution may be attributed to the chain-referral sampling strategy—the informants' inability to reach women at certain age groups. It also suggests that the heroin epidemic might have affected a certain age cohort more than others.[15]

Among women in the study, forty-nine women (54 percent) had married, but only 18 percent of the sample remained married at the time of the interviews. Among married women twenty-six of them (29 percent) were divorced, three of them (3 percent) were separated from their husbands and four of them were widowed (4 percent) and. Even though the women were mostly over 30 years old, a high proportion of them (46 percent) never married. Among the married women, thirty-nine of them (70 percent) had at least one child.[16] Two other women each had one child but were not married.

Among the women heroin users in the study, the percentage of middle school attendees (45 percent) was the same as that of high school attendees if including technical secondary school into the high school category.[17] Only one woman, 49 years old, who dropped out of elementary school, was illiterate. However, the school drop-out rate was as high as 11 percent among the samples.[18] Compared to an official report from the Kunming Bureau of Statistics (2006), the percentage of women subjects in the study who received their high school diploma was much higher than the general population average (16 percent), even after excluding three high school drop-outs. However, the percentage of college graduates citywide (8 percent) was much higher than the sample; only one woman in the study attended college, but was forced to drop out because of her family's financial constraints.[19]

The history of drug use by women ranged from one year to nineteen years (mean=11.83). Women with a history of more than five years of heroin use were equally distributed, but the number of women who had less than five years of heroin use history is much less than the other categories. The theoretical sampling strategy has helped the study to identify this pattern during interviewing; however, the chain referral sampling has limited the study's ability to include younger women heroin users into the study.

Women subjects' drug-use status at the time of interviews was quite diverse. Among nine daily drug users (10 percent) six of them (67 percent) had reduced doses. The occasional drug users (30 percent) only used heroin irregularly, ranging from several times a week to a few times a month. Women in treatment (18 percent) only included those in voluntary drug treatment programs, and were mainly from the newly developed methadone treatment program. Although most of them still used heroin frequently at the beginning of their treatment, they only used the drug occasionally by the time they were interviewed. Whereas twenty-seven women (30 percent) had not used heroin within six months, 59 percent had just been just released from compulsory drug treatment programs and 15 percent had just finished voluntary drug treatments. For women who had quit heroin for more than six months (12 percent), abstention ranged from seven months to five years.

Although over half of the women had a job and a steady income before their heroin initiation, their addiction to heroin had rendered them barely able to maintain a legitimate job, or to locate a new job once they were

Table 2.1 Demographic Characteristics of Women Heroin Users (N=90)

Age N (%)		Marital Status N (%)	
<25	3 (3%)	In marriage	16 (18%)
25–29	13 (14%)	Divorced	26 (29%)
30–34	36 (40%)	Separated	3 (3%)
35–39	21 (23%)	Widowed	4 (4%)
>40	17 (19%)	Single	41 (46%)
Ethnicity		Religion	
Minority nationalities	16 (18%)	Christian	3 (3%)
Han	74 (82%)	Buddhist	5 (6%)
		Muslim	6 (7%)
		No religion	76 (84%)
Educational experience		Drug use history	
Elementary	7 (8%)	1–5 years	9 (10%)
Middle school	41 (45%)	6–10 years	25 (28%)
High school	34 (38%)	11–15 years	27 (30%)
Technical school	7 (7%)	16–19 years	29 (32%)
College	1 (1%)		
Employment status		Drug use status	
Self-enterprise	1 (1%)	Daily user	9 (10%)
Coach	1 (1%)	Occasional user	27 (30%)
Service industry	3 (3%)	In treatment	16 (18%)
Clerk	7 (8%)	Non-drug users (<6 months)	27 (30%)
Drug-related program	7 (8%)	Non-drug users (>6 months)	11 (12%)
Jobless	71 (79%)		

addicted. The unemployment rate of women at the interviews was as high as 79 percent.[20] In the case of women who had a job, they were much more likely to work for drug-related community programs, or as clerks for small companies. In the latter case, they found employment either because of their family's social connections or based on their friends' referrals. It was almost impossible for them to secure a job by themselves in the increasingly competitive job market in the country.

The Follow-up Study

This study was originally proposed as a dissertation project in 2005. While working in the field, conducting face-to-face interviews with women heroin users, making field observations and chatting with the women's male partners and family members, I became determined to publish the work to draw attention to the devastating nature of heroin use and its impacts on these women's lives. Right after the completion of my dissertation in the spring of 2008, my proposal for a follow-up study was funded by my current institution, thus enabling me to make my second field trip to Kunming in the summer of 2008.[21]

The decision to carry out a follow-up study was based on several reasons. First of all, the follow-up study was designed to add a longitudinal feature to the initial project. I wanted to chart the changes in women's drug-use careers over a period of three years. Second, it would allow me to examine the impact of new drug treatment programs and changes in legislation on women's drug-use careers over the three-year period.[22] When the data was collected in 2005, the methadone drug treatment program was offered in Kunming for only two months. A few women participated in the program at the time, but no obvious impact was observed on account of the short period of time. Third, by going back into the field I could verify the reliability of my initial data. Fourth, I wanted to gain deeper insight into the income generating activities of the women heroin users, in particular, their involvement in prostitution and drug dealing. New data collected through interviews and field observations could supplement the initial sample, and thereby enhance the study's validity and generalizability.

After my fieldwork was concluded in 2005, I still kept frequent contact with several of my respondents, via phone or email. Although the snowball sampling strategy utilized by the study imposed a great challenge to the follow-up study, I was quite confident as to the possible outcomes prior to my departure to the field. Still, I was uncertain about the number of respondents who would come back for the follow-up study. With respect to further data collection on prostitution and drug dealing, I was also not sure how far I could go on the mere basis of promises by key informants, given the legal consequences of these illegal activities.

Indeed, in the beginning, it was quite difficult to locate again the women I had originally interviewed, due to of lack of information about their real identity. To overcome the initial difficulties, I decided to take three steps to reach out to the women subjects: first, I relied on my key informants who were also participants in my study in 2005—they were my most reliable resources; second, I was able to use the office at the community drop-in center for the follow-up interviews. Because the center was still a gathering place for drug users, those women subjects who were willing to participate in the follow-up study could easily find me there once the news of follow-up interviews began to spread.[23] Third, I asked women subjects who came back for the re-interviews to take my message back to their friends who had also been participants in 2005. Restricted by my budget constraints, I was finally able to re-interview women heroin users from my initial sample. The questionnaire for these respondents was similar to the original interview protocol, with a focus on the changes in their drug-use careers. Unlike the first data collection, the re-interviews with women were conducted in a very relaxed and friendly atmosphere from beginning to end.

As stated earlier, another objective of the follow-up study was to deepen my understanding of women's engagement in drug dealing and prostitution. With the assistance of my key informants and the chain-referral sampling strategy, I was able to recruit more women heroin users for my study. These women participated mainly in the drug dealing business (N=25) and prostitution (N=16). As shown in Table 2.2 and Table 2.3, except for their educational background, for which the percentages were quite similar in all categories, the women in the two groups showed distinct differences on other variables. In the case of women involved in selling drugs and prostitution, the age group between 35 and 39 years constituted the highest percentages. However, more women heroin users who engaged in prostitution belonged to the younger cohort, between 30–34 years of age (25 percent), than those who were dealing drugs (8 percent); they were also much more likely to be single (50 percent vs. 36 percent). With respect to women's drug-use history, the former group had a much shorter drug-use history and were less likely to receive the re-education through labor sanction (31 percent vs. 56 percent), the most severe punishment for illicit drug use in China at that time. In terms of the women's drug-use status, those dealing drugs had a higher likelihood of being daily users (40 percent vs. 13 percent) whereas those who were sex workers were mostly likely to be receivers of the methadone treatment program (69 percent vs. 40 percent).

During the follow-up study, only re-interviews and a few new interviews were conducted in the community drop-in center. Several reasons led to my decision to change the interview location. Among women drug dealers, only those who sold small quantities made frequent visits to the center (to solicit customers or to sell drugs). Unlike small quantity sellers, none of the more involved women drug dealers had ever visited the center before; they were unwilling to associate with other drug users (unless they were best friends)

Table 2.2 Demographic Characteristics of Women Drug Dealers in 2008 (N=25)

Age N (%)		Marital Status N (%)	
		In Marriage	6 (24%)
30–34	2 (8%)	Divorced	8 (32%)
35–39	12 (48%)	Separated	1 (4%)
40–45	9 (36%)	Widowed	1 (4%)
46–50	2 (8%)	Single	9 (36%)
Ethnicity		Drug dealing history	
Minority nationalities	4 (16%)	Before 1990	1 (4%)
Han	21 (84%)	1990–1995	10 (40%)
		1996–2000	12 (48%)
		After 2000	2 (8%)
Educational experience		Drug use history	
Elementary	2 (8%)	11–15 years	3 (12%)
Middle school	17 (68%)	16–19 years	11 (44%)
High school	2 (8%)	>20	11 (44%)
Technical school	3 (12%)		
College	1 (4%)		
Drug related sanction		Drug use status	
Compulsary drug rehab	21 (84%)	Daily user	10 (40%)
Re-education through labor	14 (56%)	Occasional user	3 (12%)
Drug possession	2 (8%)	Methadone treatment	10 (40%)
Drug trafficking	3 (12%)	Non-drug users (>6 months)	2 (8%)
No drug related sanction	2 (8%)		

whom they believed would jeopardize their drug selling businesses. Except for a few frequent visitors, the women heroin users who mainly engaged in prostitution generally did not want to expose themselves at the center's new location. Having known each other for years, my key informants put a great deal of trust in me; I also placed great trust in them—for the concern of my personal safety. They knew that I would make every effort to protect the women subjects' interests. Based on the above considerations, I decided to use a variety of settings for the new interviews, including tea houses, parks and women heroin users' homes.

Table 2.3 Demographic Characteristics of Women Heroin Users in the Sex Trade in 2008 (N=16)

Age N (%)		Marital Status N (%)	
		In Marriage	4 (25%)
30–34	4 (25%)	Divorced	3 (19%)
35–39	8 (50%)	Widowed	1 (6%)
40–45	4 (25%)	Single	8 (50%)
Ethnicity		Sex venue	
Minority nationalities	2 (13%)	Nightclub	5 (31%)
Han	14 (87%)	Dance hall	9 (56%)
		Nightclub/Dance hall	2 (13%)
Education		Drug use history	
Elementary	2 (13%)	5–10 years	2 (13%)
Middle school	10 (63%)	11–15 years	6 (38%)
High school	3 (19%)	16–19 years	6 (38%)
College	1 (6%)	>20	2 (13%)
Drug related sanction		Drug use status	
Compulsary drug rehab	14 (88%)	Daily user	2 (13%)
Re-eduation through labor	5 (31%)	Occasional user	3 (19%)
		Methadone treatment	11 (69%)

The women who mainly engaged in prostitution were generally very relaxed during the interviews—they were aware of the purpose of the study before they came for the interviews. In contrast, although they had been given information by the key informants regarding the nature of the study, the women drug dealers —especially the more renowned ones—still remained very alert to the surroundings during the interviews, and chose their words very cautiously. Although the relationship of trust between these women subjects and my key informants played a key role in these interviews, a brief explanation of the purpose of the study and my initial contacts with them were all very critical in gaining their trust. For the purpose of the follow-up study, all new interviews aimed primarily at collecting information about women's illegal practices and how these illegal practices interacted with their drug-use careers. Similar to the initial data collection, all interviews took about one and a half hours, and were recorded on a digital recorder. The consent form in Chinese translation was given to subjects before each interview was conducted and stipends for the interview were offered right after the conversations.

Guided by my key informants, I was able to make a couple of field trips to drug-selling hot spots (located in the Northern Train Station area), local dance halls, and nightclubs (see detailed discussion in Chapter 5). Due to budget constraints, my visits to the entertainment venues—in particular to the upscale nightclubs—were limited. On a few occasions, my key informants very kindly invited me out to dinner or to their homes. A few interviews with women who engaged in sex services were conducted on such occasions. These field trips were of great value to the study. They gave me opportunities to observe the illegal drug market at the street level, to witness how women heroin users made quick money from sex services performed at downscale dance halls, and to observe their actual living conditions. Most importantly, these opportunities helped me to relate the women heroin users' accounts with real world settings and to understand them in context.

Data Analysis

Whereas quantitative research utilizes statistical tools for data analysis, qualitative analysis is not strictly limited by technical rules. As Patton (2001, 433) suggests, "There are no absolute rules except to do the very best with your full intellect to fairly represent the data and communicate what the data reveal given the purpose of the study." The analytical process for qualitative research is quite judgmental in nature, and depends more on the researcher's intellect and creativity. Thus, researchers are viewed as the instrument of qualitative studies.

Although qualitative inquiries do not necessarily follow stringent rules, some techniques for qualitative analysis have been developed. According to Maxwell (2005, 96), these procedures entail reading and thinking about data, writing memos, developing coding categories and applying them to data, and analyzing narratives and contextual relationships. Both inductive and deductive reasoning is involved in data analysis but these are employed differently during different stages of the research analysis (Strauss and Corbin 1998). These analytical strategies have been used as the primary guidelines for the current study. The data analysis began right after the first interview or participant observation was complete —I listened to the recorded interviews right after I came back from the field, made brief transcripts and coding, and wrote memos containing observational, theoretical and methodological notes. These preliminary analyses are important because they facilitated further sampling and analysis. As mentioned earlier in this chapter, I revised my interview questions constantly, applying theoretical sampling with emerging themes from my data.

Because the study employed a ground theory approach for data analysis, the focus of analyses evolved as the research developed. During the initial data analysis process, making inductions by deriving concepts, propositions and dimensions from data is the primary task. This initial data analysis essentially involves a combination of two distinct processes:

data categorizing and data connecting, also referred to as the two stages of data analysis: examining and comparing the material within categories; comparing material across categories (H. Rubin and R. Rubin 1995, 251). By using data categorizing and connecting, the study is able to develop theories from data categorizing based on similarities, and to interpret the meanings of these findings in context. As suggested by Strauss and Corbin (1998), once the theories emerge from the data, making deductions—verifying the emerging theories—naturally becomes the main theme of the study (Strauss and Corbin 1998). In this finalizing process, identifying and analyzing negative cases were also concerns of the study—it not only shows intellectual honesty, but also adds credibility to the findings of the study (Patton 2001).

Compared to quantitative research, data analysis in qualitative studies tends to be more time-consuming. Applying appropriate coding strategies during the data analysis process is the major theme for qualitative research, and has been proved to be critical. The current study followed the steps in grounded theory coding as suggested by Auerbach and Silverstein (2003, 35): raw text —relevant text —repeating ideas —themes —theoretical constructs —theoretical narratives —research concerns. The whole purpose of coding is to derive theories from the raw data and interlace the theoretical insights of the researcher with these emerging theories—reflecting the research concerns of the study.

Validity and Reliability

The validity threats of the current study are related to both the nature of the study and the methodology used to collect the data. Heroin use is prohibited in China, and heroin users' income-generating activities are subject to administrative or criminal sanctions; topics related to sex services and HIV are sensitive to women. The nature of the study itself, therefore, poses inherent challenges to the study's validity. Unlike quantitative research, which can rule out validity threats through the research design itself, qualitative research usually can address the validity issue only after the studies have been carried out.

Although no strategies can ever eliminate all validity threats, they will certainly enhance the credibility of the study (Maxwell 2005). The present study has taken several steps to deal with validity threats, both during the research design and in the course of fieldwork. First, to decrease the pressure on women with respect to social environment, the study located female subjects from the communities in Kunming rather than from compulsory drug treatment programs operated by law enforcement agencies, or voluntary treatment programs staffed by medical and other professionals. Second, the decision to recruit informants was made during the research design itself. Informants (particularly key informants) not only "play a critical role in the recruitment of research subjects," but also "add its credibility and legitimacy on the street" (Goldstein et al. 1990, 88). Referred by their drug friends, the women subjects generally showed very satisfactory cooperation during interviews.

Meanwhile, the study set up several procedures to ensure validity during the interview process: (1) Informants and interviewees were informed in advance that they would be paid a stipend for their participation. This was expected to have a great potential to increase women subjects' incentive to participate in the study (Dunlap and Johnson 1999); (2) the face-to-face interviews were conducted in a private space within the community drop-in center for drug users, without the presence of other parties[24]; (3) interviewees were clearly notified that any information having the potential of exposing their identities would not be recorded or written down; (4) interviewees were convinced that the investigator was the only person who would fully review all the information, and (5) interviewees were invited to respond in the Yunnanese dialect, if they so desired.

The most challenging issues during interviews were topics related to women's income-generating activities, in particular women's involvement in drug dealing and sex services. After a few initial interviews, I realized that the women's character, and the way that these questions were approached, both played important roles. Women who were extroverts were more open. They often provided me with details about their illegal activities regardless of the nature of the offenses. In contrast, in the case of women who were introverts, or socially inexperienced, it usually took a longer time for the disclosure of sensitive issues. Realizing the differences among women subjects, I altered my interview strategies on a case-by-case basis during my fieldwork. In general, I always asked indirect questions first, normally about women's family and school lives, rather than direct and straightforward ones related to the sensitive topics. Based on my observation, when the women began to show interest in certain topics, they usually had a lot more to say about related points. Initially, they might have felt reluctant to touch upon some dark areas in their lives, but if they felt that there was no way to hide their secrets, they eventually gave in and provided me details about those topics. In general, the interviews offering women's own accounts, and the participant observation I conducted gave me a unique position to process more information about the women subjects from different angles.

Validity issues have been given a great deal of consideration in both quantitative and qualitative research because they are related to the credibility of the conclusions. Due to the nature of qualitative methods, however, qualitative researchers often resist the quantitative explanations of reliability (Neuman 2003). How to interpret inconsistency in these resources then becomes a major concern. To the qualitative researcher, both consistency and inconsistency from different data sources are equally important. To some degree, a lack of consistency is not a major problem in itself. Rather, the causes creating the inconsistency will be quite revealing to further inductive reasoning (Patton 2001).

The current study uses in-depth interviews with women heroin users, inquiring into their significant life events before and after heroin use. These interviews are retrospective in nature. The accuracy of the retrospective interview is often challenged. However, it seems to be the only meaningful way to examine past events among hidden populations when no official records can be accessed (Fetterman 1998). Regardless of the dramatic nature of illicit drug use, previous research has shown that heroin users did not have a problem with recounting significant events in their drug-use history if the interviewers were experienced, familiar with drug-users' culture and well prepared (Ball 1969). The research also indicates that drug use itself is not a threat to the study's reliability (Day et al. 2004).

Although the women in the study were at various stages of drug use, I did not observe that they had problems in recalling important life events. Analyses of women's accounts rarely revealed inconsistencies. However, women in withdrawal are substantially distracted. Two women who used heroin on a daily basis showed withdrawal symptoms during the interviews. One of them even vomited right in front of me.[25] The interviews were resumed when the symptoms went away. To aid interviewees in recalling more accurately, the proposed interview questions focused on a series of important life events occurring before or after heroin use, rather than only on numerical details.

Limitations of the Study

The current study is primarily focused on ninety women heroin users in Kunming. The findings from the current study can only be applied to women heroin users in the sample. Specifically, the study has several limitations. First of all, the study was conducted in Kunming, only one city in the southwest of China. Because of its proximity to the Golden Triangle —the major heroin source for Mainland China—the illicit drug market is rampant in Kunming, more than in any other major metropolitan area. Women in Kunming have geographic proximity to the underground drug market and can obtain heroin at a low price. Thus, the prevalence and pattern of heroin use among women in Kunming is not proposed as a model that would apply generally to women in other urban areas in China. Secondly, the research subjects, women heroin users, were primarily recruited from local communities of Kunming by a snow-ball sampling strategy. Such a sampling strategy has certainly limited the scope of the current study. It determines that findings from the study will not even necessarily represent all women heroin users in Kunming. Thirdly, in-depth interviews were the major source of data collection. The interviews were conducted only among those willing to be interviewed. Naturally, those women heroin users who did not show interest in being interviewed were not included in the study. Whether any career differences exist between these two types of women heroin users is uncertain, and therefore might be a factor affecting the generalizations of the current study.

3 Family, School and Post-School Life

Family, the first social institution in women's lives, played a vital role during their growth—particularly from childhood to early adolescence. In the literature of substance abuse, familial structure and stability are of salient importance to women's drug use (Platt 1988). As suggested by research, parental characteristics and parental child-rearing practices were both essential to women's development; the former was mediated by socialization of parental controls (Kandel 1980). While parental child-rearing practices are the primary sources for the building of children's self-control (Gottfredson and Hirschi 1990), the recent study also indicates that "parental efficacy"—a combination of parental control and parental support, is more effective on reducing youth crimes (Wright and Cullen 2001).

Women's experiences in school was found to play an important role in the development of delinquency prior to heroin use. Academic incompetence and early delinquent acts were correlated—women who were mostly underachievers in school were more likely to join like-minded company in school or in society (Hirschi 1969). The adverse school environment may have provided women with more opportunities to meet delinquent peers and get involved in delinquent acts (Sommers, Baskin and Fagan 2000). Compared to young males, young females seem to preserve themselves more easily from the negative influences of peers; however, such a conclusion is true only when young girls have a strong attachment to their parents, or a commitment to their future (Mears, Ploeger and Warr 1998). Furthermore, the lack of supply of social capital in women's schooling has restricted women's future options both in the job market and in personal affairs (Coleman 1988).

The objective of the study is to explore women heroin users' drug-use careers in China's changing society. Before embarking on a full discussion of women's drug-use careers, this chapter seeks to examine those pre-existing factors in women's lives that render them prone to the heroin culture. Life history interviews with women subjects have enabled this study to explore the impact of family, school and peer influences present in the lives of women heroin users prior to their drug use, and to determine how these factors interact with each other to contribute to women's early delinquent behaviors.

THE ROLE OF FAMILY

Research shows that family structure affects a whole range of childhood behaviors, and has a particularly significant influence on the early educational performance of children. With rapid socio-economic development and the transformation of people's values in the reform era, particularly toward marriage and divorce, family structure in China underwent significant changes. Corresponding to these changes, the number of children who are living in single-parent families increased dramatically As shown in Table 3.1, although most of the women (68 percent) in the study had lived with their biological parents during their childhood, nearly one third of them (29 percent) lived with only one of their parents due to parental divorce (12 percent) or death (17 percent). Moreover, on account of the One Child Policy, introduced in 1979 in China, the likelihood that the women were the only child at home (11 percent) increased if they were the first child to be born to their families in the late 1970s and thereafter. Still, many other families were unaffected by this policy if they had already had more than one child before the new policy was firmly implemented in the country. Thus, the majority of the women grew up in families with at least two children.

As Table 3.1 indicates, in terms of occupation, the women's parents were more likely to have labor jobs (72 percent [father] vs. 68 percent [mother]). There was a high likelihood that the women's mothers were housewives (21 percent). Regardless of the socioeonomic status of the women's parents, however, very few of the women in the study (N=5) had deviant parents; two of these parents had histories of heroin abuse prior to the women's own heroin use.[1] The low substance abuse rate among the parents can be attributed to the fact that illicit drug abuse emerged largely in the late 1980s, in particular among the younger generations. The data clearly shows that the women's siblings, rather than their parents, were more likely to be heroin users (15 percent vs. 2 percent).[2]

The interviews with women heroin users suggest that women's relationships with their family, particularly with their parents, were crucial during their growing years. Women who perceived their parents in positive terms were more likely to refrain from status offenses and early delinquent acts; in contrast, women who were neglected or rejected by their families were more likely to show disobedient behavior. As indicated in Table 3.1, among women in the study, four types of relationships with their parents were identified: Twenty-four women (27 percent) had good or satisfied relationships with both of their parents; thirty women (33 percent) had poor communication with one or both their parents; eight women (9 percent) had an extremely distant relationship with either one or both of their parents; twenty-eight women (31 percent) were overindulged by one or both of their parents (if the former, they normally had a good relationship with the other parent). Although those who were denied gratification, as well as those who were overindulged were much more likely to display ungoverned behavior,

Table 3.1 Family Characteristics of Women Heroin Users (N=90)

Family structure (at age of 18)	(%)	Father's occupation	(%)
Both parents	68	Professional	7
Parental death	17	Business owner/ manager	6
Parental divorce	12	Military cadre	14
Adopted	3	Peasant	1
		Laborer	71
Number of siblings		Mother's occupation	
No sibling	11	Professional	4
One sibling	33	Business owner/ manager	2
Two siblings	28	Military/cadre	5
Three siblings	17	Peasant	6
More than three	11	Laborer	62
		Housewife	21
Addicted family members		Relationship with parents	
Brother	12	Good relationship	27
Sister	3	Lack of communication	33
Mother	1	Poor relationship	9
Father	1	Overindulgent	31
None	82		

lack of communication with parents was also a major issue confronting many of these women—an issue that was largely ignored by their parents.[3] The study found that women's relationships with their family were closely related to their family structure and to parental child-rearing practices. Women who had problems with their parents were more likely to be from broken homes, or where physical abuse was frequent. The following section will offer a detailed discussion of the characteristics of women's families and their influence on women's lives:

Family Conflict/Break-up

While family break-up has profound influence on young girls, the quality of parental relationships also plays a critical role. Serious conflicts between parents often resulted in families breaking up; however, break-ups did not occur in all families where there were serious conflicts. Consequently, long-term heated quarrels and fighting between parents produced the same trauma on young females. Although only eleven women (12 percent) experienced parental divorce before reaching the age of 18, eighteen others (20 percent) reported frequent quarrels and fighting between their parents.[4] Women felt scared and unwilling to stay at home when parental conflicts increased in intensity. They said:

> Fen: My parents often had furious quarrels. My brother and I were scared all the time. Sometimes I felt that they would divorce, but nothing ever happened. For this reason, I didn't like to stay at home.

> Lin: The relationship between my parents was getting worse day by day. They fought with each other constantly. I hated going back home.

> Yuan: Since I was a small child, my parents have been quarreling and fighting. I was always in a state of fright when they started. I didn't want to live with them. After I quit middle school, I began living in an apartment with my boyfriend.

Although not all unhappy marriages ended in divorce, families with frequent and intense conflicts were more likely to break up. Eleven women's parents finally divorced before the women reached the age of 18. The parents who were younger in age were more likely than older parents to seek divorce, a phenomenon that reflects the escalating divorce rates in China and highlights significant changes in Chinese family structure in recent decades. Parental divorce signifies a turning point in young females' lives. After divorce, almost all the women's parents remarried. Three women were able to stay with one of their parents: two women with their mothers and one with her father. All others—even those as young as a year old—were handed over to their grandparents. These women virtually grew up in families without the presence of either of their parents; the parents only acted as their financial support. Lacking frequent contact with parents, women were deprived of psychological parenting in their families (Johnson, Dunlap and Maher 1998). Due to the generation gap and other reasons, young girls felt reluctant to share their feelings and thoughts with their grandparents.

Hong, 29 years old, was very lovely and sweet. She had beautiful expressive eyes. Sadly, she had an unfortunate childhood. After Hong started middle school, she was able to live with her mother. But she never grew close to her mother. She said:

> My parents divorced when I was one. I was supposed to live with my mother, but I actually stayed with my grandma. My mother was twenty when she gave birth to me. She soon remarried and I had a half-blood

> brother. My father left for his hometown in another province after the divorce. He couldn't come back to visit me very often either. He, too, remarried. I also have a half-blood sister. When I had problems, I always talked to my friends rather than sharing with my grandma.

Another woman, Yue, was in a situation even worse than Hong's. Yue, 23 years old, began to take heroin in 1999 when she was only seventeen. When she sat in front of me, she looked like a bashful high school student; she was thin and pale. Her parents divorced when she was in elementary school. Her father became her legal guardian based on the court decision. She virtually lost contact with her mother since then. She was actually living with her grandparents and could barely see her father. Her grandpa was the only person who cared about her at home, but passed away many years ago. She said:

> My grandma (father's side) prefers boys and dislikes girls. Until I could speak, she began to carry me around. My mother remarried. Every time I visited her, my grandma (mother's side) made scornful remarks because she dislikes my father, and diverted her anger to me. Nobody cared about me in the family. I was like an invisible person at home. If I had any problems, I could find nobody to talk to. For these reasons, I moved out when I was fifteen and stayed with a female friend with a family situation similar to mine.

Separation alienated these girls from their parents. They felt no connection with their parents, which fostered mistrust and engendered further communication problems. As Kai told me, even when she had a chance to talk to her parents, she always hid her true feelings and felt reluctant to tell the truth. She said, "Of every ten sentences I said, eight were lies." When the women were finally able to live with their parent, they faced new challenges in their live—difficult issues in the blended families. Na, an enchanting, 34-year-old woman, told me about her big, new families:

> My mother gave birth to me when she was seventeen. She divorced my father when I was fourteen. My stepfather is three years younger than my mother. To him, everything is about money. Because of him, my parents divorced. For this reason, I disliked him even more. My mother gave birth to another boy, and then she divorced again. She remarried a third time. I only lived with my mother half a year, and then I decided to join my father. My father also remarried; my stepmother brought her son to my family.

Comparatively, the girls from broken families got involved in more complicated family relationships, especially when stepparents and their children were involved. Even if women mostly said that they had good relationships with their half-blood brother or sister, none of them were able to build intimate relationships with their stepparents. Kai was 33 years old. She always dressed stylishly carrying a Walkman. Similar to Na, she was unable to see either of her parents during most of her childhood—they both remarried. She was very mad at her stepmother, couldn't hold back her anger. She said, "My stepmother is an evil woman. I tried to get friendly with her, but she always criticized me." Due to their family circumstances, these young girls had always been self-governing and somewhat rebellious at early age. Their internal needs for understanding and appreciation naturally led them to seek friendship from peers, either in school or in society.

Poor Parent-child Communication

As discussed in the previous section, family conflict and family breakup were reasons that apparently alienated young females from their parents. Interviews with women also revealed that poor communication with parents was widespread—one-third of the women in the study were disturbed by this issue. Women who harbored negative feelings about their relationships with their parents often did not show closeness to their parents either during childhood or later in life. The failure to sustain good communication was largely due to inconsiderate or irresponsible child-rearing practices on the part of the parents, except in cases where the parents were disabled.[5]

Jia, a 39-year-old woman, was adopted by her aunt when she was a little girl. Her character was greatly shaped by her foster parents.[6] She said:

> My childhood was repressed and solitary. My aunt was very strict with me; I couldn't even play jump rope with other kids. I went to the same elementary school where my aunt worked. After school was over I had to wait until her work was done; then I walked home with her. I never had a chance to tell her what I felt in the family. My biological parents always quarreled with each other. They lived in the same courtyard, but I was estranged from them.

Among the women in the study, Min is quite special. My conversation with her was conducted on the same day that she was released from a re-education through labor camp.[7] She had spent a year there, and had gained some weight. Her moon-like face indicated that she was recovering well. Her mother picked her up from the facility and accompanied her to the drop-in center for the interview. Min said that she had always had communication problems with her father:

> Though I was the only child in the family, I was raised by my grandma in a small city in Yunnan. I came back to Kunming when I started elementary school. My mother was fond of me but I wasn't getting along with my father since the beginning. Even if my father likes me, I feel that he would favor a son rather than a daughter. That is why ever since

> I was a little girl I was always eager to do everything well. Right now I still have problems talking to him.

Despite the improving status of women in Chinese society, male figures were, and still are the decision-makers in most families. Influenced by the traditional ideology of childbearing, some of these adult male figures still showed preference toward male children. As will be discussed in the next section, some fathers were more likely to impose physical punishments on their daughters due to their gender identity. Based on Min's own interpretation, her unruly character was certainly attributed to her father's attitudes toward her. As one of the few women in the study who was accepted at a technical secondary school, Min began to date drug-using boyfriend during her study. She was finally expelled because of her own heroin use.

The study suggests that poor parent-child communication have occurred so frequently regardless of the social and economic status of the women's parents. While women from families with economic hardship were likely to be ignored by their parents due to heavy financial burdens, women from wealthy families also complained that their parents were too busy with work to talk to them. In the reform era, modern Chinese families are also experiencing increasing pressure to invest more time in work and to reduce leisure hours at home, which may potentially increase the barriers or misunderstandings between the parents and their children.

Fei, was a 32-year-old, single woman who was accompanied by her boyfriend to the drop-in center for the interview. She had quit using heroin five days prior to our interview. Though she told me she was feeling better day-by-day, she was thin, with a pale complexion. Her voice was weak, but she had a clear mind. Fei said that her babysitters, rather than parents, had assumed parental roles in her family during her school years:

> My mother was a manager in a big company. My father was a mechanic. They were both busy with their jobs and seldom had time to take care of my brothers and me. We had two babysitters at home until I was twenty-six. One babysitter even attended parent's conferences in school on behalf of my parents.

Poor parent-child communication, something that could occur even without the knowledge of the parents, was the most common problem that young females encountered. In the beginning young females felt neglected or ignored by their parents, and they were then reluctant to share their thoughts and feelings with them. Unsurprisingly, such responses would then drive young females to seek emotional support elsewhere. Meanwhile, as several women pointed out during the interviews, their parents were mostly laborers and did not receive much education, which created potential barriers between young girls and their parents. For these reasons, young girls had diminished expectations of being understood by their parents.

Physical Punishment

Chinese people have long believed that how they educate their children is a family affair. Following this traditional line, Chinese authorities do not actively intervene in the area of domestic violence by parents against their children even at the present time, if no significant physical injuries are incurred. Physical punishment imposed by parents is quite a common practice among Chinese families. Eleven women (12 percent) reported frequent incidents of physical punishment by their parents during their childhood and (or) teenage years. These incidents comprise mainly physical abuse together with verbal abuse. No sexual abuses were identified among women subjects in the study, showing a sharp contrast with research findings in the Western literature.[8]

Physical abuse at home was mostly caused by the girls' indifference to their studies, playing truancy, staying out late or smoking. Women were given more physical punishments (mostly) by their fathers than by their mothers: 55 percent by their fathers, 18 percent by mothers and 27 percent by both parents. Women whose parents were laborers were more likely to report physical abuse than those whose parents were professionals, successful businessmen or cadres. Women generally lacked legal knowledge to protect themselves due to Chinese cultural traditions and limited resources available in China.

Ming, a 39-year-old woman, still stayed single. When the interview was conducted, she had just been released from a re-education through labor camp. She did not show much happiness about her release. Rather, she was anxious about her future. She told me that she did not have much interest in her studies—despite what her mother had done with her:

> During my childhood my father worked in Kunming and my mother stayed in the country. I lived with my mother when I started elementary school. She forced me to study, but I didn't have the will to do it. I stayed back in the seventh grade and stayed back in the eighth grade for three years. My mother was very strict. She always whipped me if I didn't study. She never asked what I thought. I had a stubborn and ignorant character and never felt that I was wrong, which led to more beatings.

Another woman named Li, had beautiful almond eyes. Beyond her sweet looks, she was the kind of person who liked to be adventurous. She was one of the girls with persistent delinquent behavior during school years. Her delinquent behavior began as early as elementary school because she had lost interest in her studies. She was often severely punished by her father for these reasons:

> I started smoking in sixth grade. I bought my own cigarettes when I was in middle school. If my father found any cigarettes on me, he beat

> me up. To separate me from my friends in the society, in my second year in middle school, my father sent me to live with a relative in a small town. Nothing changed me. I dated a police officer there and lived with him when I was a senior in high school. After I graduated, I came back to Kunming and still played with my old friends. When I came home late, my father forced me to kneel on the washboard. I thought, I played one day, he beat me once; I played five days, he still beat me once. Why don't I just play a couple of days more?

Whereas Ming and Li were punished by their parents for their disobedience, sometimes women were beaten even for small things or for no justifiable reason. Chun, a 29- yearold woman, explains that her mother treated her very differently from the way she treated her younger sister: always satisfied with her sister, but mad at her. She said, "One time I came back late, my mother whipped me with knitting yarn and my hands were paralyzed for three days." Chun could not control her feelings when she was talking about the unfairness at home. Tears welled up in her eyes.

As shown in the last section, young girls were not always favored by their fathers or grandparents. The old tradition that "a son is better than a girl" is still rooted in some families and influences parents' attitudes toward girls. Several women were abused by their fathers partly because of their gender. Lan was short, with close-cropped hair. Raised in a single-father family, she had a strong and decisive personality. She said:

> I have two brothers and one sister. My father prefers sons more than daughters. My little brother always fought with me. My father beat me even when something was my brother's fault. I have one elder sister. She protected me all the time. For this reason, we always got beaten together, but this rarely happened to my brothers. Very often we girls had to bend our knees on the ground with our brothers standing by and watching.

Bin was 34 years old, born in a Muslim family with one brother and three sisters. Compared to many other women of similar age in the study, she looked older than she actually was. She was the youngest child, but was confronted with enormous frustration at home. She attributed it to her father's character and her sex identity: "My father's work as a porter was so exhausting that he always had a bad temper. He likes boys better than girls. Sometimes a box was suddenly thrown and would hit me on my back."

Physical punishment in women's families had significant life consequences. Violence had failed to change the young girls' behavior as their parents had hoped. Rather, they became even more disobedient than before. For example, Chun moved out from her home right after she graduated from high school; Bin ran away and began living with her boyfriend since the time she was barely sixteen. Consequently, childhood victimization is expected to increase young females' likelihood of using alcohol or drugs later in life (Travis 1995).

Economic Hardship

Parental absence due to parental death was surprisingly high among women. As introduced earlier in this chapter, fifteen women (17 percent) lost at least one of their parents before they were 18 years of age. Except one woman who had lost both parents, the loss of the father appeared frequently in this sample: father (71 percent) vs. mother (29 percent). According to the Yunnan Statistical Yearbook (2005), the mortality rate in Yunnan Province has long been one of the highest in China. Even after a significant decrease in 2004, the mortality in Yunnan still ranked third in the country in 2005.

Among the women who lost one parent to disease or accident, none of the remaining parents were re-married. In contrast, those parents who divorced all remarried sooner or later. One possible explanation might be age differences between parents in these two groups: parents in the divorce group were much younger than those in parental death group. The younger generation generally has a more liberal attitude toward remarriage, and also has more opportunities to find new partners. Economic hardship was prevalent among single parent families due to parental death and parental divorce (prior to the remarriage of parents). Most single-parent families with low incomes, especially those with several children or those who lived in rural areas were confronted with real economic difficulties. Young females had to assume the economic burden of the family; in a few extreme cases, they dropped out of school due to poverty.

Two of the women grew up in single-parent families in rural Yunnan. They endured more economic hardship than those women from single-parent families in Kunming. Tong was one of the three women in the study who claimed to be a lesbian. She had lively round eyes and dressed like a cool boy: one-inch short hair; shirt tucked into casual pants with a cell phone hanging from the belt, sneakers on her feet. She was young but sophisticated. When she was only three, her father passed away. She began to sell things to support her family as early as during her elementary school days. After she finished elementary school, she quit her studies.

Living in even worse conditions than Tong, Ying finally chose to run away from her home in a remote village. Ying wore a short-sleeved, almost translucent shirt that was very revealing. Her hair partially obscured a long, faint scar on her face. She was pleasant and composed. She spoke frankly and told me she truly regretted her decision to leave her family and home town because of all the things happened afterwards. She said:

> I was born in a small village. My parents were peasants. My father died when I was two. My mother planted tobacco and raised pigs to support our three children. When I was fourteen, one day I helped my mom sell

> tobacco at the market, and she only gave me a few cents for my whole day's work. I felt that my feelings were hurt. As a result, I stole 80 yuan ($22) from my mom and headed for Kunming. I thought, if I could only escape from my family, I didn't care if I lived or died.

Economic hardship forced young girls to leave school earlier to help support their families or change their own lives. Limited financial resources in the family often meant that the girls, in particular the eldest daughter, had to bring in income while their brothers could continue their education. Zhen was a 36-year-old woman, wearing a faded white cardigan. She came to the interview with her 4-year-old son, who was dressed up and carried a nice backpack. Zhen regretted the sacrifices she made for her family—giving up her studies after finishing middle school in order to support her family.[9] However, she said that her brother and sisters all look down on her.

Although economic hardship was more likely to occur among families with parental death or divorce, two women, Qing and Wei, whose parents were both deaf mutes, were confronted with extreme difficulties during their childhood.[10] Qing was 40 years old. Her painful childhood experience had made her an independent woman at a very early age. Speaking about her childhood, Qing said:

> When I was one year old, they divorced. Before my mom remarried, we have been living with my grandma and my uncle's family for a long time. My mother had no income, but took care of my uncle's children and did house work. My uncle and his wife looked down on my mother and me. My grandma was nice but could do nothing to help our situation. I didn't even think about continuing my studies. I just wanted to get a job and make money. I was assigned to a factory right after I graduated from middle school at age fifteen.[11]

Facing economic hardship, most of these women and their families chose to work hard to improve their families' financial situation. As an exception, Yun's family acted differently. Yun was a 34-year-old married woman whose hair was dyed light yellow. Her nice clothes and self-confidence indicated her that she was in a very good economic condition. But after Yun's father was arrested for opium trafficking when she was only three, her parents divorced. Her joyful childhood was turned completely upside down. She said, "Due to our economic hardship, my mother made many boyfriends, or, using the common expression, she sold herself, to get money. My mother and my two brothers began stealing things from the factory my mother worked."[12]

As discussed in Chapter 1, while China's economic reform has created enormous opportunities for people to become rich or improve their economic conditions, families without good education or social resources are not able to make significant changes in their lives. In urban areas, the number of people living in poverty has greatly increased since the economic reform.[13] Young females have abandoned their studies and, have instead looked for jobs, which has caused them to be immersed into street culture and the adult world by an early age—resulting in significant negative effects on their lives.

Spoiled Daughters

In contrast to women with economic hardship, twenty-eight women (31 percent) said that they were spoiled by at least one of their parents. The study found that women's birth sequence within a family was a significant factor affecting their parents' child-rearing practices. Except for two women from wealthy families, the remaining twenty-six women were either the only child, or the youngest child in the family. Indeed, over half the women in the study were either the only child (11 percent) or the youngest child (47 percent) in the family—the ones who are often overindulged by their parents. This indicates that, even in large families, girls who were the youngest were in a better position to gain affection from their parents. None of these women were from a divorced or single-parent family. This further suggests that family stability is also a significant factor in parents' child-rearing practices.

While wealthy families and (or) families with a secure social position are more likely to offer strong financial support and opportunities to their daughters, other families may exhaust their resources to satisfy their daughters' needs and spoil their child emotionally. Regardless of family background, the data reveals that the most distinguishing characteristic of these spoiled daughters is their self-centeredness. They were more likely than others to act in a self-serving manner.

Qiong was a pretty and graceful 28-year-old woman from a wealthy family. Her family owned a large company, and she was the only woman in the study who had served in the military. When she was in school, she made all kinds of friends, both in and outside of school. She told me:

> I have one brother. Our parents have doted on us all the time. Since my father started his business very early, my family has been very wealthy. When I was little, I got 2 yuan (about $5) as allowance every day. My father always went away on business trips and would return every week or so. My parents were so busy that they never cared about the friends I made. My friends ate, slept and played at my home. Most of these friends were street wanderers and had their own reasons to stay with me.

Besides giving money, families with good social positions were likely to provide their daughters with other opportunities. Dan was short and had cropped hair. She was married and had a 6-year-old son. As the youngest child at home, she was spoiled by her parents, but was completely out their control. Unlike other girls who rarely found stable work, Dan did not appreciate what her parents did for her. She said:

> My father was a cadre in the government, and my mother was a manual worker. As the youngest child in the family, my parents have doted on me. My brother has a master's degree and still wants a doctorate. I didn't have much interest in school. Whatever my parents said, I couldn't study well. After I graduated from middle school, my parents arranged a job for me in a factory. I did not like the job because it did not pay well. I worked there for a few years, and then I resigned and opened a hair salon with my friend.

Similar to Dan, Bin was also the youngest child in her family. Her father served in the military and her mother was a teacher. Bin had an angular face painted with thick white powder, which made her bright red lipstick more startling. She wore a chemise that exposed her arms covered all over with prominent scars. Though it was summer, she wore leather pants and boots. Her voice was extremely coarse due to heroin use (snorting). She told me that her parents had always satisfied her needs, but she never took her parents' words seriously. She said, "Since I graduated from middle school, I have played with my friends and done nothing for about eight years. When I was twenty-four, my parents opened a shoe store for me. But I did it for fun."

Fan was a graceful 32-year-old woman. Her long hair curved loosely over her shoulder. She said she had been a beauty in school, but heroin had taken away her looks. Fan's father owns a big family enterprise. Although she was not close to her mother, she was spoiled by both her father and grandmother (from her father's side) who had absolute authority in the family. When her father began to spend less time with her, she became very irritated. She said "I missed the college entrance exam because I wanted to make my father angry and disgraced him on purpose." After she graduated from high school, she moved out to live with her friends.

Unlike women from families with apparent problems, spoiled girls were not motivated to study hard or work hard because they could always depend on their parents. Typically, they developed strong, self-centered, arrogant and emulative personalities—these characteristics eventually increased the young girls' chances of challenging tradition—rebelling against their families. Most importantly, as suggested by Nagin and Paternoster (1994), such characters will potentially weaken the conventional attachments and commitments that would have deterred them from deviance and crime.

LIFE IN SCHOOL

As discussed in the previous chapter, among women heroin users in this study, slightly more than half only attended elementary school or middle school. Among the seven women in the study who only attended elementary school (including three drop-outs), two younger women are from rural areas, while the five women from Kunming were much older (between 39 and 49 years of age). This implies that the women from Kunming with the lowest education were concentrated in the older age group.

Most of the women in the study, when young, lacked purpose and commitment to their studies. Though no delinquent acts are identified during the school years, the rate of early delinquent behaviors is significant. Ten women (11 percent) dropped out from school at different levels, but only two of them quit their studies on account of heroin use. Eighteen women (20 percent) reported that they were either occasionally or regularly truant while enrolled in school. Smoking is highly prevalent among women in the study. While 48 women (53 percent) reported that they started smoking prior to age 18, half of them were occasional or regular smokers while they were students. Drinking was also practiced by some young girls during their school years, but only occurred in gatherings or parties. A heavy drinking habit was likely to occur in the case of the few women who had a family history of alcohol abuse. Among women in the study, ten women, including two school drop-outs, tried heroin while they were still students at school.

During the interviews, women mostly said that they were not highly motivated to study, and did not perform well in school. The combination of lack of interest and poor performance together became the major factor driving many of them to discontinue their studies after middle school.[14] Only a few women were forced to quit school due to their family's economic hardship. Women's attitudes toward studies, and their performance in school were strongly influenced by family, school related factors and women's individual capabilities as well.[15]

Ju, whose parents were alcoholics, began to drink while she was in third grade. She became a cigarette user when she was in middle school. She was also good at playing mahjong and spending money.[16] With pre-existing family problems, finally it was school that provided young girls opportunities to meet more troublemakers. Xiaoling, a 30-year-old girl with large black eyes, was adventurous and a natural leader. Her experience illustrates how a young female got involved in truancy, smoking, drinking and early dating during her school years. She relates:

> When I was seven, my parents divorced. I stayed with my mother, and my father left for his hometown in a different province. As the only child in the family, I wanted to be the best in everything. I'm always a leader. My family was wealthy at that time. I had money in my pocket every day. I shared all my money with my friends in school. After they used my money, they had to listen to me. If I said "Let's skip school," almost all the boys in the class would follow me. If I said, "Let's drink beer," almost everyone drank until drunk; if I said, "I don't love you,"

> I mean that I do not care whether you commit suicide or not. You're screwed.

Lin was short with shoulder-length wavy hair. In contrast to her petite figure, Lin was also a tough girl with street smarts. Like Xiaoling, Lin, is also the only child in her family. Her father was an official working for the local government and her mother was a worker. Because of frequent quarrels and fights between her parents, Lin hated staying at home and grew increasingly rebellious, which directly reflected on her performance in school. Lin told me about her school days:

> My mother worked in a cigarette factory, and there were always cigarettes at home. I started to smoke back in elementary school. Sometimes I even smoked in class. I began to skip school in the elementary years. I began to drink when I was in middle school. I often got drunk. I liked hanging out, singing and dancing with my classmates.

While Lin's early undisciplined behavior in school originated from her resistance to her family, her continuing engagement in these activities caused more troubles for her school life:

> When I was in middle school, I was put in a class for those who didn't like to study–several students used drugs. There were only seven girls in the class. The teachers thought we were all garbage and didn't care how we played with each other in the class so long as the police weren't called to the school. I abandoned myself to despair. I did whatever I wanted to do. I had a lot of boyfriends. I switched from one boyfriend to another very quickly.

With the economic reform, the higher education system was resumed in China in 1978. Before the extension for higher education in 1997, however, only very limited number of high school graduates were able to continue their higher education. Due to high competition, a tracking system (school tracking and class tracking) was widely adopted in the country, which resulted in students falling behind in elementary school being grouped with incompetent students. Although family factors played a very important role in motivating and encouraging women in their studies, the quality of school education had direct impacts on students' performance.

Yu was 28 years old. She dressed in a low-cut, short-sleeved blouse with her plumpish curves exposed. She was an honest and open-minded girl. Yu was one of the few who expressed a strong desire to study, but felt frustrated by the chaos in school. She said:

> My parents were both laborers. My mother's work was to make concrete blocks —It was very hard work. I really wanted to be a good stu-

> dent for them. Unfortunately, almost nobody in my class liked to study. Our classes were in chaos. Sitting in the classroom was like being in a disorderly meeting–everyone was talking. I was in the last row of the classroom and could barely hear what the teacher said. Several female students were using heroin by that time. Eventually I gave up my efforts and joined them.

Yu described the disorderly students she went to school with, but relationships with teachers also affected the paths of several women. Yi was an eye-catching girl wherever she went. She was tall and thin, like a fashion model. When I met her, she was wearing a green chemise and short skirt with a black, dressy hat. Although Yi was only 30 years old, she already had a sixteen-year history of heroin use. Yi began to use heroin when she was only fourteen—the youngest of all the women in the study. Nobody could tell that she was a cancer survivor who suffered from oophoroma.[17] Yi told me that because she did not get along with her home-room teacher, she had gradually lost interest in school. Once she graduated from middle school, she decided to discontinue her studies.

Besides family and school related factors, the study found that women's perceptions about themselves also played a role in how they performed in school. As several women proudly announced during the interviews, "Most of the women who used heroin were charming girls who were at the top of fashion." Tian, a 30-year-old woman, was an athletic-looking woman who once was a champion in a provincial swimming competition. She had tattoos on her upper arms. On her left arm, there were two long scars which resulted from street fighting during her school years. Tian had no desire to study and was always involved in fights while in middle school. Tian explained her reasons, "At the time I was young and pretty, and very self-confident about my beauty. I felt that girls like me needed only a couple of words to survive in society." Towards the end of my interview with her, she expressed her desire of marrying a rich man and changing her life.

Increasing consciousness of being beautiful in their teen years had not only made the young girls give up their efforts to study, but had also driven them to indulge in social life with young boys and men at an overly early age. Yuan was a 30-year-old woman with large liquid eyes, and pleasing curves. She was still a glamour girl. Regrettably, she told me that she was an HIV carrier. She said:

> I made some bad friends and always stayed out when I was in middle school. I thought I was prettier than other girls and had better grades in school. The more boys asked me out, the more my vanity was satisfied. I began dating schoolmates and going to dancing halls in the last year of middle school. Soon I started making friends outside of school and dropped out of middle school.

Early dating was also frequently reported by other women. Among women in the study, thirteen of them (14 percent) began dating while they were students. With a high frequency of early dating, three females began to live with their boyfriends while they were in middle school or high school. Li dated a police officer and cohabitated with him for half a year when she was a senior in high school. She explained that her intimate relationship with the man was for fun and out of curiosity. Under similar circumstances, Ju, a 33-year-old woman, got pregnant when she was a senior in high school. She delivered the baby before she reached the legal age to marry. Wei was 28 years old—the only one in the study who attended college, although she quit in her third year. At the time of the interview, she was still a dance partner in an upscale nightclub. Wei revealed a different reason for cohabitating with a man while she was still in middle school. She wanted the money:

> My parents are both deaf and mute. My father is a butcher. My brother assisted him. My father likes gambling. After he lost all his money, my brother also lost his job. My brother then began to use heroin. To support my family, I began working in the dance halls while in middle school. I met a man there. He was married and more than twenty years older than me. He had a respectable job and a good income. I began living with him since I was a senior in middle school. While living with him, I didn't have to worry about money.

Eventually, problems in school, whether in academic performance or in personal relations, were major factors that drove young girls out of their student lives to immerse themselves in society at an early age.

Although problematic issues were observed in school life, family influences were also heavily involved in turning the women away from normal pathways. Being in single parent families, being neglected by parents or not having good communication with them were major issues in this regard. When these young girls grew up, therefore, peer influence began to play an important role in their lives, together with the increased influence from their intimate relationships, particularly in the case of those girls who engaged in early dating.

POST-SCHOOL LIFE

Regardless of factors that affected women's efforts in studies, women's performance in school finally determined whether they had further opportunities to continue their education. The lack of commitment to their studies and increasing negative peer influences, led many of these young girls to leave the formal educational system. Leaving school is a significant event in the life of a youth, in that it not only increases risk-taking in those with pre-existing risk-taking behavior, but also reduces their future employment options (Sullivan, 1989).[18] After these young girls left school, those who had status offense behavior intensified that behavior. Even for those women who did not display such behavior, their risk in associating with delinquent kids and deviant adults significantly increased.

With the economic reform, young women in China have received increased opportunities to work in wide-ranging areas in society. Nevertheless, young girls who do not have a high level of education are still not in a good position to find a well-paid job, unless they can take advantage of their parents' financial resources or social connections. Restricted by their education level, women's early occupations were highly concentrated in the service or manufacturing industries with only a few exceptions.[19]As a common theme, women in the study changed jobs frequently due to the nature of their unrewarding jobs, which demanded hard work for low wages.

Post-school life was a turning point for these young females. After leaving school, many of them began to associate with people in society, especially young males, who had much influence on their anti-social behavior than friends of the same gender (Warr 1996). Women's education and their limited occupational opportunities predetermined that the people they connected with came from similar backgrounds. With expanding social networks, non-smokers quickly developed smoking habits, occasional smokers became regular users. Prior to heroin use, sixty-four women (72 percent) had smoked either regularly or occasionally. The number of women who drank also increased, though they still reported drinking mostly in a group setting rather than as a personal habit. Thus, smoking was quite prevalent among women heroin users in their post-school lives, but habitual drinking was not.[20]

Another significant factor in the post-school life of these young females concerns the issue of dating. The early dating rate among women in the samples was high: twenty-two women (24 percent) dated men before the age of 18; nine of them started their relationships with men soon after leaving middle school. Before initiating heroin use, twenty-six women (29 percent) had left home and typically lived with their boyfriends.[21] Only two women dated men with college degrees; all other women dated men having similar occupations as their own, such as small business owners, manual workers or people without stable jobs. Unfortunately, several women dated street wanderers.[22]

Fen was a 34-year-old woman, whom I could barely associate with heroin use. She always looked placid and was modest in her dress and behavior whenever I met her in the drop-in center. She had a very graceful manner of smoking and liked playing mahjong with other people in the entertainment room. Unfortunately, she was partially deaf due to her heroin use. I had to speak loudly so that she could hear me. Fen was one of the few women in the study who was always a "three good" student in school.[23] Her life began to change after she dated a street wanderer. He was violent towards her, but she was unable to get rid of him. She was sobbing when she mentioned her father who had passed away a few days before the interview. She regretted what she had done to her family, even though her father beat her severely for her disobedient behavior. Fen said:

> After my boyfriend's parents divorced, he became a street hustler. He always used bad language, and got in fights. He wasn't even nice to me. He told me to obey him and threatened to beat me up if I left him. We were always hanging out in karaoke clubs, or dancing with his friends. Even after my father whipped me with a belt, I still went back to him and his friends.

The violent threats from Fen's boyfriend were the primary reasons for her remaining connected to him for several years. Some other women, however, just completely lost themselves while dating men. Ni was an elegant, 33-year-old woman whose looks were astonishing even after sixteen years on heroin. In contrast to her charming and peaceful appearance, her stubborn love for her first boyfriend—a street hustler—greatly changed her life:

> I was so spoiled by my parents. I never learned to cook until now. I started making friends outside of school when I was thirteen. I liked the feeling of being cared for (by my man). I went to a secondary professional school and was assigned to a big local hospital. I gave up my job as a nurse because I didn't care about other things while dating with my boyfriend. I just liked being with him. Until he was arrested for larceny and sentenced, I separated from him.

As mentioned earlier, Wei cohabited with a married man while she was a middle school student. Three other females dated married businessmen after they left school. Having relationships with married men was vehemently condemned in the early era of the economic reform; women involved in such affairs were referred to as "*the third party*," nowadays termed "*Xiaosan*." However, when it became a general social phenomenon, and quite widespread in society, many young women considered this an accepted path toward a better material life.

Song, a 38 year old woman, looked emotionally depressed when I met her for the first time—she had just been released from the compulsory drug rehabilitation center that very week. Song had straight cut hair, always wore sneakers and clothes that were not colorful. Though she admitted that her sexual orientation had changed (she was now a lesbian), because of the dreadful economic conditions prevalent throughout her childhood in a single-parent family, as a young woman she had dated wealthy businessmen in order to live a life of luxury. Song told me that when she was nineteen, for more than half a year, she had dated her boss, the owner of the store where she worked. Soon after, she lived with a wealthy man from another province who was doing business in Kunming. Not only did he rent a house, employ a house-maid, and pay for Song's routine expenses, but he also gave her an allowance every month.

In sum, women's lives prior to heroin use played an important role in their initiation into heroin use. Women's experience with family and school profoundly impacted their lives not only during school years but also during their post-school lives. Problematic issues with family and school were the major reasons that drove some of these young girls' to associate with delinquent peers in school and in society. Most importantly, women's early delinquent behavior, in all likelihood, led some of them to deviant and criminal behaviors further down the road.

DEVIANT AND CRIMINAL BEHAVIOR

As discussed in the previous section, a large portion of women in the study engaged in smoking, drinking and early dating both in school and right after leaving it. However, only sixteen women (18 percent) had displayed serious deviant or criminal behavior prior to their heroin use. Two of them came from a family with parental deviant behavior.[24] In most cases, the women themselves either displayed disruptive behavior during their school years, or had male partners who were involved in illegal activity. While the illegal activities the women were involved in include commercial sex service, gambling, selling drugs, harboring drug dealers and using violence, engaging in the sex trade was very typical practice.

Commercial Sex Service

After liberation, the central government began a campaign to eliminate the sex industry, and eventually closed it down in 1957 (He 2002). As overseas/foreign investments moved into the eastern coastal areas (mainly Guangdong) in the early 1980s, the sex industry reemerged with flourishing nightclubs, karaoke bars, dancing clubs and beauty salons. Overseas businessmen were the initial customers of sex businesses. With a quickly expanding sex industry throughout the country, males from all social sectors in China have been involved as customers in prostitution (Jeffreys 2004). The booming sex industry in China gave great temptation to young girls who wanted to make quick money and had no legitimate means of doing so. Lack of caring from their families was also a contributing factor.[25] The characteristics of prostitutes have changed quickly, too. Female sex workers come from both rural and urban areas; they can have little or no education or college degrees (He 2002).

Among women in the study, a significant number engaged in commercial sex services after they initiated heroin use, while only eight of them (9 percent) were involved in commercial sex prior to heroin use. Among these women, while one woman who worked as a *mami* (female pimp) was married, all others were single women. Though all these women provided sex services to their clients, they preferred to call themselves *zuotai hostesses*—a term with similar meanings as *sanpei xiaojie* ("Miss three-accompanies") [26] In China, the term *zuotai hostess* or *sanpei xiaojie* is used to refer to women who provide escort services in entertainment venues, but who do not necessarily have intercourse with men. However, people understand that the term *zuotai hostess* is actually a substitute for the term prostitute, because these women mostly offer all sexual services once they are indeed at the venue.

Of these seven women, two came from rural areas of Yunnan. Poor living conditions in their hometowns motivated them to move to Kunming. Their new city life gave them a quickly expanding network of acquaintances from diverse backgrounds; the dramatic difference in income between conventional jobs available to them and money earned illegally finally attracted them to sex work. Naturally, the habit of hard work they had learned from their rural lives gradually gave away to the lure of what they were told was easy money. The two women Ying and Shan struggled with themselves for a short period of time before finally deciding to join the commercial sex industry. Ying said:

> When I came to Kunming, I knew nobody. I began to work in a small restaurant making meat buns. My salary was only 100–200 yuan ($25–$50) a month. Soon I met a girl from my hometown. She had dated several boyfriends by that time (She died of heroin later). One time, a man who was a friend of hers invited me out. I firmly said no. She then asked me, "Do you want to stay poor forever?" I struggled with my conscience, and finally decided to go out with her: she taught me all the skills needed to being a *hostess,* including dancing and flattering the men.

Similar to Ying, Shan was also from a rural part of Yunnan. She had dark skin and looked stronger than other women. Her father was a schoolteacher and her mother worked as a laborer in the fields. Although she had a good relationship with her parents, she said that her life in the countryside was kind of boring and she could not map of her future. While she was lucky to find a boyfriend who worked as a police officer in Kunming, she could not resist the temptation of making money. She said:

> Working in a small dress store, I was only earning about 150 yuan ($18) a month. The girlfriend of my boyfriend's friend told me how to make more money. She was working in a nightclub behind her boyfriend's back. While I really worried about what would happen if my family or my boyfriend knew the truth, after tussling with myself for several days, I decided to follow her example. Shortly after, I could earn 3,000–4,000 yuan ($360–480) per month. Sometimes it was possible to make 7,000 yuan ($840).

For Ying and Shan, participation in the sex trade not only brought them fast money, but also a new lifestyle—one that involved smoking, drinking and troublesome social values they never experienced before. Yuan also worked in a nightclub as a hostess after she dropped out of middle school. She said "I earned 1,000 yuan ($173) a day for about two years. I couldn't spend all the money. Many *hostesses* working in the dance hall were taking heroin. One day I bought heroin from them out of curiosity." Yuan's experience further illustrates how life in the sex industry drove women to the heroin—prone subculture—associating with heroin-prone peers and having quick money.

Different from the above young girls, Liqun was the only married woman in the group. She was a 35 year old woman with long hair dyed a dark brown. Although the mother of a ten year old girl, she still looked young and pretty. She once worked as a *mami* (female pimp) in a nightclub after she had separated from her husband who went out boozing, singing and playing mahjong almost every day. Her job was to assign hostesses to different clients, and she took a percentage of the service fees. She confirmed that among the hostesses, many were heroin users. Working with hostesses, she could not reject their invitations to use heroin with them.

As discussed in Chapter 1, the flourishing of China's sex industry was a by-product of China's social and economic reform. Women's involvement in the sex industry resulted from their desire to be in hot pursuit of economic gains when legitimate opportunities were blocked off. In order to pursue better material lives, women set aside the potential risks of being exposed to the deviant subcultures associated with the commercial sex industry. The prevalence of heroin use among women hostesses, and drug dealing in entertainment venues (based on women's accounts) have changed their perceptions about heroin and provided them with easy access to the drugs.

Drug Related Crimes

According to the Criminal Law of P. R. China, drug dealing is strictly prohibited; criminal responsibility for heroin dealing or trafficking is determined by the quantity of drugs involved; the death penalty might be imposed on whoever sells or traffics more than 50 grams of heroin.[27] Regardless of the harsh punishment, some women get involved in drug dealing after they begin using heroin. But only one woman—Yun—was selling heroin prior to her own heroin use. Her participation in selling the drug was largely related to her father's business in illicit drugs.

As shown in an earlier section, Yun grew up in a single-parent family during most of her childhood. After her father was released from prison for drug trafficking, a new avenue was open to her, a 14-year-old girl. She said:

> My father opened a small grocery store, but he still ran the drug selling business. I thought, I had a father with money —I didn't need to study any more. My father might think we three children didn't have money

> so he gave us heroin to sell. I often danced with boys, and changed my male dancing partners quite often. While dancing with boys, I had lots of fun and heroin was easily sold out. At that time, people were simple and pure, unlike in present times, men always wanted straight sex. By the time I was able to do this business without much difficulty.

Yun was arrested by the police several times, but was always released because of her father's position as a government informant. On one occasion, she had more than ten grams of heroin on her when she was arrested. While she awaited prosecution, her father rescued her by selling a big dealer's name to the police. She was soon released without any charges at all. Yun's initial purpose was to obtain money by selling heroin. But almost inevitably, dealing in the drug finally led her to using the drug. Yun sadly said that she had lost contact with her father for several years, and did not even know whether he was still alive. Her tone revealed respect, rather than hatred, for her father.

According to the Criminal Law of P. R. China, harboring drug traffickers is subject to criminal sanction.[28] Among women in the study, two women, Lin and Kaili once harbored drug traffickers who had trafficked large amounts of heroin in Kunming. Consequently, Kaili and Lin both became addicted due to the harboring of drug traffickers. Both Lin and Kaili's connections with drug traffickers were through their male partners. Lin's husband was sentenced to a juvenile detention center for larceny, where he met a big drug trafficker. Upon their release, Lin's husband allowed the drug trafficker to stay in his home trafficking drugs. Kaili's boyfriend (current husband) had no criminal history at all. Kaili told me that the friend of her boyfriend, a drug trafficker, was from Xiaguan, a small town belonging to Dali—one of the most important heroin distribution sites in Yunnan Province. She said:

> My boyfriend and I opened a small restaurant and lived together in 1989. His friend (we both knew him) from Xiaguan trafficked heroin to Kunming. He was a big trafficker and never sold less than 100 grams at a time. He stayed with us for over three months. During his stay, he showed us how to mix heroin with tobacco, and smoke it. When he left, my boyfriend and I were both addicted. He promised to come back, but he never did.[29]

Both Kaili and Lin were aware that these friends were trafficking over 100 grams of heroin, but they and their partners opened their homes to the traffickers and allowed them to keep drugs there for months. When Kaili and Lin talked about their experience with me, neither one said that they were hesitant to harbor drug traffickers. Regardless of their differing backgrounds—Kaili was a hard-working woman, but Lin had been delinquent since the time she was in school —neither considered what they had done as a serious crime. And with heroin available at home, it was almost irresistible for them.

Violent Behavior

Among women in the study, only three had been involved in serious violent behavior prior to heroin use. As a matter of fact, the women were all involved in weapon use. Consequently, Ru and Yan had seriously injured their victims. Among the three women, Tian and Ru had persistently displayed violent tendencies during their later teen years. As Tian said, "I wasn't afraid of picking fights on the street. When I saw people with knives, I would confront them rather than run away. I was overly confident but sometimes ended up in the hospital." Similar to Tian, Ru was a very irritable person at that time and always carried knives or other sharp things with her.

Ru, a 37-year-old woman, was short and small with no make-up, and wearing a typical housewife's dress. I could not believe that the woman sitting in front of me was once charged with voluntary manslaughter. As the youngest child and suffering from septicemia, Ru was spoiled by her family during her childhood. However, her violent behavior eventually changed her life. Ru related:

> I acted like a boy until I reached 18. After I graduated from middle school, I was on the job-waiting team of my parents' work unit[30]. One time I had an argument with a workmate in my team. I stabbed him five times in his stomach (and also in other places). In the stomach alone, he needed eighteen stitches. I was charged with intentional homicide and was sent to the juvenile detention center for three years because of my age.

For Ru, serving time in the juvenile detention center was a major turning point in her life. She made many friends when she was there and learned bad habits from these friends. Many of the friends she made in the juvenile detention center became her business friends later on. With them, she was also on her way to heroin. Unlike Tian and Ru, Yan did not have any violent behavior prior to an incident in which she stabbed her ex-boyfriend. Yan wore red trousers that looked dirty on the edges. Because Yan was still taking heroin irregularly, her face was yellow and her hair was dry and messy. Her little boy, a 3-year-old boy, came with her. He was cute, but had temper tantrums. Her ex-boyfriend was a manual worker who always used violence. On one occasion, when he hit Yan's head against the wall, Yan picked up a knife and stabbed his leg. Unfortunately, the artery on the leg was hit and injured. Yan's initiation into heroin use was related to this incident:

> While he was hospitalized, one of his friends came to visit. He told us that heroin can stop pain and gave some to him for free. I didn't stop

> my boyfriend from doing this because it was my entire fault. After he took the heroin, his pain disappeared. It was a miracle, just like an elixir. After watching him using heroin for nearly two months, I had increased curiosity and followed him.

Gambling

Mahjong which is played as a group entertainment activity, originated in China. Since mahjong was often played as a gambling game, it was banned after 1949. With the economic reform, playing mahjong regained popularity in China. People liked playing mahjong for both its entertainment and its gambling aspect. People usually bet only small amounts of money, which is quite normal in China. However, based on the current administrative law, playing mahjong that involved large amounts of money was subject to administrative sanction.[31] Among the women in the study, many liked to play mahjong. However, Xue, a 36-year-old, was the only woman who started gambling by playing mahjong prior to heroin use. She then got heavily involved in a new fashion in gambling —baccarat —operated by the underworld. Her gambling habit smashed a would-be marriage. She told me:

> I liked playing mahjong. Every day after my boyfriend went to work, I would join my friends. He worked for a transportation company and had a very good income. He gave me all his salary and only kept his bonus. Almost every day I had some 2,000 yuan ($240) to spend. Later, a club opened for baccarat. I lost over 200,000 yuan ($24,000) there. My boyfriend gave me another 50,000 yuan ($6,000) to open a stock account, but I spent the money gambling. Eventually I couldn't get back all that I had lost and had to separate from him because of objections from his family.

After separation from her boyfriend, Xue began to date a man who shared her love of gambling and liked hanging out with people in society. With her new boyfriend, Xue began to meet a new crowd of people—several of them were heroin users. It is clear that if she had not been involved in gambling, she would have formed a family with her boyfriend who had a legitimate job and good income. However, her overindulgence in gambling had totally changed her life.

In sum, women's serious deviant or criminal behavior was mostly gender related or drug related; women's involvement in violent crime was extremely low, and none of the women were involved in property-related crime. Additionally, and in contrast with Western studies, this sample of women revealed a low overall rate of participation in deviant or criminal subcultures prior to heroin use.

CONCLUSION

A review of women's lives from their childhood to post-school indicates the importance of family and school, in either aggravating or mitigating women's delinquent and other anti-social behavior. In particular, women's families acted as the primary social instrument that exerted an influential impact on women's lives both at home and in school, especially from childhood to early adolescence. Although not all women grew up in a family with apparent problems, women who were neglected, rejected or physically abused at home were more likely to show early anti-social behavior.

Family, as a link between the macro social forces and the micro world of children, its structures and processes, is interwoven with significant social changes (Elder 1994, 11). In the reform era, Chinese families as a whole have undergone significant changes in several areas: First, with increasing divorce rates, the number of broken families has been rising dramatically in Chinese society: more young girls are living in a single-parent family or in households without the presence of parents. Second, with rising urban poverty, families with poor economic outlook have increased in numbers in urban areas, which has limited young girls' opportunities for further development. Third, under the growing economic pressure, parents have to spend more time on their work and less time on childcare and support. Lastly, within a fast-changing society, youth are more hospitable to new ideas while their parents are more likely to resist these changes. These emerging issues in Chinese families are no doubt creating new problems and challenging many Chinese families more than ever. To a certain degree, this study reveals that the experience of women heroin users within their families is typical of that of many other women in the country.

Because illicit drug use is an emerging social issue in China, almost all women in the study were only the first generation of heroin users in their families. Due to this reason, the intergenerational transmission of conduct norms of illicit drug use witnessed in many inner cities of the United States (Dunlap et al. 2002), was almost exclusively absent among women in the samples. Meanwhile, childhood victimization, as highlighted by drug-use studies in the United States, was only partially supported by the current study—involving physical and verbal abuse. Sexual abuse was not observed in this study. The social and cultural differences between the two countries might be the possible reason for these divergences.

The second theme that emerged from the data was the experiences the women had in school. Most of the women were underachievers. Only a few of them had a good academic record. Most young girls were not strongly motivated to study, due to a lack of sufficient family and school support. Failure to pursue further education beyond the nine compulsory years was also triggered by vicious competition at the college entrance exam—only a very limited number of students could gain opportunities for higher education. The less competent students, like women in the study, feel that time invested in studies was not well rewarded. Therefore, many of them became more realistic about their lives—discontinuing high school study and getting a job.

While hanging out with peers, usually classmates to begin with, these young girls developed an extended social network, particularly with young adults in society. They were exposed to adolescent deviant behavior, such as smoking, drinking, early dating, cohabitating with men, and pregnancy. Indeed, since the 1980s, an increase in juvenile delinquency has been witnessed throughout the country (Bakken 1993). Peers of these young girls acted as instigators into deviant behavior, especially when families failed to function as potential barriers (Warr 2002). Because many of these women were involved in intimate relationships with men by an early age, both peers and their intimate relationships had considerable impact on their maturity during late adolescence or early adulthood. Only a very small portion of women engaged in serious deviant/criminal behavior prior to heroin use, and women's socialization with peers and the influence of their families and male partners assumed substantial importance.

In conclusion, women's immersion into the world of heroin did not occur overnight. In the changing social context of Chinese society, women's family, school and peer relations all play important roles. Consequently, family-related problems were more likely to weaken the bonds between these young girls and their parents, disrupt their academic achievements and therefore increase their susceptibility to peer pressure. The prevalence of deviant behavior among women in the study had prepared them with both social norms and opportunities to participate in the heroin-prone subculture.

4 Initiation into Heroin

In addiction studies, scholars who study drug use by adolescents, or drug use in the general population, often take the social learning approach to understand drug initiation (Akers 1991), viewing "set" and "setting" as important variables for this learning process (Zinberg 1984). Studies of male drug users have consistently documented that male drug users experimented with drugs for sensation seeking or due to peer pressure. Differing from mainstream research, two themes emerge from the studies concerning the causes of women's initiation into illicit drug use: victimization and women's social relations.

Studies on women's initiation into drug use have consistently proposed victimization of women as a defining attributor, which differentiates women's experience from that of men (Inciardi et al. 1993; Kassebaum 1999; Sommers, Basin, and Fagan 2000; Bloom et al. 2003). The immediate consequences of childhood abuse may involve physical or psychological trauma. The history of trauma not only impairs women's normal development in childhood, but also extends these negative experiences to adulthood. Victimization of women both during childhood and adulthood, including physical, emotional and sexual abuse, is linked to illicit drug use. Illicit drug use by women, however, was largely interpreted as a way of self-medication—coping with trauma and resisting victimization (Chesney-Lind and Rodriguez 1983; Miller 1986; Inciardi et al. 1993; Bloom et al. 2003; Chen et al. 2004). However, these studies did not intend to explain why women were much more likely to choose illicit drugs when there were, in fact, other options available to manage personal trauma. In addition, the extent of victimization among women drug users varies with studies, suggesting that not all women drug users came to illicit drugs with a victimization history. A reasonable question raised here is: what would be possible reasons for women who do not have victimization history to initiate drug use?

The relational theory proposed by Miller (1976) has also been applied to studies of woman's addiction. Studies based on relational theories gave weight to relationships in women's lives, and viewed drug use by women as a direct result of passive responses to life events. Deriving from the relational theory, two important social relationships were viewed as leading women into illicit drug use: family relationships and intimate relationships with men. Although both men and women are affected by family members' drug use, addicted women were more likely to report family members' drug use than their male counterparts (Greenleaf, 1989; Bourgois and Dunlap, 1993; Inciardi et al., 1993; Chesney-Lind and Laidler, 1997). In particular, the influences of intimate relationships in regard to drug use by women appear in two ways: attempting to keep an intimate relationship (Richie 1995) or facing the failure of a relationship (Pohl and Boyd 1991; Bloom et al. 2003). These arguments have been challenged by several accounts. Some scholars in particular suggest that a woman's initiation into illicit drug use need to be understood within a much broader social context, one of multiple relationships, because women are actively engaged in a variety of social activities just as men are (Rosenbaum 1981; Maher 1995; Hamid 1998; Sterk 1999).

The current study, being exploratory in nature, examines factors considered by both these approaches to explore women's initiation into heroin use in China. While the previous chapter discussed the lives of women heroin users prior to drug use, the present chapter seeks to examine the process of women's initiation into heroin use, in particular the social and personal factors that contribute to it, and to identify patterns of initiation among the samples.

POPULARITY OF HEROIN IN KUNMING

As indicated in Chapter 1, heroin use in China in the reform era originated in Yunnan Province, with Kunming, the capital city, a major witness to early heroin use. Because the new drug epidemic in China began with heroin, the majority of women in the study did not have a transition from other illicit drugs to heroin. Rather, they began their drug-use career directly with the hardest drug—heroin. Only eight women used opium prior to heroin use; three others who began using heroin after 1990 had prior experience with other illicit drugs.[1] As discussed in Chapter 3, most of the women in the study were either regular or occasional smokers; alcohol abuse was atypical among them, while a small portion had never smoked before they used heroin. This pattern shows both similarities and differences with studies of heroin users in the Western countries—heroin users invariably took "gateway drug" before beginning heroin (Inciardi, McBride and Surratt 1998; Kandel and Yamaguchi, 2002).[2]

The data indicates that women's recruitment into heroin use was directly related to the popularity of heroin in the area, in particular, from the late 1980s to the early 1990s when there was increasing heroin trafficking in Yunnan. Table 4.1 shows women's initiation into heroin use year-by-year. Among ninety women heroin users in this study, initial heroin use was recorded as early as 1986, but two of the women used heroin at Ruili, a border city in Yunnan near Muse, Myanmar—a major drug producing area. Beginning in 1988, the number of women who reported using heroin witnessed a quick increase over the following three consecutive years. The number of women heroin users who initiated heroin during this period comprised nearly half of the total samples—significantly higher than at any other time period. Overall, nearly 60 percent of women began to use heroin before 1992. After 2000, the number of women who initiated heroin use decreased sharply. These findings suggest that the period from the late 1980s to the early 1990s was a critical stage for women's heroin use among the study samples, one marked by a rapid increase in size. It also suggests that many women in the study used heroin at a very early stage of the epidemic. It is important, therefore, to examine how and why heroin became such a popular drug at this time among these pioneers.

To answer these questions, the tripartite model—drug, set and setting—proposed by Zinberg (1984) is a valuable instrument in identifying patterns

Table 4.1 Women's Initiation into Heroin Use by Year (N=90)

Year of Initiation	Frequency	Percent	Cumulative Percent
1986	3	3.3	3.3
1987	1	1.1	4.4
1988	9	10	14.4
1989	18	20	34.4
1990	10	11.1	45.6
1991	4	4.4	50.0
1992	8	8.9	58.9
1993	4	4.4	63.3
1994	4	4.4	67.8
1995	6	6.7	74.4
1996	5	5.6	80.0
1997	2	2.2	82.2
1998	5	5.6	87.8
1999	3	2.2	91.1
2000	1	5.6	92.2
2001	3	3.3	95.6
2002	0	0	95.6
2003	2	2.2	97.8
2004	2	2.2	100.0
Total	90	100.0	

of women's initiation into heroin use in China, including its initial effects, women's internalized norms about drugs, and the role played by social and physical settings. Based upon a comparison with later cases, findings indicate that women who used heroin during or before the early 1990s showed a pattern distinct from that of women who followed later; analyzed in light of the three determinants above, the early drug users did not have much knowledge about heroin, they lacked internalized norms to resist heroin use, and had more opportunities of witnessing other people using heroin in public or semi-public gatherings.

As discussed in Chapter 1, the prevalence of heroin use in Kunming is linked to its proximity to the border areas of Yunnan Province. Heroin use began to emerge with the reform era, and can be partially attributed to the increasing number of ports between China and other southeastern countries, in particular Myanmar. The increase in the number of ports, together with the economic reform and open-door policies aimed at advancing China's economy, created f new economic opportunities in the border areas of Yunnan. The job status of women after leaving school was closely related to their level of education—26 percent of them worked in the service industry or in factories, many of them became the forerunners in the economic reform by opening small family businesses (32 percent).[3] Although none of them launched out as entrepreneurs, these family businesses yielded very good returns, sometimes as high as several hundred thousand yuan annually. Many of these women can be considered real winners at the beginning of the economic reform.

Three women initiated heroin use as early as 1986. Two of them, Ning and Xia, started their heroin use while doing business in Ruili.[4] Another woman, Ling, said that she began to use heroin in Kunming. Ning and Xia's accounts confirmed that heroin use was very prevalent among people who were doing business in Ruili at that time; heroin was very cheap and easy to find. Ning, a 40-year-old woman, was very sophisticated. Because she visited the drop-in center quite often over a period of time, I was able to talk to her frequently after my interview with her. As one of three women who began using heroin in 1986, she proudly said that she knew a lot about early heroin use in Yunnan and was glad to share her experience with me:

> I started my business in 1981; by 1986 I was selling goods between Ruili and Guangzhou (Guangdong Province). I heard about No. 4 from my business friends. At that time, I didn't know its name as heroin. Heroin was very cheap, and it was popular among business groups in Ruili. If you spent dozens of yuan ($2.68), you would get one gram of heroin in Ruili; two yuan ($0.54) would buy the same amount in Myanmar.

Hanging out with business friends, and having easy and convenient access to heroin in Ruili, Ning felt it was inevitable that she should use heroin. She continued:

> At that time, I liked to gather with my business friends. They laced cigarettes with heroin and smoked it. It happened quite frequently that someone lighted a cigarette and passed it to others in the group; both men and women mixed together. A widespread cliché was "Take heroin, and get everything you want." If you wanted money, money would fly all over the sky. I didn't know any bad things related to using it. And I was so tempted to use it.

As stated by Ning and other women in the study, "Take heroin, and get everything you want" was a widespread cliché among heroin users at the time. The cliché became so attractive, because of a growing demand for lives with more money and pleasure following the economic reform. Although women knew about the negative aspects of opium due to the long tradition of its use in the province—several women had generations of family members who used opium before the liberation in 1949—they knew nothing about heroin. With the increasing popularity of heroin, women found themselves unable to resist using heroin due to the influence of their social and physical environment.

Xia, 43 years old, was short and thin. Unlike most other women in the study, she had no make-up on her face and dressed as ordinary housewives of her age. This quiet woman in front of me began heroin use in Ruili in 1986—the same year as Ning. She said:

> I was doing family business in Ruili at that time since both my husband and I had relatives there. My husband only had a short stay in Ruili, but I lived there for five years. I earned lots of money—several thousand dollars a year—and didn't know how to spend it. Those business friends described how wonderful and comfortable No. 4 could be. I was full of curiosity. I didn't think much about it when I first accepted the cigarette they gave me.

Ning and Xia's accounts convince us that heroin use was very popular among business people at the time, which is consistent with official reports. The prevalence of heroin use among this group may be explained by two factors. Although the price of heroin appeared to be low at the time, it was still expensive for the general population, earning low wages, to maintain a drug habit. Heroin's popularity among business owners was thus related to economic reasons, but also to changes in ideology as well—as a group that became rich first, business people were forerunners in pursuing materialism and popular culture.

Ling was the only woman who started using heroin in Kunming in 1986. Unlike Ning and Xia, Ling made her living by accompanying and entertaining wealthy businessmen. She was only 44 years old, but she looked much older than her actual age—deep furrows lined her brow, and she was sloppily dressed. I was hardly able to connect her with her previous experience.

Ling had wandered the streets since she was a teenager. Her name was quite popular in the street. On account of this, she could not finish her elementary school. She told me how she initiated heroin use:

> I began to use heroin in 1986. At that time, I was hanging out with some big bosses at luxury restaurants, playing mahjong all day long. They gave me tips of 100 yuan ($26) for accompanying them and also invited me to smoke heroin. The heroin was kept in small penicillin bottles. They laced heroin with tobacco. Though I didn't use it daily, after a couple of months, I was hooked.

Although Ning said that she had never heard about heroin in Kunming until 1987, Ling's practice suggests that heroin might have been used in a few upscale entertainment venues in Kunming earlier than 1987—a different setting from the group gatherings in Ruili.[5] Once again, it was the business group, family business owners that took the lead in heroin use in Kunming as it did in Ruili. At the time, large private enterprises had not yet come into being. Because earlier businessmen were mostly men, it is assumed that early heroin users were more likely men than women. Based on interviews with women, it appears that only a few women in the study used heroin before 1988.

Fang, a 36 year old woman who was near-sighted, was the only woman who initiated heroin in 1987. Recently, having abstained from heroin use for four months, Fang was a very dedicated staff member at the drop-in center. Back to 1987, Fang was running a fruit business and had a boyfriend who was a heroin user. Fang told me that she had used heroin earlier than many others she knew. Based on her observation, heroin use in Kunming gradually gained popularity after 1987, when the social environment accepting the culture of heroin use emerged. She said: "When I first started using heroin, nobody in my courtyard (of about fifteen households) used heroin. Slowly, people in my neighborhood started to use it. I had more friends who became heroin users."

According to interviews with women heroin users, women's first heroin use during the initial heroin epidemic was more likely to occur in public areas. The marital status of women influenced the types of group activity they were involved in: while young girls often took their first try in a dance hall or a karaoke lounge, married women mostly initiated their heroin use at a mahjong table, while dining out or in a gathering at home. After the economic reform, the new entertainment venues emerging in China provided more choices for people (both men and women) to spend their leisure time and pursue popular culture. Jingyi, who had long, dark, shining hair, began heroin use in 1989, at the age of 20, after frequent visits to dancing clubs. She recalled that dancing gained popularity in Kunming in the mid-1980s.

When dance halls emerged in China, it was not a widely accepted form of entertainment for the public, because people tended to be more conservative after the long years of constraints imposed during the Cultural Revolution.

Naturally, the business owners and young people who liked hanging out became major participants in chasing popular culture which was greatly influenced by the Western way of life. Lingling, who had a spinal deformity—the only inherently disabled person in the study, initiated heroin use in 1989 when she was twenty-one. She told me, "After I took over my mother's job in a factory in 1986, I began to learn the ways of the world. I went out, having fun, playing and dancing. I knew more and more people."[6]

Some other women who liked playing mahjong initiated heroin use with their mahjong friends —so-called *pai you*. As introduced in Chapter 3, mahjong, as a group entertainment activity, was repealed after 1949, because people often used it for gambling. After the economic reform, playing mahjong became fashionable and gained popularity in both urban and rural areas. Among women who often visited the drop-in center, many were mahjong fans. Na was 34 years old and single. She had a boyfriend who used heroin, but she was lured to heroin by her mahjong friends in 1989. Like many other women in the study, Na's initiation into heroin was also related to her life experience prior to heroin use. She said:

> My home in Kunming was in the downtown area. My mother liked playing mahjong so I grew up at a mahjong table. I liked playing mahjong in my neighborhood. My *pai you* were all older than me and most of them were men. They often smoked cigarettes with heroin. I tried it for one time, but I didn't like that kind of feeling. Later on, I won 800 yuan ($215) from a *pai you* who paid me with 10 grams of heroin. He advised me how to divide the heroin into small bags and sell to others. I was tempted to get the money, but I failed to sell any of them. I began to use that heroin while playing mahjong with them.

While the economic reform and the ensuing dramatic social changes greatly challenged the conventional social values of Chinese society, the government's narcotics control policies lagging behind the emerging social issues significantly contributed to Kunming's heroin epidemic. As witnessed by Fang and other women, "By the time, the cops knew nothing about heroin. If they found heroin on you, they returned it to you." Hua gave me a vivid description of the illegal drug market in the early 1990s. She said that in certain blocks in the Northern Train Station area, the entire street was full of drug sellers—just like a drug wharf. The chaos of heroin selling in this area during the same time period was also witnessed by Lin: "Those Yi-minorities held heroin in their hands, soliciting customers on the street. If one street seller spoke to the customer, 'Buy mine, 40 yuan ($11),' another seller would respond by, 'come on; buy mine, only 30 yuan ($8).' "

Heroin use originated with business people, and therefore, there was a widespread belief that only those who had big money (*you qian*) were able to use heroin. As stated by Mei, if someone used heroin in Kunming in 1989, other people were likely to say admiringly, "You are so rich!" Thus, heroin use for women was not only for fun and entertainment, but also for status, and enhanced one's reputation among extrovert peers. Using heroin made one fashionable rather than a "junkie" in Kunming at that time. The development of this popular culture in the city not only fostered a heroin-prone attitude but also promoted social identification attached with drug-using groups (Anderson 1998, 250).

Tingting, wearing black, framed glasses to correct her myopia, looked like a school teacher. When I first met her, she seemed very depressed because she had been released from re-education through labor several weeks ago. Tingting was once a successful businesswoman. Her parents were both senior military officials, which created in her a need of superiority that led her to use heroin to compete with others. She said:

> I graduated from secondary professional school in 1988. I only worked half a year in a company and then started my own business. At that time, I was young, proud, arrogant, and curious about all new things. Many people around me were using heroin. I had more money than they did. Why can't I use it? After I used heroin, my vanity was completely satisfied. I just happened to step into society at the wrong time.

The large amount of readily available heroin in Kunming combined with the absence of virtually any formal legal controls on its use during this initial stage, inevitably led to a spike in heroin consumption. Without legal constraints, many women took heroin use for granted. Women internalized their rationales for using heroin thus: "I spent my own money and hurt no one else." The lack of information about heroin and its consequences is also a major factor that should not be ignored. Although women admitted that they did know heroin use was not a good thing, they did not know just how bad it was.

Moreover, women heroin users' lives prior to heroin use were also playing an important role in leading them into a social culture favorable to addiction. Women who had a history of deviant or criminal acts before they used heroin were much more likely to pursue local popular culture due to peer pressure. But for some other women, as Tingting's experience reveals, their individual lifestyle and personality were facilitators in this process.[7] Taking heroin was viewed as a fashion—being the cool ones in a group of friends. Smoking was a popular method of using heroin at that time, which was a great temptation to women who were mostly already smokers. Because of these reasons, heroin use quickly spread through Kunming in the late 1980s and continued through the early 1990s.

SOCIAL PROCESS OF INITIATION

The previous section highlights the emergence and popularity of heroin in Kunming from the late 1980s to the early 1990s, and underlines the importance of "set" and "setting" in women's initiation. Except for these background factors, the study concludes that the most influential factors leading to actual contact with heroin were women's social relations prior to their heroin use. These social relations distinctively affected women's pathways to heroin, including their reasons for heroin use, the company in which initiation occurred, the location of their first attempt at using the drug and their experience with heroin. With a few exceptions, all women were with other people when they used heroin for the first time. Even women who first tried heroin by themselves, did so under the influence of their significant others—normally drug-using male partners.

Table 4.2 shows women's initiation into heroin use according to social relations. Mixed-sex friends (31 percent) played the most important role in their initiation into heroin, regardless of the women's marital status; female friends (27 percent) were important to both single and married women.[8] A woman's marital status did determine how she was affected by other social relations. Women with a history of marriage hardly ever began heroin use with a male friend, boyfriend, or family member; in contrast, single women were more likely to be led to heroin use by these social relations.[9] These findings strongly indicate that women's initiation into heroin use was influenced by the social worlds to which they belonged, as is suggested by previous research (Rosenbaum 1984; Maher 1995).

The age distribution of heroin initiation is also quite different among single and married women.[10] As indicated by Table 4.3, at the time of heroin initiation, sixty-three women (70 percent) had never been married, and twenty-seven women (30 percent) had a marriage history. The women's ages at initiation range from 14 to 39. Even though a large percentage of women used heroin before age 20, they mostly began using heroin after they left school. The majority of women (74 percent) in the study initiated heroin use at or before 24 years of age (mean = 21.96), which is quite similar to the research findings from the United States and Australia.[11] There is hardly any initiation into illicit drugs after age 29. Single women (mean =

Table 4.2 Women's Initiation into Heroin Use by Social Relations (N=90)

Relation	Single	Married	Overall
Mixed group	18	10	28
Female friend	16	8	24
Boyfriend	16	1	17
Male friend	9	1	10
Husband	0	6	6
Family member	4	1	5
Total	63	27	90

Table 4.3 Women's Initiation into Heroin Use by Age (N=90)

Age at Initiation	Single	Married	Total
14–20	35	0	35
21–24	25	7	32
25–29	2	11	13
> 30 years	1	9	10
Total	63	27	90
Mean = 21.96			

19.56) had a much earlier initiation into heroin than married women (mean = 28.14). In the case of single women, 95 percent of them initiated heroin at or below the age of 24 whereas only 26 percent of married women did so. In contrast, among women who began heroin use at or above age 25, the majority of them (87 percent) were married.

A comparison of initiation of heroin by single and married women indicates that while the single women were more likely to be frustrated with issues in their families, the married women had considerable marital problems.[12] Among married women, only fifteen were living with their husbands at the time of initiation: six women were divorced, four women were separated from their husbands and two of them were widows. Among women who remained in their marriages, only two of them had no significant marital problems. However, regardless of women's marital status, whether they eventually initiated heroin or not was determined by their social relations and situational factors.

Initiation in a Mixed Group

Taking women in the study as a whole (Table 4.2), 31 percent of women were initiated into heroin in a mixed-sex group, indicating that both single and married women were likely to be introduced to heroin by mixed-sex friends. However, although initiation occurred in a mixed-sex group, the initiation location, company and motivations were different for single and married women. Single women were likely to be initiated into heroin in entertainment settings, typically in dance halls, karaoke lounge etc.; parties seemed to play an important role. Unlike single women, married women were almost exclusively small business owners. They mostly initiated heroin in associations or gatherings with business peers whom they knew well. While the importance of familiarity and trust between initiates and inviters was observed in the previous study (Waldorf et al.1991), the current study suggests that it was only relevant to married women in the study. Due to the opportunistic nature of these meeting, single women contemplating heroin in such settings might not necessarily know all the people in the group well, not even, perhaps, the inviters, only a few people in the group might be trustworthy friends.

Fen, a single woman when she initiated heroin use in 1989, was actively engaged in group activities with her boyfriend—a street wanderer. She told me:

> With my boyfriend, I was very outgoing and busy with many activities. We went to karaoke clubs, dancing and singing, or played at hotels with his friends. These friends often mixed heroin with tobacco to smoke. It seemed like that they always had as much heroin as they wanted. After a while, I became curious about their drug use. When we were invited to use it, we didn't take it seriously.

Since the economic reform, new entertainment venues such as dance halls and karaoke lounges emerged in Kunming, as in other metropolitan areas. Single women who began heroin use within a mixed-sex group shared some common characteristics—they were all actively involved in social gatherings with peers. Early deviant behavior, such as smoking, drinking, early dating, and running away, was highest in this group than in other groups. Tian, mentioned earlier for her participation in street fighting, associated with delinquent peers that eventually led her to heroin. She said:

> When I was in middle school, I had a best friend who had an elder sister. She made many friends in society, and was very *zhuai (*cool). Everybody called her "big sister." We played with her all the time. While we were playing together, she always sat there smoking heroin. One day, she asked me to have a try. I sucked (the cigarette) about four times. I felt dizzy and wanted to throw up. She asked me to finish the cigarette to get a true feeling. I did what she wanted me to do.

Just like Tian, most of these women used heroin after they had observed their friends using it for a couple of times, or for a while. Women said that they used heroin because of increasing curiosity, and through wanting to keep pace with their friends while hanging out.[13] Women said that "If you don't use heroin, you aren't our *wanyou* ('play fellow')," was a popular cliché among sociable youths at that time. Naturally, the women wanted to be part of it. In the case of women who initiated heroin at or before the early 1990s, a lack of knowledge about heroin was also a contributing factor. Young girls simply followed their instinct without further thinking about the consequences of heroin use. Comparatively, married women were more likely to be motivated by curiosity rather than peer pressure. The majority of these women had troubling issues in their marriage at that time, such as the death of a husband, divorce, domestic violence or an undesired intimate relationship, which apparently became a contributing factor in their heroin use. The initiation of the women into heroin normally occurred at a mahjong table, or at a meeting with business friends, either at their own homes or at friends' homes.

Caiyun was a small business owner when she initiated heroin in 1989. She was 45 years old and divorced her husband seven years ago. She was cohabitating with her boyfriend who was more than ten years younger than her. She told me how and why she began to use heroin:

> After I married, I ran a small restaurant; my ex-husband managed a business with his family. My husband liked gambling and never listened to me. He was so introverted that I couldn't even have a quarrel with him. Several business owners working near my restaurant were using heroin, and in the beginning, I persuaded them not to take drugs. But I was so disappointed with my husband; I wanted to get rid of my problems through heroin. I then joined them.

Like Caiyun, Qing was once a small business owner, a smart and hard-working person. She started her relationship with her husband at the age of 17, but divorced him when her son was just over one year old. Her initiation into heroin was then under way. She said:

> My ex-husband was very brutal. He liked to use weapons and always beat me up without reason. Even his parents feared him. Once he slashed my hands with a knife. We divorced eight months after we got our marriage certificate. After I divorced, I always stayed with my business friends. I knew they used heroin together and advised them not to use drugs. Since I was so depressed, they persuaded me to take drugs to forget my troubles. I finally accepted it.

The preceding analysis reveals that in the case of single versus married women, initiation into heroin within a mixed-sex group occurred in different physical settings and for different reasons: single women took heroin for fun, out of curiosity and due to peer pressure, within more diverse social groups and in wider physical settings. In contrast, married women had more restricted social relations—family related or work related friendships. Therefore, their initiation into heroin was mostly a result of the influence of business peers and was spurred on by family related problems.

Initiation with Female Friends

The number of women who began taking heroin with female friends (N=24) comprises the second largest group in the study. In contrast with women who initiated heroin with mixed-sex friends, women in this group shared some common characteristics in their heroin initiation regardless of their marital status. They were almost exclusively invited by their female friend(s) who had close relationship with them. Except for two sex workers, they did not generally associate with people who liked hanging out in society. Nor did they frequent entertainment venues. Their first heroin use occurred mostly in private rather than public settings, such as either their own home or that of their friend. Curiosity was the major reason for these women to initiate heroin. However, peer pressure was not a factor affecting their initial decision. Instead, heir close and continuous contact with female drug-using friends increased their curiosity about heroin.

Yangliu was a 33-year-old woman with freckles scattered on her pale, rather expressionless face. Her curiosity was aroused as she observed her best female friend repeatedly using heroin. She said: "Seeing one of my best friends using heroin right in front of me a couple of times, my resolve began to waver." Similar to Yangliu's experience, Chun began heroin use with several of her best female friends in 1996. She said:

> I rented an apartment with my schoolmates after I graduated from high school. At that time, three or four of my best friends were using heroin. They all learned about it from their boyfriends. I knew a little bit about heroin's effects, so I was strongly against it. But after they played with heroin in front of me for a while, I felt increasing curiosity. When my life also became troubled (with family and money problems), I wanted to numb myself with heroin.

As suggested by Chun's experience, women initiating heroin use in the mid-1990s had gained more knowledge about the negative effects of the drug, because of increased propaganda, by both central and local governments. This indeed increased their struggle against heroin initiation. Chun finally could not resist heroin on account of both curiosity and the pressure in her life. This further suggests that curiosity alone might not be a sufficient cause of heroin initiation. Besides family-related issues, as illustrated in Chun's experience, women's relationship with their male partners at the time of initiation was also found to be influential. Lan once had a strong dislike for heroin use. But when Lan was going through a difficult time with her boyfriend, she was ready to change. Lan said:

> Before I used heroin, I was living with my boyfriend (her ex-husband) and had a discussion with him about our marriage. One time, he suspected that I had a relationship with another man, so he beat me. I took a bottle of sleeping pills to commit suicide but was rescued. When I was very unhappy with my relationship with my boyfriend, one of my best female friends (a heroin user) invited me to stay with her while her husband was away on a trip. Since I was very depressed, I started to use heroin with her within two weeks.

Like Lan, women who used heroin on account of troubles in their intimate relationships mostly said they had experienced first love or true love with their boyfriends or husbands. Three women committed suicide because of crises occurring in their relationships before they tried heroin. Ying was one of them. Ying used a wrist guard to cover her left wrist despite the hot weather. She showed me a large area of deep scars from wounds she inflicted on herself after her boyfriend separated from her. She said, "After I separated from my boyfriend, I began to hit the bottle. Almost at the same time, I learned how to use heroin from a female friend—who I've known for years." Although Lan, Ying and several others had easy access to heroin prior to their heroin use, they did not begin using the drug until deep depression from their intimate relationships entered their lives.

These women's experience convinces us of the important role women's family relationship and intimate relationship play in their initiation into drugs. It also illustrates the differences between women who began heroin use with female friends, and women who did so with mixed-sex friends. The experience of these women also suggests that changes in narcotics control policies have greatly shaped women's perceptions about heroin. During the early stage of the heroin epidemic, with little knowledge of the dangers of heroin, many women blindly followed others without realizing the consequences. However, with increased awareness about the negative aspects of heroin use, the answer to the question whether women would eventually initiate the drug, was determined by the frequency of their exposure to heroin use and their mental state at the time of the initiation.

Initiation with Male Partners

Among married women in the study, six of them divorced, two were widows, and nineteen of them remained in their marriages before they initiated heroin. Among all women who initiated heroin with their male partners, six of them began heroin use with their husbands or ex-husbands and seventeen women tried heroin with their boyfriends. Women who initiated heroin use under the influence of their male partners were both young and middle aged.[14] Like the women who initiated heroin with female friends, these women were rarely involved in deviant or illegal conducts. As they were in an intimate relationship with their male partners, women in this group were all initiated into heroin use at home. The male partners were mostly employed as laborers, or business owners; all of them were heroin users. They developed their heroin addiction either before, or after, entering into relationships with the women under discussion.

Although the male partners used drugs themselves, they generally discouraged the women from taking heroin, with only a few exceptions.[15] While women admitted that they also had increased curiosity to heroin after observing their male partners' drug use for a period of time, they mostly initiated heroin use because of increased frustration out of their partners' drug use. Some women intended to act as role models for their drug-using partners, by showing them how to get rid of drugs easily—eventually they all failed to do so. These women themselves became hooked on the drugs. The study indicates that over half the women in this group claimed that their boyfriends or husbands were their first lovers, suggesting that intimacy between women and their male partners is also a crucial factor in heroin initiation.

Qiangwei, a 29-year-old woman, was delicate and quiet. She attempted suicide in order to prevent her boyfriend—her first lover—from using heroin, before she finally joined in his habit. She had dark brown spots on both arms as a result of her initial methadone treatment. When Qiangwei was asked whether she thought about separating from her boyfriend at that time, she said, "Never." Qiangwei gave me details about her initiation:

> I was a good student in school. No one would ever imagine that I use drugs now. I began dating my husband in high school. He attended college, but I didn't. After he graduated, he worked as a translator in a large company. He began to use heroin after one year of work. To stop him from using heroin, I tried different ways to commit suicide: I took large amounts of sleeping pills, drank panaplate, and cut an artery. When all these efforts failed, I used heroin with him.

Whereas single women overvalued their relationship with their first lover, the quality of marriage was important to married women. Meijuan was a very fashionable woman. She had a well-groomed appearance and was full of self-confident. However, when Meijuan accidentally saw her husband using heroin with a young girl, she did the same thing as Qiangwei—she attempted to commit suicide.[16] After Meijuan had made every effort to help her husband, she realized that nothing would change him. Then she began to use drugs herself, though at the time, she didn't even know how to smoke.[17] In cases such as this, the decision to take heroin was not made out of a desire to connect with a drug-using partner, but had no other choice if they remained in the relationship.

In general, women's male partners played very inactive roles in women's initiation into heroin. They did not want their women to use it. In some cases, they threatened or committed violence against the women's attempts to take the drug. However, women with drug-using male partners found it almost impossible to stay away from heroin indefinitely. Meiru's experience is a good example. Meiru, 32 years old, was still single after she had lived with her boyfriend for thirteen years. Unlike most women in the study who initiated heroin by smoking or inhaling, Meiru (and Meijuan, too) injected heroin at her first time with the drug. Meiru said:

> My boyfriend began to use heroin after we dated for two years. He quit many times, but always came back again. He is my first lover. I never thought about leaving him; I might be too silly and single-minded. When he and his friends got together, the most frequent topic they

> talked about was drugs. After we had lived together for five years, I began to try heroin myself. I couldn't really smoke, so I picked up the remaining drug in the syringe he used, and injected it into my vein. Our friends cracked jokes that I became addicted on the leftovers.

Unlike women who initiated heroin within a mixed-sex group or with a female friend, none of these women were motivated by immediate situational factors. The intimacy between these women and their boyfriends and their long-time exposure to the heroin use in a family setting was a prevailing factor in their initiation. If the women could not break off their relationship with drug-using male partners, they were destined to use heroin sooner or later. For example, two women (Ping and Weili) began to take heroin with their ex-husbands after they were divorced. Whether women have the wisdom to handle their intimate relationships is apparently a critical issue.

Initiation with Male Friends

Women in this group were mostly of a young age group at the time they began heroin. Of the ten women who initiated heroin use with a male friend, all except Lin were single. This indicates that young, single women were more likely than married women to socialize with men in social settings. As in the case of women who were introduced to heroin by their mixed-sex friends, all women in this group were outgoing and active; most of them showed early deviant behavior. Their relations with the male friend who introduced heroin to them did not need to be close. These males were either someone they knew, or a friend of their partners. The settings of the first try were mostly in public areas, though occasionally initiation occurred in private settings as well.

Like women who used heroin within mixed-sex groups, these women's first try was quite accidental; however, the big difference between these two groups was that these women were not under peer pressure to use heroin. Mei was lured to use heroin by a male she knew in a dance hall. She said:

> I liked to play with friends when I was in school. After I graduated from middle school, I spent more time dancing and playing mahjong. I knew these things weren't so good, but I didn't realize how bad they were, either. One day after my father beat me I went out to dance with my friends. In the dance hall, a guy I knew invited me to use heroin. Since I was feeling so bad, I picked it up. Afterwards, he was always looking for me.

Although physical punishment by Mei's father was a direct stimulus to her first trying heroin, Mei's lifestyle significantly increased her chances of being close to heroin-prone youths. Before she used heroin she did not know many other users. But after she started she realized that almost all of her friends were using heroin. It was simply a matter of time before Mei eventually used heroin. Just like what happened to Mei, troubles in women's lives were often the triggers to try heroin.

Yue, a young girl, came from a broken family and lacked care from her family after her grandfather died. She moved out at fifteen, and shared an apartment with a female friend who had a similar family background. Her heroin use began with her sympathy for a boy, who she did not know well, but who also came from a broken family:

> In my last year of middle school, I moved out and lived with a female friend. My studies got worse, and finally I was unable to continue my studies after middle school. I began selling beer in a dance hall, and making money by dancing with others. I made many friends, both boys and girls. One day, a male friend asked to stay in my apartment for a couple of days. I kept him. After a few days I knew he was taking heroin. He said that it was fun and invited me to have a try. I did as he instructed. Afterwards we fell in love.

Another woman Meiyu, was a young woman with a sallow, slack complexion. She wore a red sweater that only made her look more faded. Occasionally she lisped out her words. She told me that after using heroin, she began to lose her memory and her thinking slowed. Before she used heroin, she liked hanging out in society and making money as a dance partner because of the lack of caring at home—her father, a businessmen, was heavily involved in gambling; her mother was also busy on running the family business. Meiyu's heroin use was related to her acquaintance with a male drug trafficker from Kaiyuan, Yunnan, who she met in a dance hall.

Among these women, four initiated heroin use together with their boyfriends. The male friend who introduced heroin to them was, in all cases, a friend of their boyfriends. These women's boyfriends were either small business owners, or men who liked playing in society. Without exception, all the women were living with their boyfriends at the time of initiation, which provided them an ease environment for drug use without the possibility of being identified by their parents or other family members. Initiation generally occurred in a public setting, and occasionally in their homes. Compared to women who initiated heroin use with a male friend of their own, none of these women connected their first try to any pressure in their lives. They just felt that it was quite normal for them to use heroin together with their boyfriends. As Ni told me, "I've always been dependent on my men. My second boyfriend was doing business. When his friend brought heroin to us, I didn't take it very seriously, even though I knew it might lead to addiction."

Initiation with a Family Member

Among women heroin users in the study, only five initiated heroin on account of family members (from both immediate and extended family).[18] In two cases heroin use was influenced by the woman's father or brother, while three others initiated heroin with relatives in the extended family, including an uncle, a cousin, or a nephew. Although more women in the samples had relatives in extended families using heroin, they admitted that they were not affected by the drug use of these relatives due to lack of frequent contacts with them. Among these women, Buo was the only married one. The others were single. This suggests that family influences on women's drug-use behavior might be more significant in the case of young girls who lived with their parents.

Among these five women, three tried heroin due to increasing curiosity. As indicated in the previous chapter, Yun's initiation with heroin took place on account of her drug selling business, an opportunity provided by her father (a drug dealer) when he was released from prison after eleven years of incarceration. At her father's direction, Yun began to sell heroin with his two brothers. In the course of drug dealing, Yun started to use heroin, so did her brothers. Like Yun, Jun's father was also a big heroin dealer. Jun was a 32-year-old woman with a chubby face. She was a voluble person with a loud voice. In contrast to Yun, Jun did not get involved in her father's drug-selling business. She did not even think about using heroin until the day her cousin suggested it, and she had become increasingly curious:

> My father got liver cancer in 1988, so he used heroin to control the pain. When he couldn't afford to use it, he began selling it. He often brought big chunks of heroin home. My cousin was a *wanyou* (playgirl). She asked me to steal my father's heroin. My father often divided heroin into small bags, so I took a little bit from each bag. Since he was a big dealer, he never realized I was stealing from him for nearly two years until his death. My cousin taught me how to smoke heroin.

Unlike Yun and Jun who had deviant parents, Fei came from an affluent family. She was spoiled by her parents, having nothing to do at home after her high school graduation. Her heroin use was related to a special occasion at her uncle's home. She said:

> Both my uncle and aunt used heroin. I remembered my uncle used a plastic bag to carry his drugs. Since my parents weren't always at home, my brothers and I were taken care of by two babysitters. After I graduated from high school, my mom didn't want me to work. The money she gave me was more than others' salary. Having nothing to do at home, I always visited my uncle's home. One day I caught cold and felt

> stomach pains. My uncle taught me to smoke heroin. He offered drugs to me for free for a while. Shortly after, I became addicted.[19]

Fei was not the only woman in the study to claim that her first try with heroin was to treat painful symptoms. Buo, the only married woman in this group, was pale-faced, short and thin. Her eyes were droopy. When she spoke fast, it seemed as though she was out of breath. She was hospitalized many times due to her reaction to heroin. Her parents were both senior officials in the military, unfortunately her mother passed away when she was still a child. After Buo married, she had a very poor relationship with her husband, but was very close to her relatives. Though she was very depressed by the relationship with her husband at the time, her reason for using heroin was to release the pain: "When I felt uncomfortable on several occasions, such as when I had a cough or menstrual pains, my cousin gave me heroin to relax. I gradually lost control of myself."

Indeed, in the previous groups, women were also occasionally advised by their female friends or boyfriends to use heroin for relief from stomach pains, tooth pain and even weight loss. Quick relief from their symptoms increased women's curiosity about the magical quality of the drug. Such experiences finally led these women to use heroin. Lacking medical knowledge and ignoring the consequences of heroin use were contributing factors in women's initiation. These factors were more prominent in the case of women who initiated earlier in the heroin epidemic.

CONCLUSION

As shown in this chapter, women's initiation into heroin use involved a socialization process, in which both sociological factors and factors related to the individual contributed significantly. The experience of women heroin users in Kunming suggests that women's initiation into heroin use in Chinese society has both similarities and differences with studies conducted in Western countries. While pre-existing social and cultural characteristics contribute to these differences, China's changing society is a major factor.

Women's initiation into heroin in Kunming was closely linked to emerging and increasing drug trafficking in the area. Interviews with women indicate that heroin was highly accessible in Kunming until the late 1990s. In particular, heroin overflowed in the communities and neighborhoods of Kunming in the early 1990s.[20] Due to the fact that China was closed to the international world for decades, the heroin epidemic in China was greatly delayed in comparison to those in the United States, Western Europe and other Asian countries, where the epidemic reached its peak in the 1970s. But China's open-door policies in the reform era opened the country, which was no longer immune to the global trend of illicit drug use.

As discussed in Chapter 1, since the economic reform, the economic status and social values of the Chinese people have changed greatly. With better economic status, women are involved in more social activities than before. Women's roles both in family and society have been expanded. Among women in the study, the early heroin users were almost exclusively business owners. Women heroin users in the study show distinct differences from women heroin users in urban areas of the United States, who are primarily from disadvantaged social groups in poor neighborhoods. However, at the early stage of China's heroin epidemic, lack of knowledge about heroin and its consequences led women to pick up the heroin habit usually without realizing its possible dangers. With cultural infiltration from Western countries, young followers took heroin for fun, for fashion and to be cool. A favorable social culture for heroin use quickly formed in the city. Both "sets" and "settings" favorable for illicit drug use began to emerge.

While women were motivated to use heroin out of curiosity, single women who were active in outgoing activities, were likely to use heroin due to peer pressure. Women's initiation into heroin involved a wide range of social relations.[21] Over half the women in this sample began to use heroin within a mixed gender group or with female friends.[22] Women trying heroin in a mixed-sex group constitute the largest group in the study. This suggests that nowadays Chinese women are as widely involved in social activities as men. While it was typical for women to use heroin while facing the frustration or failure of a relationship, women also used heroin for the purpose of acting as a role model for their drug-using partners, and not simply to feel a greater connection with them. While both single and married women were frequently under the direct influences of their male partners; single women were also likely to be introduced to heroin by male friends.

Finally, women's initiation into heroin use is a co-product of their times and their individual dispositions. Women's lives prior to heroin use played an important role in their initiation into heroin. The study identified significant differences in the motives that led single and married women into heroin use: single women mostly had frustration with their families, while for married women, the problematic issues in their marriage became outstanding. The individual drug user's pathway to imitation varied, depending on which stage of the drug epidemic she/he belonged to.[23] Women who initiated heroin use at or before the early 1990s, when heroin began to dominate the streets, showed a pattern distinct from that of women who used heroin afterwards, and in particular, from women who used heroin in more recent years. While the availability of heroin, the opportunity to try it, and women's willingness to use the drug have been always critical for their initiation into heroin, as suggested by Stephens (1991), the social milieu favorable to such practice plays an equally important role.

5 Continued Use and Crime

The transition from initial experimentation with drugs to stabilized daily practice is a significant change in drug-users' careers. After the experimentation stage, some drug users may stay away from drugs whereas others may increase their use of drugs and eventually become addicted to them. A review of the literature indicates that, except for a few studies on female drug use, the large body of research documented is on the fast lives of male drug users from escalation to maintenance. Where women are concerned, compared with initiation and discontinuation stages, studies barely focus on escalation and maintenance. How women drug users immerse into drug-use careers from initiation to escalation and maintenance, and how they develop the necessary skills for their career transitions, are either not emphasized or ignored. Meanwhile, with an increasing demand for heroin, women's ability to purchase heroin and support their drug use becomes an inevitable preoccupation. Due to the high cost of heroin, it is predictable that women may participate in illegal activities. Based on these reasons, in this chapter, I have focused on two themes emerging during women's transition —managing drug use and taking care of business.

ESCALATION TO CONTINUED USE

As discussed in Chapter 4, initiation into heroin is only the first stage of a drug-use career. It is in the course of repeated heroin use that women begin to recognize their addiction. Due to differences in physical tolerance to heroin, frequency of use, and the dosage of the drug, the timing of addiction varied greatly among women in the study. Some women exhibited apparent symptoms after only several tries, but it took others a month, or even several months to do so. Regardless of women's knowledge about heroin use, they were mostly unaware of addiction when it finally occurred. Addiction was often recognized by women after they shared their experience with other, 'more seasoned' drug users (Becker 1953; Lindesmith 1947), including, but not limited to those who introduced heroin to them in the first place.

Addiction involves a gradual process, marked by a series of early symptoms. Most women said that during their initial trials of heroin, they did not feel well after using the drug. Nausea, headache and vomiting were quite common; only a few women reported that they experienced a truly pleasant feeling. The reason they continued their experimentation nevertheless, was largely due to encouragement from their drug-using peers.[1] As Jia said, "I didn't feel well at the beginning. Other people (drug users) told me it was quite normal. When I saw they all looked good, I no longer worried about it." Thus, women's initial worries about withdrawal were eased by explanations from peers and by their own observations of their peers' practices. Meanwhile, the fact that women persisted in trying again was also attributed to continuing opportunities. Yangliu said: "At the beginning I only smoked heroin about two times with my female friends. Shortly after, a friend of my boyfriend used heroin right in front of us. After he knew that I had tried it before, he handed drugs over to me."

In general, those who initiated heroin use before or during the early 1990s had a relatively quick escalation due to easy access to heroin and the government's lenient polices on narcotics use. Although women who began heroin use after the early 1990s had more knowledge about the drug, and sometimes were even warned by their drug-using friends not to use drugs, they were still unlikely to realize they were addicted before they exchanged information with other experienced drug users. Xiaoling, who initiated heroin use in 1992, described how she recognized her addiction:

> When I started using heroin, I felt dopey, and itchy. But wherever I scratched, I felt comfortable. One day drug friends didn't visit me; I got a runny nose and itching all over my body. I thought I was sick, so I went to the hospital. The doctor prescribed intravenous injections for me. While injecting in the hospital, I chatted with a guy next to me, and he concluded that I was addicted because he was a heroin user.

Women's recognition of addiction marked a milestone in their heroin use career. Many of these women believed a myth about heroin, namely, that if they did not use heroin very often, they would not get addicted. But once they understood that they were hooked, women were rarely able to quit drug use, including those who had been extremely confident about their ability to control drug use. At this point, women began to realize that continuing drug use was the only way for them to release the pain induced by withdrawal (Lindesmith 1947). However, whether women would continue their heroin use careers after recognition of addiction was determined by several factors, including the availability of drug-use opportunities, their conventional activities, as well as by their perceptions about drugs. While the transition from recognition of addiction to a continued drug-use career seemed uncontrollable, women, this study found that it could be interrupted by certain unintended events, in particular, women's relationship with male partners.

Seven women in the study were able to refrain from further drug use after they experienced withdrawal. Xi told me that in her case it was her dream of marriage that was the primary factor: "My boyfriend never used heroin. I wanted to marry him because I loved him with all my heart. I didn't use heroin until we broke up." To a certain degree, Xi's relationship with her boyfriend postponed her drug-use career, which was evident by her immediate recourse to heroin right after her separation from him. Jingyi, who had long, dark shining hair, was in a similar situation as Xi when she tried heroin—she was dating. Shortly after her initiation, she was busy preparing for her wedding and then got married. But she resumed heroin after she had been married for four years. She said:

> After I got married, my husband and I operated a clothes business. He stayed in Guangzhou and only came home two times a month. I felt very lonely and bored after work. One day I ran into one of my friends who was a heroin user. She invited me to use heroin. After that, she often came over since she didn't have money to buy drugs. I became heavily addicted since then.

Although women's experiences reveal that ignorance of the nature of withdrawal may lead individuals to escape addiction (Beck 1967, 175), they also suggest that women's intimate relationships with men can play an important role in drug-use escalation. Women's intimate relationships with male partners could thus influence women's heroin use in two different ways: on the one hand, they could facilitate women's continuation of drug use; while on the other hand, they could also interfere with it. The determining factor seems to be their male partners' drug-use status.[2] Unfortunately, most women in the study were not able to stay away from heroin after they showed addiction symptoms—they transited naturally from recognition of addiction to escalation and continued drug use.

METHODS OF ADMINISTRATION

The method used to administer the drug was closely connected to the women's continuation of drug use. Generally speaking, a novice almost exclusively took heroin by smoking or snorting—depending on opportunities available to them. Women might smoke heroin on one occasion within one group of friends and snort it on another occasion with other friends. Selecting or changing the method of administering the drug involves a learning process which is influenced by the social interactions between women with other drug-using peers, physical tolerance to drug use and economic reasons.

The typical drug-use route followed three patterns: 1. smoking—snorting—injection; 2. snorting—injection; 3. staying with snorting for the entire drug use carreer. This finding was consistent with research findings in the

United States, where injection was identified as the predominant route of heroin administration and snorting or smoking heroin occurred to a lesser extent. Smoking heroin was attractive to women in the initial stage of drug use because the majority of them were regular cigarette smokers. A few women who had never smoked cigarettes before they used heroin, began by snorting, or in rare cases, by injecting heroin on the very first occasion. With increasing dependence on heroin, smoking was eventually replaced by snorting and/or injecting. However, like smoking, snorting was costly and inconvenient for daily use, and therefore did not remain the method of choice for long.

The majority of the women tried the intravenous route and stayed with it. Their initial reason for trying the intravenous route was a combination of two factors: more intense and pleasurable effects gained from intravenous injection, and economization of the amount of heroin required. Once women got used to this method, they found it very difficult to stop due to increased physical tolerance. Only ten women (11 percent) had never injected heroin on account of a short drug-use history, or because they were uncomfortable with needles, fearing pain or pinholes. Women were generally tempted to inject heroin based on descriptions by their drug-using peers about thrilling experiences in store. They mostly injected heroin in private settings—either their own homes, or those of their drug peers, rather than in get-off houses.

Xiaoling had smoked heroin for three years but had never snorted heroin before she began injection. She told me why she changed from smoking to injecting:

> Once you inserted the needle in your vein, and saw blood coming out, then you pushed it back in. It was so great! You won't have a bitter taste in your mouth like with smoking and snorting. My friends who weren't injectors all wanted to try injection. A couple of my friends who had tried injection earlier helped me at the beginning. After a while, I knew how to do it by myself.

Although all of the women were aware of the risks related to injection into a vein, and especially into an artery, they still preferred to shoot the vein, due to the pleasurable sensation, rather than to do a skin pop. Ying described her first shot into an artery this way: "I could feel my blood flow all over my body; my entire body was paralyzing, like I was hit by electricity." The pleasures of heroin injection described by Ying were confirmed by some of the other women. Ming said, "When I saw blood coming out from my artery, I felt extreme itching and tickling all over her body, even in my uterus." Juan told me that she experienced warm and delicate feelings after the first shot; the smell of a delicious apple stayed in her nose for a while.[3] However, only after one year, as with many others, Juan no longer felt the pleasant sensation of heroin injection.

Although women were motivated to inject heroin for its pleasant feeling, other considerations, including convenience and economization of the drug also played a role. Li's experience was very typical of that of most women in the study. She had tried both smoking and snorting before she finally stayed with injection. She explained why she preferred injection:

> In the beginning, I smoked heroin. Cigarettes were laced with heroin. Following that, for over a month, I used heroin by snorting. Snorting wasted drugs and also was time consuming. I was working in a nightclub as a hostess. Then I began injection. Normally I got one shot right after I bought drugs. After I had done my makeup before going to work, I had the second shot. Arriving at the nightclub, I got another shot. After I came back home, I probably had my last shot. It varied every day, ranging from five to eight shots. I felt injection was very convenient for me.

To make the transition to injection, women must learn injecting skills from experienced drug users, either their male partners (if any) or other drug-using friends.[4] The interviews revealed that most women did not view the switch to injection as a symbolic change in their drug-use status, because it was quite a common practice among their peers.[5] Suzhen, 40 years old, had a long scar along the corner of her mouth, the result of an accident during her withdrawal. She started to inject heroin after snorting it for six years upon the suggestion of one of her best friends, herself a drug user. Suzhen relates:

> She helped me to open a pinhole in my arm. I then followed that pinhole to inject drugs. Even a little bit off that pinhole, I wouldn't get the right shot. I knew I got it right when I saw the dark blood. I was scared at the beginning. But a short time later, I did it by myself. Normally I injected a smaller amount of the drug than I needed in snorting because people often overdose. But if I couldn't go to sleep at night, I had to snort heroin again after injection.

As revealed from Suzhen's experience, taking heroin by injecting and snorting at the same time was quite a common pattern in order to reach an intensive high. For the most part, women's male partners were their primary recourse for help; it was only when women's male partners were absent due to separation or incarceration that women's drug-use friends became the people they relied on. The timing of women's apprenticeship with heroin injection varied with individuals. Sometimes, women were able to inject by themselves after just two or three tries.

During my interviews with the women, I was quite surprised to learn of another reason for injecting heroin. Several women were advised by their peers, and even by doctors, that injecting would afford an easier means for future abstention. Ming had snorted heroin for two years before injection. She tried to quit several times, but all efforts failed. When she was in voluntary rehab, the doctor suggested that she come back after using heroin by injection for one month. Ming injected heroin for a week before revisiting the voluntary rehabilitation facility. However, after she completed her treatment in voluntary rehab, she had lost interest in snorting, but had turned into a heroin injector.

Most women in the study began to inject heroin when they reached the most intense point of their heroin use, when they faced the problem of the high cost of drugs. Injecting actually lowered the dosage at the beginning, but it went up again with increasing addiction. Injecting heroin eventually took women into a stage of burn out—women called it *shang da yin*. As Ying noted:

> At the very beginning I snorted heroin because I had money. After six years, I didn't have that much money. I began to inject heroin. Soon after, I became a heavy user—*shang da yin*. Every day I used heroin when I took my meals: morning, noon, and afternoon. Only when I was on heroin, did I have the strength to make money. The maximum dosage for the day was two grams per day. The frequency varied with needs: from seven shots to over ten shots. My femoral artery was punctured on two sides. I did the same thing on both my arms. I didn't think about it too much when I did it. I just wanted to relieve the momentary pain.

After women had injected for a period of time, the intense, pleasurable sensations of injection gradually diminished, and the difficulties of injection increased. The most difficult issue was to locate veins.[6] As Kaili said, "Eventually, I couldn't locate veins. Even if I followed the old pinholes, I had to shoot many times before I got the right one." During my follow-up study, I visited two women's homes and was able to witness their injection routine. It took both of them more than one hour to get the shot right. Unfortunately, they both needed more than one shot per day, which made these injections one of the most troublesome aspects of their daily routines. Due to these reasons, women quite often changed their drug-use technique periodically, typically going from injecting to snorting, then from snorting back to injection in order to re-sensitize their reaction to drugs. The consequence of change was an increase in dosage. Xiaoling pointed out:

> When I felt I lost the good feelings of injection, I switched to snorting. When I lost interest in snorting, I changed back to injection. Typically I changed back and forth within a month. But if I only used one gram per day by injecting, I had to increase the dosage to one and a half gram for snorting in order to reach the same intensity. When I changed back to injection, the dosage had also to be increased. No matter whether I was injecting or snorting, I always kept it to three times a day: morning, afternoon, and evening.

DRUG AVAILAILITY

The availability of drugs has a direct impact on drug-users' careers (Faupel 1991). As shown in Chapter 1, heroin abuse emerged in Yunnan in the late 1980s, following which the amount of heroin trafficked to China steadily increased. With the launching of national narcotics control policies in the early 1990s, local law enforcement conducted frequent and severe strikes against drug trafficking. These strikes were normally made prior to the "International Day against Drugs" and major Chinese holidays, such as National Day and the Spring Festival.[7] In general, at the present time, opportunities for purchasing heroin from the drug selling hot spots, such as the Northern Train Station area, are significantly reduced from what they had been in the 1990s. According to interviews with women heroin users, although these strikes temporarily restrained accessibility to heroin, once the strikes were over, everything went on as before. On the other hand, though, opportunities for purchasing heroin directly in the street have notably decreased in recent years. Still, the NST area was the primary location to go to fulfill an urgent need for drugs, as for example, if the usual drug dealer was arrested or short of supply. Minority nationalities, typically Yi, Hui, and Weiwuer lived in cheap hotels, or rented apartments from which they sold heroin.[8] They often assigned pregnant or nursing women, or even children, to make the drug transaction. Women complained that the police, who were often stationed at drug-selling hot spots looking for opportunities to arrest buyers, often left visible sellers alone.

During my first fieldtrip in 2005, I observed Yi women, wearing their traditional costumes, sitting in groups beside the major traffic routes in the NTS area. Almost all the local people knew they were soliciting customers for drugs. However, when I returned to Kunming in 2008, they were no longer stationed there. Instead, they hid themselves in the secluded streets known by drug users and by local policemen as well. Guided by my informant, who participated in my follow-up interviews in 2008, I was able to visit one of these new drug-selling spots. During one of my visits, I witnessed a drug transaction between a woman drug user carrying a baby on her back and one of the Yi women drug sellers. My informant told me that although undercover policemen were in nearby places observing the Yi women drug sellers' transactions, they would not arrest the female buyer as she had a baby with her.[9]

Other issues related to the availability of heroin were changes in its price and quality. Whenever the local police carried out a hard strike on drugs, the price of heroin went up. In general, women heroin users have witnessed an increase in its price, and a reduction in its quality, particularly in recent years. When interviews were conducted in 2005, the price of heroin of the highest purity had increased to about 300 yuan ($37) per gram, in contrast to about 100 yuan ($18) per gram in the early 1990s; the price of heroin of low purity ranged from a few dozen yuan to about 100 yuan ($12). During the time of my conversations with the women drug dealers in 2008, the price of heroin had increased to about 450–500 yuan ($63–70) per gram; the retail price was much higher, ranging from 500–700 yuan ($70–98).[10] The diminishing purity of heroin was also observable. As explained by Xiaoling:

> Compared to drugs in the 1990s, the quality of heroin has deteriorated now, and its potency is not what it used to be. For example, before, if you bought 0.5 yuan's worth, you felt dopey. But today, even if you spend one yuan, you won't get the same feeling. Before, if you took one gram you wanted to hit your head on the wall when you *duanyao* (quit drugs), but now even if you took two grams a day you won't do that. One gram of heroin of good quality lasted for four to five hours, but the effect of bad quality heroin lasts only two hours.

In addition, women purchasing heroin from dealers in the NTS area were also likely to get bad quality heroin or even a fake product. As Li stated: "Heroin in the NTS area was cheap and convenient, but you had to learn how to tell the quality of drugs. One time, my friend and I bought fake drugs—a big limestone." Along with the aforementioned issues, women also identified two major changes in heroin-related transactions: drug sellers were reluctant to give heroin on trust as they had before, and the amount of drugs buyers could ask for at a time was limited. As Xiaoling sadly said:

> Right now, you couldn't even get a few yuan's worth on credit. These changes occurred around 1998. Before that, if I didn't have enough money to pay for drugs, dealers would say, "It's only a couple of drugs. Just take it." They could give you drugs on credit even when they were worth more than several hundred yuan. I could also ask for 10 or 20 grams each time. But right now I can only get one or two grams.

As a result of these changes, women were under increased pressure to make full payments for their daily drug purchases, and they had to maintain frequent, generally daily, contact with drug dealers, which could potentially increase their risks of being arrested. Women attributed these changes to stricter enforcement of narcotics control policies.

DRUG PURCHASE

After initiation, with the need for heroin increasing, women heroin users had to find ways to obtain the drugs.[11] The most serious threat associated with heroin purchases was the risk of being arrested. Women generally complained that, in recent years, arrests of drug users had become more frequent than before. The police widely used drug sellers and drug users as informants to arrest other drug users; women drug users referred to this practice as *maima* —"selling the horse." Since most women drug users were in a network of addicts, *maima* became a real threat to their drug-use career.[12] Meanwhile, a special task force—a plain-clothes criminal investigation division—the first one of its kind in China, was established by the Kunming Municipal Public Security Bureau in 2004. These police officers dressed in civilian clothes, acting as bicycle repairers, rickshaw pullers, or shoeshine persons, in appearance far removed from regular police officers. Many women told me that these officers in disguise were the real threats to their daily heroin routines and several of the women were arrested by these undercover agents.

Compared to asking a dealer by telephone to supply drugs, purchasing heroin at an on-site visit was obviously more risky. Very often, women were arrested on their way to procuring the drugs, or on their way back with the drugs, or even at a drug dealer's home. For these reasons, women were less likely to purchase heroin from the street, rather, they relied heavily on their connections with specific drug dealers to get their daily supplies. Without exception, all women admitted that they made some basic mistakes at the beginning of their drug-use careers. Mei told me "When I entered the drug dealer's home, the police were already there. I still handed over the money, and was arrested right away." With increasing experience, however, women learned how to minimize their risks of being apprehended by the police. For example, women who had small children always took them along for drug transactions because the police were unwilling to arrest a mother with a little child.

To minimize the risk, most of the women tried to maintain stable connections with certain drug dealers. Women themselves admitted that locating drug dealers and obtaining drugs involved a learning process. As Xuan said, "Purchasing drugs was pretty much self-taught. When you got on drugs, you began to know many people in this circle." In particular, women's experience in mandatory rehabilitation facilities provided them a widening social network of drug users and drug deals. Juan told me, "I got to know some people selling drugs in Changpo.[13] They gave me their phone numbers and I called them when I was out. "

Purchasing heroin by making a phone call sounds like a convenient and easy method for women to use. But not all women could actually avail of this fast and low-risk service. Essentially, where, and from whom, women could get drugs was based on their ability to get drug money. As Ying said, when she had plenty of money to spend, drug dealers sent heroin to her in minutes. After she ran out of money, she had to go back to the street to get drugs. While the quality and quantity of drugs were primary concerns during the purchase, the majority of times only women in good financial shape could purchase heroin of good quality. In Juan's words:

> The quality of heroin has several levels: *yiya* (one quarter) priced at 30 yuan, 40 yuan, or 50 yuan. If you weren't familiar with the drug

> sellers, you paid 50 yuan, but might only get the quality of a 40-yuan heroin. So many things are blended into heroin now. Since I always had good relations with the sellers—paying money on time and having long-term relations with them, I don't worry about the quality.

As revealed in the interview with Juan, when purchasing heroin the quality of the drug was one concern and its quantity was another. All the women realized that they could not expect a full amount of drugs from the sellers—because the drug market was a seller's market. Still, good financial resources gave women a better position to be treated well. As Lan said:

> If you purchase 0.5 gram heroin, good sellers gave you 0.4 gram, but a bad seller only gave you 0.3 gram. I bought 5 grams every time. These friends (drug sellers) all knew I had money to spend. With people like me, who never owe money to dealers and purchase drugs all the time, the dealers won't scrimp on drugs. But if you always fell into arrears, or asked for drugs irregularly, it would be quite different.

However, frequent arrests and strikes on narcotics often made it impossible for the women to secure their connections with drug dealers. During the strikes, drug dealers generally remained in hiding, and did not respond to phone calls. Therefore, securing heroin during hard strikes was a critical issue for women addicts. Maintaining connections with at least two drug dealers became a common practice. An in-person visit to the NST area was the last resort, when drug dealers could not be located by any other manner.

Because most women felt it was a headache to search for drugs, those who had good financial resources could ask other drug users to go find the heroin in exchange for being allowed to keep a small amount for themselves. In the case of those who had drug-using male partners, the burden of purchasing was naturally taken over by the men. However, due to the risks inherent in the transaction, or on account of involvement in other illegal activities, the women's male partners had a greater chance of being arrested. Once the men were arrested, the women had to look for drugs by themselves or quickly locate another male partner.

ILLEGAL ACTIVITIES FOR DRUG MONEY

To support the cost of drugs, a regular, stable and substantial economic source is required. Generally speaking, women who were in business and those working in the sex trade were able to pay their drug expenses from their savings, sometimes even for several years. However, spending their savings, selling property and even personal belongings might help women for a short period of time, but would not sustain their heroin habit for long.

For those young girls who did not have any personal savings to spend, or property to sell, cheating family members (especially parents) and friends, sometimes even stealing from the former, provided a source of money at the beginning of their addiction. These tricks could not be played for long, either. Unlike male drug users, women's gender identity opened another avenue for them to get funds for drugs—support from male partners.[14] As Hua said, "Since I have known my boyfriend, I do not worry about money. He could get money every single day by stealing or robbing." However, only a few women (especially those with distinctive beauty) were able to rely on the male partners through their entire drug-use careers.

When women had finally exhausted all possible legitimate resources available to them—family, male partners and friends—they had to choose between quitting drugs and finding other ways to get money. Studies indicated that women drug users were as busy as their male counterparts in taking care of their business to maintain their drug habits. Many women drug users engaged in different types of income-generating activity at the same time (Rosenbaum, 1981; Anglin and Hser, 1987; Denton and O'Malley, 2001). Compared with male drug users, women drug users are more likely to commit nonviolent and income-generating crimes, including prostitution, property crime and drug dealing (Rosenbaum 1981; Hser, Chou and Anglin 1990; Chesney-Lind and Laidler 1997; Willis and Rushforth 2003). Women's previous deviant or criminal behavior is expected to have significant influence on their income-generating activity.[15] In particular, illegal activity prior to drug use by women provides them with skills and easy access to the local criminal subculture.

In contrast to previous studies, only a small portion of women in the current study had engaged in serious deviant behavior or committed crimes prior to their heroin addiction. After their initiation into heroin, however, their engagement in illegal activities significantly increased, and was mainly concentrated in three areas: illegal sex service (46 percent), shoplifting/stealing (31 percent), and drug dealing (19 percent). How these women, who have never participated in illegal activity prior to drug use, initiate illegal activity to support drug habits, has remained largely unexamined by previous studies. Thus, it will be very important to explore how women drug users develop criminal skills to engage in street crime, and with whom they associate to practice these skills.

Illegal Sex Service

As revealed in previous studies, participating in sex services is more appealing to women drug users because it is a relatively easy and quick way to get money; sex work was also the "only consistently available option" for them (Maher and Daly 1996; Chesney-Lind and Laidler 1997). Among the women in the study, forty had been hostesses and one had once been a *mami* following their initiation into heroin. This group includes eight women who had previously participated in the sex trade. As Mei said, "People had no choice when they were on heroin. Men stole bicycles and young pretty girls got money by being hostesses." To gain a deeper understanding of women's participation in the sex trade, during my follow-up study in 2008, I purposely interviewed sixteen women heroin users who were mainly engaged in prostitution. Field observations at local nightclubs and dance halls were made as well. As Table 2.3 indicates, while a small portion of women were still on heroin (32 percent), over half of them were in methadone treatment. Many of these women were over 35 years old (75 percent) and they mostly carried out their business in dance halls (56 percent), with a relatively low percentage doing so in nightclubs (31 percent). To maximize their income, two of the women chose to work in the dance hall during the day, switching to the nightclub at night.

Among women in the study, young girls normally began their illegal activity by providing sexual services, including, but not limited to prostitution. Although this illegal practice provided women with the steadiest income, most women did not go into this business until they had exhausted other options. In general, women struggled with themselves before making the final decision to engage in such activity. Tian and her boyfriend were truly in love. Her boyfriend had tattooed her name on his arm. While her boyfriend was incarcerated, Tian had to make money on her own. Tian's experience was very typical of women in the study:

> My father firmly pronounced that he wouldn't give me money for heroin. Actually my parents weren't able to afford my heroin use. Their monthly salary was about 2,500 yuan ($450). Even though I wasn't heavily addicted, I needed one gram every three days, which cost me about 200 yuan ($36). As a young girl, what could you do without money? I felt that my parents just let me do wherever I wanted. I began to be a hostess. I could earn at least 100 yuan per night. With good clients, I might make 200 or 300 yuan.

Although the decision to become a hostess was related to a women's inability to support her drug use, there were also strong indications of peer influence on this resolution. Almost without exception, women got involved in the sex trade under the influence of, or on an invitation from their female drug-using friends. Women might initially struggle with their decision; however, the temptation of gaining quick money, as seen from the experience of their peers, finally became irresistible.

Mei and her husband were both heroin users. Unlike other drug-using men, her husband was not able to make money on the street. Although a housewife for years, Mei finally threw herself into the business with the encouragement of her best friend:

> Many of my friends were hostesses. A best friend of mine went to dancing halls every night. Seeing that I had no money and did nothing at

> home, she invited me to go with her. She showed me all the details of the business with men. I didn't like those places. I felt so embarrassed when I saw her dancing with those men. My friend blamed me, "You're here for money. Look at you. How could you make money?" Gradually, I got used to the situation.

Mei claimed that her husband did not know she earned money by being a hostess. Indeed, many drug-using male partners did not actually care how their women obtained money when they were desperate for drug money. Some of them relied completely on the women to secure their drug money. Thus, if their male partners were heroin users, women's involvement in sex services was unlikely to lead to the breakup of their relationships. Regardless of men's attitudes toward their women's engagement in the sex trade, women felt more comfortable admitting they were *zuotai* madams (hostesses) rather than *chutai* (prostitutes). Women felt reluctant to admit that they engaged in prostitution with their clients. Although, in the beginning, women tended to resist going out with clients, with increasing heroin use and growing demands for money, women eventually gave up on themselves. In the words of Wei:

> At that time, *zuotai* brought me about 200 yuan ($28) per night, but was still lower than *chutai*. One day I served a client from a Northeast province who liked me very much. He took out 10,000 yuan ($1,800) and invited me to go out with him (to have sex). After I said "No" to him, he increased the money to 30,000 ($5,400) yuan. I still rejected him. Finally, he was very disappointed and left. With my increasing addiction, however, I started to go out with those clients who invited me.

Three types of entertainment venues in Kunming provided opportunities for women to get involved in sex work: upscale nightclubs, downscale nightclubs and low-priced dance halls (which locals refer to as "*momo dance halls*").[16] None of the women in the study solicited customers in the street (so-called *zhan jie girls*, or street girls). In fact, the street girls in Kunming were mainly middle-aged women from rural areas (either from Yunnan or other neighboring provinces). Because the majority of women in the study were natives of Kunming, they drew a distinct line between themselves and the street girls.[17]

During my follow-up study the women told me that in recent years, the upscale nightclubs were operated more like a company: women clocked in before 8:00 PM in the evening and any inexcusable absence was subject to a penalty fee of 50 yuan ($7.20). They dressed in seductive uniforms and were called upon for services based on their previous sales achievements.[18] Women working in these places could earn 300 yuan ($42) for accompanying clients, including singing, dancing, and playing cards while drinking. If they provided immediate sexual intercourse (women called it *kuaican*—"fast food") inside the private room of the nightclub, they could get another

300 yuan. If they were invited to go out and spend a night with their clients, they might earn at least 500 yuan ($70). In contrast, women working in downscale nightclubs made much less money even though they provided the same services. Finally, women working in the *momo* dance halls were at the bottom of the sex trade ladder, but they could go to work whenever they wanted (pimps were not involved).

During my fieldwork in 2008, I made several trips to these *momo* dance halls. *Momo* dance halls open three times a day, in the morning, afternoon and evening. The early morning opening hours are mainly for senior folks doing their morning exercise. During the afternoon and evening opening hours, however, all the women were there for the purpose of soliciting clients. The admission fees are as low as just a few yuan. Unlike other dance halls, these places turn their lights off when the music starts. Using a cell phone, or even lighting up a cigarette, are strictly prohibited by the security guard. Because there is no dancing at all in these dance halls, intimate touching, oral sex and sexual intercourse are the real reasons that attract male clients—all performed in the darkness with the music playing (each song lasts about 10 minutes).

It was great humiliation with very little monetary reward for the services the women had provided. The service fee for each song was 10 yuan ($1.45), which allows intimate touching. The extra services, such as oral sex or sexual intercourse, required additional payment, but it was merely 30–50 yuan. Among the women in the study, those who could not make money in the nightclubs had no choice but to join this illegal business. They all felt ashamed for engaging in it. During the few minutes of short breaks between songs, the men walked past and examined the women who lined up on one side of the dance hall. If they liked what they saw, they quickly grabbed the woman's hand and dragged her to the central area of the dance hall, to disappear, within a few seconds, into the darkness.

While nightclubs could bring women more money than the low-priced dance halls, all the women, irrespective of the entertainment setting they worked in, had to learn certain strategies to adapt to their environments.[19] Xiaoling, who had always worked in upscale nightclubs, said: "If I stayed longer at the same place, I'd have more frequent visitors. If they liked you, they asked for you by name next time. I didn't need to spend too much energy with them." However, the women I interviewed in 2008 complained that, with the passage of time there were no longer such easy ways to make good money, on account of the increasing demands from men and the rising numbers of women in the sex trade.

The women sadly said that the men were not satisfied unless they had tortured you by all means to maximize their pleasure. They also said that if you felt you could not tolerate certain things, other girls were more than willing to step forward. During my fieldtrip to these dance halls, I was truly astonished by the intense competition among the women—only a quarter of them (from among over one hundred girls) were picked out by the men at each round. To remain competitive, the women working in the nightclubs must accept the fact that they might be touched sexually by men in front of the other girls and clients, and they might have to perform strip dances and provide immediate sex service.[20] It would certainly appear that the more tolerant they were, the more money they could make; yet this was not always true. Women working in dance halls had to endure extremely difficult situations in return for little money.[21]

Regardless of all the difficulties they confronted, there is no doubt that sex services provided them with quick and convenient money. The age and beauty of the women predetermined the types of service venues they could enter. In general, women's age was a determining factor affecting their continued work in upscale nightclubs. Lei, 36 years old, was tall, with long, straight hair flowing down her shoulders. She said: "If you are eighteen or nineteen, it's all right. But if you are over thirty, it wouldn't fit you well. You can still be there, but you can't get money and you have to pay transportation fees." Jing who was 38 years old, expressed the same view: "After I passed the age of 27, I felt I was not competitive with those young girls." Increased heroin use eventually also made some women lose the opportunities to make good money. With diminishing opportunities, many of them who previously worked in upscale nightclubs sought recourse in *momo* dance halls, or came out to make money on the street. Ying felt great stress due to the changes brought about by her heavy drug use:

> When I was young and pretty, wherever I went, my clients always loved me. These men spent their money on you because you were charming. With increasing drug use, I lost my beauty. Right now I am unable to make money in nightclubs. I can only dance in those *momo* dance halls. Sometimes, security guards wouldn't allow me to enter, because they could easily tell I was a drug user.

Making a living as a sex worker had a lower risk of being arrested by the police when compared to other street crimes. Only few women were taken into the police custody because of engaging in prostitution. However, this does not mean there was no risk at all. Searches of entertainment venues, especially during police raids, increased the pressure on women operating in such businesses. During my follow-up study, one of these *momo* dance halls was struck down by local law enforcement and publicized in the local media. However, at the same time, at least a dozen similar dance halls continued undisturbed, which implied that these strikes merely picked their targets selectively, rather than systematically.

Property Crime

The number of women committing property crime was second only to those involved in illegal sex services. Twenty-eight women had engaged in property related crime, mainly shoplifting and stealing (women referred to it as "*zhua-jie*" in Yunnanese slang), either occasionally or over a long period of time. As discussed in the last section, the age of the women significantly influenced which income-generating activity they could be involved in. Young girls rarely ventured into property crime as a primary financial source; if they did, it was only occasionally, and as a supplement to their daily income. In contrast, for women who were unable (or unwilling) to make money from sex services or drug dealing, property crime became a major theme in their lives. They mainly concentrated on shoplifting, and to a lesser extent, on stealing. The targets were primarily brand name stores, supermarkets, grocery stores, or portable property available on the street (electronic or regular bicycles).

Unlike their ambivalence towards making money through sex services, most women—even the bravest ones—experienced real fear about stealing. As stated by Faupel (1991), the learning process for drug users was not limited to getting off and coping, but also included hustling. Studies on women drug users generally recognized that women drug-users' street hustling required both "technical and social skills and street smarts" (Sterk 1999, 63). In contrast to the findings of previous studies, the current study revealed that where property crimes are concerned, a male partner, crime group, or association with other men was atypical.[22,23] Women began their initial practice by observing or assisting others—normally female drug-using peers. Hands-on training from other women helped them overcame their initial fears, and learn how to select suitable targets and develop the skills necessary for shoplifting/stealing. Women's initial fears disappeared also with increasing experience. As Congshan said, "Gradually I didn't feel guilty at all; I felt like I was picking out my own things."

Lin showed early delinquent behavior while she was in school. Regardless of her disobedience, she did not get involved in street crimes until she began to use drugs. It was from one of her best female friends that she learned how to steal. She told me how she started:

> One day my classmate stole a dress and treated me to heroin. She said, "Don't laugh at me. I have no choice." I replied, "I won't laugh at you because I might do the same thing." She advised me not to take things of little value because it won't bring in good money. Even if you stole goods worth only 20 yuan, you'll still be arrested for the theft. I thought, "I'm using drugs, but I won't owe anything to my friend. The next day, I'll do something and treat her."

Lin's first attempt was very successful, and it quickly built up her self-confidence. She continued:

> The next day I went to a small store located on a busy street full of different types of shops. I put my hands on a handbag priced at 800 yuan ($145). When I saw that two salespersons didn't pay attention

> to me, I grabbed the bag and made two big steps to the gate. I was so scared; I ran all the way back home. I sold it for 100 yuan ($18). When I had money in my hands, I knew I could do it. The next day, I visited another store and did the same thing.

It is worth mentioning that with the economic reform, a variety of shopping malls, brand name stores and supermarkets emerged and mushroomed all over the city, providing increasing crime opportunities for women heroin users to commit property crime. As Jun witnessed:

> Between 1997 and 1999, many new stores and supermarkets were opened in the city. It was quite easy for us to make money from these places. I always went out with my drug-using friends. We were empty-handed when we left, but we returned with two or three heavy trash bags in hand. We could make 500 to 600 yuan ($60–70) per day sometimes, and always at least 200 to 300 yuan ($24–36).

Though fearful at first, most women quickly grasped the skills required to commit property crimes on their own. Of all the women who had committed property crime, two women's experiences were very impressive. Qing was the most skillful and successful shoplifter and Tao specialized in stealing electronic and regular bicycles. While their ages and family backgrounds differed, they were both very resolute persons and very proud of their ability to make money. Neither one had been caught by the police for committing property crime; nor did they engage in other types of illegal activities during their drug use careers.

When I interviewed Qing, she had been released from Changpo less than a month before. She looked very healthy and strong. By shoplifting, Qing not only supported the drug habits of her boyfriend and herself, but also paid for her son's everyday expenses and pocket money. Qing was very proud of her ability to make money. She said:

> I never spent more than three hours to get money I needed for the day. Sometimes it was even less than one hour. Others hardly made 50 or 100 yuan per day. For me, making 1,000 yuan a day was quite normal. I could secure at least 500 to 600 yuan per day. I only visited those brand name stores. I always dressed up myself when I made my trips to these places. No one doubted that I was a common customer. I not only supported my boyfriend's and my own drug use. I also gave money to my son—at least 50 yuan a day until today (he's working now). I also assisted others who couldn't make money on a given day. So they all respected me and flattered me.

Although shoplifting was mostly preferred by women, some women engaged in stealing portable property on the street. Tao, a 28-year-old woman, was quite open and without pretension. Unlike most of the others, Tao's initial stealing activities were carried out with her boyfriend, but shortly after she worked independently. She was very skilled in choosing potential targets:

> If you went to a community with all new housing buildings, you'd see that many people left their bicycles and electronic bicycles in front of the building for their convenience. Especially when people were decorating their new apartments, they were careless. One day I stole four electronic bicycles (each has a market value of about 3,000 yuan). If there were no electronic bicycles available, I chose expensive bicycles. If I had no other choices, I stole ordinary bicycles, which were only worth 30 to 40 yuan on the black market.

Compared to being a sex worker, stealing was more risky. Even if women were afraid of being apprehended by security guards or the police, they were seldom subject to serious penalties due to the low value of the stolen property. Security guards rarely reported thefts to the police if the women were able to pay fines. However, if the women were sent to the police, and heroin was found on them (or they were identified as heroin users), they were likely to be transferred to compulsory drug treatment centers at the officers' discretion.

The women knew how to take advantage of their gender identity to deal with this hurdle. Lin, a woman with street smarts, recognized that people could do nothing serious to her because of the low value of her stolen goods. One day she was caught in a brand name store and the salespersons wanted to beat her. She stopped them by saying "You'd better take me to the police, don't use violence here." She said to me "What should I be fearful of? Nothing was serious." As for those women who had small children, they employed different tactics. As Juan told me:

> I was caught in the mall more than ten times, but received nothing more serious than a summary fine. After I was caught, I cried and acted shamelessly. On two occasions, they asked me to pay a fine and called my family. My mother came in with my little child. She said that she had no money at all. They saw how small my boy was, and they reduced the fines. My little boy could always worm me out of the situation.

Still, a few women were never able to make it in the stealing business on their own. They were only able to work within a group of people, but then could not expect a good share of the stolen goods. Mei told me, "I only pretended to be a customer to hide my friends' stealing from view. When we divided money, I got less than the others. But without my friends I couldn't do anything." Women's characters evidently play a role in the type of illegal activity they get involved in, as well as in the role they play in these activities.

Where property crime is concerned, a related issue is how women cash in the stolen goods. There were a variety of sites in the city where women could get immediate cash; these sites were well known by drug users and other street people, and were concentrated in the Northern Train Station area. Business owners not only paid cash for stolen goods, but also provided skills and tools for further crime. As Tao said, when she sold her first stolen bicycle to a person known as a fence for stolen bicycles, she was given some tools and taught how to open bicycle locks.

Drug Dealing

Because drug dealing in China is subject to severe criminal sanctions, it was a very sensitive issue for women heroin users. Although several women candidly told me about their drug dealing business in great detail, even before I asked any questions, most tended to avoid talking about it, and answered my questions rather briefly. Seventeen women in the study admitted that they sold heroin after they became addicted to it. But only one of them admitted that she was once a big drug dealer—selling heroin over hundreds of grams. All others simply bought more drugs from drug dealers than they needed for their personal use, and then divided the rest into small bags to sell to other users.[24]

Due to the fact that only a relatively small number of women admitted to having engaged in selling drugs, it was uncertain whether these numbers revealed the true picture of women heroin users' roles in the drug trade. For this reason, during my follow-up study, I decided to locate more women heroin users who were in the drug selling business. Although it is indeed very challenging to locate women drug sellers, through the efforts of my key informants I finally reached twenty-five female drug dealers who were heroin users. Except for one woman, who had dropped out of the business because she was suffering from advanced AIDS at the time of the interview, all others were active drug dealers.[25] As Table 3.1 shows, the drug-use status of these women dealers varied: except for two women who had not used heroin in six months, women who were daily drug users constituted the same high percentage as those in methadone treatment (40 percent). This group does not include those who used heroin occasionally (12 percent). All the women had extensive drug use and drug-dealing histories. Only five of them (20 percent), however, had been sanctioned for drug-related crime.

In terms of the scale of women's drug selling businesses, although it is not difficult to distinguish between the top dealers and those selling small bags of heroin, it is hard to differentiate between women dealers whose businesses were in the middle range—the drug selling business always went up and down with changing opportunities. According to one of the top dealers, a middle-sized drug dealing business should involve transactions of at least one hundred grams or more. However, based on available information, it is hard to draw a distinct line between those who were selling

100 grams and those whose transactions involved 200 or 300 grams. Even the mid-range women dealers themselves had no clear idea as to their exact level in the hierarchy of their selling networks. For these reasons, as shown in Table 5.3, the study categorizes women's drug selling businesses according to three levels: Four top women drug dealers were in the large, wholesale business, involving more than 500 grams of heroin (Tier 1); twelve women's businesses involved amounts ranging from at least 50 grams to 500 grams, both wholesale and retail (Tier 2), and nine others were selling small bags directly to drug users (Tier 3).

Due to the nature of drug selling, as indicated in Table 5.1, women drug sellers were more likely to run the business in the form of a partnership, typically with their male partners (also heroin users.). Only ten women (40 percent) in the follow-up study managed their business alone, and over half of these were Tier 3 dealers. This pattern is quite different from women's involvement in property related crime where they rarely associated with

Table 5.1 Women's Roles in Drug Selling Business in 2008 (N=25)

Types of Business	Women's Roles in Business	N (%)
(Tier 1)		
Over 500 grams (N = 4) [a]	Partnership with boyfriend	1 (4%)
	Assistant of boyfriend	1 (4%)
	Husband as an assistant	1 (4%)
	Partnership with stepsister	1 (4%)
(Tier 2)		
50–100 grams (N = 12) [b]	Partnership with boyfriend	6 (24%)
	Partnership with husband	2 (8%)
	Run the business alone [c]	4 (16%)
(Tier 3)		
Less than 50 grams (N = 9)	Partnership with boyfriend	2 (8%)
	Partnership with husband	1 (4%)
	Run the business alone	6 (24%)
		25 (100%)

Notes:

[a]In the past, two other women drug dealers had trafficked more than 1,000 grams of heroin. One of them had to downgrade her business to the Tier 2 level because of a serious disease, while the other one was forced out of the Tier 1 business after she divorced her husband who ran the family drug trafficking business. After her divorce, her husband was sentenced to death, but the penalty was suspended two years. She was now selling small bags of heroin.

[b]Tier 2 women drug dealers mostly distributed more than 100 grams of heroin. It excluded two women who downgraded to selling small bags.

[c]One woman employed a *mazai* for her business.

their male partners. Regardless of the partnership, women rarely relied on their male partners to run the business (except one Tier 1 women dealer who was an assistant in her boyfriend's business). Rather, they worked as co-workers with their male partners, with a clear division of labor. As the women indicated, they wanted to ensure that they would be able to continue the business by themselves in case their male partners were arrested. What is more, one Tier 1 woman dealer told me that she did not want her husband to have a hand in this drug selling business simply because he was not intelligent enough. Her husband only assisted her in business by using his role as a top underworld figure.

As explained in Chapter 3, according to the penal code in China, trafficking illicit drugs may be subject to the death penalty. Criminal sanctions imposed on drug dealing were a serious concern, but were not necessarily decisive factors in deterring women. Lei, who had sold small bags in the past said: "No matter whether you're taking or dealing heroin, you could be arrested. Even if drug dealing doesn't last long, you can make some money through it." While women who had a bigger heroin business might not be as at ease with potential criminal sanctions as Lei was, as a matter of fact, their perception was that small bag sellers actually faced more risks of being arrested.

Most of these Tier 1 and Tier 2 women drug dealers told me that the local police recognized them, and knew what they were doing, but could do nothing further for lack of hard evidence—unless they were caught red-handed with the drugs. For this reason, the women believed that connections with the local police were essential for operating the business, as they could easily downplay or dismiss the cases if they were arrested. Even for Tier 3 dealers, establishing a good relationship with the local police station was also essential. One of these small dealers told me that once she was arrested, she could call her "insider" (*neixian*) in the local police station to bail her out. In return, under other circumstances, mostly during police crackdowns, the local police asked the women to sell other drug dealers' or drug-users' names to them. Of course, the women said that they would never do what the police expected of them, except for self-protection.[26]

As a Tier 1 dealer explained, you must have strong ties with both *heidao* (the underworld) and *baidao* (the police) to run a drug business. Several women drug dealers' male partners themselves were top underworld figures or had a reputation in the street. In case unexpected things happened, several women drug dealers (Tier 1 and Tier 2) had pre-arranged with their *mazai* to be the scapegoats. *Mazai* are men who work for the larger drug dealers, and have a trusted relationship with them. The women dealers normally gave them a very good share of their daily revenues so as to secure their loyalty. Two women told me that their *mazai* had been arrested and sentenced, but none of them sold the women's names to the police. In contrast, several other women who also trafficked drugs in large amounts, would rather work the business all by themselves (with their male partners or alone). They believed that having a *mazai* was itself an indication of a big drug selling business.

All women drug users knew that selling drugs could bring them good money, but for various reasons they did not put this knowledge into action. More realistic reasons why women did not engage in selling drugs were their restricted social connections with *shangxian* (the upper level drug dealer) and *xiaxian* (the lower level drug dealer). Most women were in a situation such as that of Yan. She said, "I only knew people selling small bags, and I had no connections with big dealers. I don't have many drug-using friends either and it's hard to find buyers." Therefore, except for unusual courage and insight, women's pre-existing social connections with the dealer and the buyer are determining factors for them to be prequalified for the drug business. In addition, running a large drug business involves a considerable amount of money—a large amount of capital for investment is also required.

According to my conversations with the women, as well as my observations, women who engaged in the drug dealing business were all sociable and determined persons who were outgoing and liked making friends. To maintain a safe and stable drug selling network, women needed to be very skillful in handling relationships with both the seller and the buyer. Some women drug dealers had their *mazai* working on the front line, including making drug transactions and handing relationships with the police, while the women themselves remained behind the scene to avoid risks. In contrast, other women drug dealers preferred to run their business on their own behalf.

Regardless of the scale of the women's business, one of the keys to surviving for a long time in this risky business was the women's ability to evaluate short-term profits and to assess potential risks. Though recruiting new *shangxian* and *xiaxian* were both risky, the more crucial factor was, comparatively speaking, how to control *xiaxian*. For Tier 1 and Tier 2 women dealers, the credibility of their *xiaxian* was more important than the total number of *xiaxian*. For example, they always put a potential *xiaxian* to the test, verifying whether he/she was trustworthy, before they got involved in large drug transactions with them. In general, Tier 1 dealers had no connections with Tier 3 dealers, not to mention the end customer, namely, the drug users; Tier 2 dealers had both wholesale and retail businesses, but their retail transactions only targeted wealthy business owners who always asked for heroin in a large amount for their own use. In contrast, women who were selling small amounts of drugs had direct daily contacts with drug-users; they were more likely to be economically motivated. The experience of Congshan, a small bag seller, was very typical of that of drug dealers at her level. She said: "My daily income from drug selling had to cover all my expenses, including drug use, food, taxi fares, and spare change." This partially explains why Tier 3 dealers were more likely to be arrested by the police.

In terms of women's connections with *shangxian*, all women at Tier 1, and some at Tier 2, had direct contacts with drug traffickers from the source areas in Yunnan Province, including Ruili, Xundian, Xiaguan, Baoshan, etc. If it was a new business with unknown *shangxian*, a visit to the source site and an examination of the drugs beforehand was a must. Then they used the bank to forward the deposit. Even these women dealers all acknowledged that this operation could potentially put them in jeopardy but they had no better choices. The sellers were responsible for trafficking drugs to Kunming. After the deal was made, then the rest of the drug money would be paid by cash right up front. Once trustworthy relationships were established, drug traffickers sent their *mazai* (or went themselves) to deliver the drugs to Kunming on a regular basis at a designated place, or, on rare occasions, to the Tier 2 dealers' residence.[27] These women said that they preferred to conduct business with "*laobiao*"—a nickname meaning "fellow-villager" directly from the sources, in particular the Hui Nationality, who had the reputation of not selling off other drug dealers. Comparatively speaking, women were suspicious of the local folk in Kunming, who were considered unreliable and sneaky. At the bottom of the drug selling trade hierarchy, Tier 3 women made all-cash transactions with their *shangxian* (Tier 2 drug sellers) and *xiaxian* (heroin drug users).

As discussed earlier in this chapter, opportunities for selling and purchasing drugs in the street gradually diminished with increased narcotics control in the city. With the wide use of cell phones in China, women drug dealers conducted their daily business exclusively by phone—receiving orders and arranging drug delivery. Bigger women drug dealers told me that they used secret codes to exchange information with drug traffickers and buyers, and carried several cell phones simultaneously. As a common practice, the women would not accept phone orders from strangers. Xuyan, who was a Tier 2 drug seller, described how she made the transactions:

> After I got a phone call, I then asked the buyer to meet me somewhere. I always delivered the drugs by myself. If I had other people doing that for me, it might suggest that I have a big business. When I met with the buyer, I seldom took the drugs with me. I hid the drugs somewhere, for example, underneath a brick or flower pot. Once I got the money from the buyer, I then told him/her where the drugs would be.

While the small bag sellers tried to cover their everyday expenses through their daily business, the bigger women dealers had made some huge profits far beyond their daily needs. Many of them mentioned that they were thinking about leaving the business, but nobody actually knew if, and when, they would be able to stop—the great profits from the heroin business will always remain a temptation. Despite lots of cash in hand, however, these bigger women dealers, unfortunately, could not buy any property, nor even a car, under their own names. Instead, they had to find temporary places in the city and change their locations frequently. Several of them invested the money in legitimate businesses operated by their close friends or family members and sometimes in illegal activities as well, such as gambling. Two of the bigger women drug dealers told me that they even gambled away several hundred thousand yuan a day, but they were not upset about the losses, they were simply spending the quick money they had gained from the drug dealing business.

The increasing heroin traffic and the growing population of drug users in Kunming created more opportunities for drug sales. Almost all the women dealers in the study entered the drug selling business upon becoming addicted to heroin. While supporting their own habits might have been their original intention, the large profits from the drug selling business led some of the women to consider more prospects. Women's roles in the drug market varied, from low ranking street sellers to high ranking drug lords, which demonstrate women's increasing stakes in the illicit drug trade in the research site. Because these women, especially the bigger dealers among them, could manage their heroin use in a controlled manner (or received methadone treatment in the recent years), there was no indication that women's drug use was an interfering factor in the running of their business.

Other Crimes

As previously discussed in this chapter, women heroin users in the study were more likely to engage in sex services, property crime and drug dealing following their initiation into heroin. Aside from these particular illegal activities, six women also engaged in other illegal businesses, including extortion, robbery, arson and gambling, to maintain their drug careers. Though the number of women heroin users in this category was small, their illegal activities had significant social consequences.

Two women in the study, Na and Lingling, were involved in extortion.[28] After Na separated from her first boyfriend in 1993, she lost the financial source for her heroin use. Although she knew some of her friends were doing "*ge zhu*" by that time—extortion of money from rich people, she did not think about it until she was desperate for money.[29] This scandalous activity targeted men who were looking for prostitutes. After luring them to a pre-arranged cold-drink store, young girls then ordered expensive fake imported wines and other appetizers. If the client failed to pay the money charged, the people who operated the store would not allow him to leave, by threatening or performing violence on these victims. One of Na's best female friends introduced her to this shabby activity. She said that she was very tempted by the quick money she made, but was upset the first time:

> When we stood in front of a luxury restaurant, a guy called us to come over. I didn't know how to respond. My friend dragged me over. We invited him to a cold-drink store to discuss the business. The man ordered a bottle of beer; my friend ordered a fake XO and peppermint

> ice for herself and me. Then she flattered the man and encouraged him to drink more. The guy even didn't get a chance to touch us, but was charged several thousand yuan. By the time he was asked to pay the bill, we already left the store by the back door.

Na told me that she and her friend both earned 500 yuan ($87) that night. She felt very excited about this new business. Her friend gave her some tips on how to make good money. After practicing several times with her friend, Na began to go out by herself. She selectively targeted men from Guangdong, other places in Yunnan, or elderly men from Kunming because they had money and were easily cheated. Although Na had sympathy for the men she met when she first began this business, she gradually got used to it. Na worked this way for two years until the media began to disclose these scandals. Having no choice, Na had to work as a hostess in a nightclub to secure money for her drugs.

Lingling, previously introduced, had a boyfriend who lived with her for over fourteen years. But she also took on a second boyfriend while her first boyfriend was in Changpo. Before she began relying on her second boyfriend, she had to find money by herself—she joined her friends, a group of heroin users (mostly males) who specialized in illegal street businesses. She said, "Once we found a suitable target, we sprayed some blood on our bare feet beforehand. We then kicked people's bikes and yelled, 'you hit me.' This business needed at least three people to work. Because Lingling was a disabled person, she was chosen to play the key role in the ruse. They knew no one wanted to get involved with a disabled person. That was how this scam worked. Lingling said:

> I always acted as a pedestrian. To get money, negotiations for compensation fees had to be operated by a *shuo ke* (someone who pretends to be a passerby). How much money we could get depended on how much money our targets had with them. Sometimes, they gave 200 yuan ($24) and sometimes just a few dozen yuan. It was easy to cheat people by this trick. After a period of time people recognized what was going on, and we lost this business.

Ni was the only woman who engaged in violent crime while on heroin.[30] No one would have connected her elegant and peaceful nature with it. She was part of a group of robbers who used beautiful women to seduce men looking for prostitutes. Ni had never engaged in prostitution like other young girls, nor did she steal goods. She said that she was very dependent on her boyfriends. After one of her boyfriends was arrested for drug use, she had two options: figure out a way to get money by herself or quit using drugs. Because she was highly addicted, and was unable to quit, she joined up with four heroin users: three males and one female. She said:

> We two girls hung out on the street to look for male visitors to Kunming who solicited prostitutes, and took them to a rented apartment, where the three males were hiding. When the man got involved with us, the males came out and threatened the guy for money. We did this two times and earned 7,000 yuan ($900). We spent all the money on drugs, and in two days the money was gone.

Shortly after, Ni was arrested for robbery and was sentenced for three years in labor camp. Right after her release, she began to live with her boyfriend (current husband), who supported her drug habit by dealing in drugs.[31]

As previously stated, Ling began to hang out on the street while still a teenager, and did not even finish elementary school.[32] She had a reputation on the street. Although her broken-down appearance was disturbing to people, she was experienced in society and had street smarts. Without any support from her family, Ling set fire to her own apartment on purpose. She said:

> I did it on purpose. I was so hungry. I picked up people's leftovers in small restaurants. Sometimes, people eating food on the street gave me what they couldn't finish. I stole eggs and cooking oil and other food from local groceries every day. See what I look like? They won't even bother to catch me because even the police don't want me there. I've got all kinds of health problems. They would just waste their time and energy.

As Ling expected, after the fire incident, her financial problems drew attention from the local government. Her neighborhood committee arranged a place for her to stay, and she also began receiving a subsistence allowance of 210 yuan ($26) per month from the government. Despite this assistance, unfortunately, Ling was still using heroin on a regular basis. During my follow-up study, I was told by my informant that Ling had lost her life in another fire she had set herself.

As introduced in Chapter 3, Xue was the one woman in the study who was addicted to gambling prior to her heroin addiction. After they became addicted to heroin, two other women also got involved in gambling: Ru even ran a gambling house with her friends for a period of time, and made some good money, which was all used to support her drug habit. The other woman, Rong, became obsessed with gambling after she married her husband, a businessman who was also a gambler. When I interviewed Rong, she had just returned, with her little boy who was only 2 years old, from her third trip to Bangshan (Myanmar), a place well known for gambling, drugs and prostitution. Indeed, quite a number of women in the study had previously visited Myanmar due to its convenient access for local people in Yunnnan Province. Rong was reluctant to tell me that her husband was arrested for gambling several months ago however her boyfriend disclosed the truth. Because of the long journey, Rong looked very exhausted, with messy hair and untidy clothes. She was also sad about losing big money during this trip to Bangshan: over several tens of thousands of yuan (about $5,000). She said she won about the same amount of the money during her first trip, and then lost over 100,000 yuan (about $18,000) during the second one. Still, Rong told me that she truly enjoyed the trip, not just for the gambling, but also for the cheap, very pure heroin that cost only about 50 yuan ($6) per gram.[33]

In sum, women's involvement in illegal activities changed according to the social networks available to them, and their ability to get money over a period of time. Even though women generally chose a primary illegal activity in order to secure their drug money, this study also suggests that women might resort to other opportunities at the same time to secure their drug money. Consequently, their illegal activities were driven by their increasing demand for drugs, which not only reduced their legitimate working opportunities, but also their illegal gains.

CONCLUSION

Whereas women's initiation into heroin use has been emphasized by the literature, their escalation into continued drug use has not received much attention. The local social context, or in other words, the cultural atmosphere favorable to heroin use, has persistently contributed to women's continuing with their drug-use careers. The current study indicates that the two defining factors in the process from escalation to continuation were, on the one hand, the women's associations with their drug-using peers and on the other hand, the strength of these relationships.[34] It is also important to note that a social learning process has occurred, linking these seemingly separate events in women's continuing drug careers.

Women's recognition of addiction was of symbolic significance in their drug-use careers. As suggested by Lindesmith (1938) and Becker (1967), knowledge about drugs learned from experienced peers convinced women that they were hooked on drugs. They learned that only through continuous drug use, would they be able to avoid the pain of withdrawal. Despite unpleasant reactions to initial heroin use, women also described the pleasure and excitement derived from it. Further drug use was continued not only to release the pain from withdrawal, but also for the purpose of gratification. Although continued drug use was driven by the inability to overcome withdrawal, women's experiences also suggest that commitments in conventional society may postpone this process (Waldorf et al. 1991). Especially important in this context were women's relationships with non-drug-using male partners.

The method women use to take the drug is of importance, and involves a learning process that changes back and forth. With increasing addiction, smoking and snorting were replaced by injecting; injecting was also occasionally replaced by snorting because of diminishing sensitivity to drugs, and for other reasons. Women heroin users transited smoothly from smoking to snorting, but had to learn the skills necessary for injection. Women's drug-using peers, not necessarily their male partners, provided them with essential training.

In the context of purchasing drugs, women were very independent if they did not have male partners to support them. For those women who fully relied on their male partners, the honeymoon did not last long due to frequent arrests. Women had to go out for drugs by themselves or find the next male partner. In the case of the small portion of women who had enough money for drugs, they employed other drug users to buy drugs so as to minimize their own risk of being caught. With the quality of heroin diminishing, women also learned that steady relations with drug dealers were a necessity to secure a steady supply and ensure drug quality.

The most challenging issue for women heroin users was how to finance their drug use. Although studies have always focused on women's illegal income-generating activities, not much attention has been paid to the process by which women moved from having legitimate resources, to getting involved in illegal activities. The current study indicates that, besides women's own savings and property, their family was the primary source of money for drugs. Women were also more likely to depend on male partners for drug money—their male partners were mostly drug users. Women began to engage in illegal activities once they had exhausted all legitimate financial resources available to them.

Compared to their lives before they used heroin, most women engaged in at least one type of illegal activity afterwards. There is an indication that women who had early delinquent or criminal histories prior to heroin addiction were more actively involved in illegal activities than those who had no such history. Women's illegal practices were mainly concentrated in providing sex services, property crimes and drug dealing, but rarely engaged in violent crimes. While women's intimate relationships with their male partners were of significance to their continuing drug use, crime partnerships (drug selling) were also likely to be organized along the lines of domestic arrangements. Meanwhile, women's associations with their drug-using peers, in particular with their female drug-using friends that provided them with constant learning opportunities to survive in their drug-use careers.

6 Desistance

While the previous chapters discussed women's initiation into heroin, and their continued drug use, in this chapter, I investigate the social and individual factors contributing to their desistance of heroin, and explore whether these factors are interrelated. As studies of illicit drug use suggest abstention and relapse is a repeated theme in the natural history of addiction (Hser, Anglin and Powers 1993). It is uncertain whether any readiness to abstain leads to lifetime abstinence. Nevertheless, the numerous relapses contribute to the final termination which is spiral in nature (Prochaska, DiClemente and Norcross 1992).

Although Western scholars have examined various factors related to the cessation of drug use, these studies have mostly focused on the general drug-use population. Regardless of differences in methodologies, recent studies are more interested in theorizing subjective factors associated with desistance (Schroeder, Giordano and Cernkovich 2007). The factors contributing to drug-users' motivation for change, or the degree of change seem to stand at the midpoint of these discussions.[1] Other scholars indicated that, due to the complexity of the issue of cessation of drug use, catalysts for change comprise only one of the three-stage desistance processes, which also includes a firm action for discontinuation and integration into new social networks (Sommers et al. 1994).

Different from the above studies, studies on women's cessation have primarily focused on gender-specific factors. It is indicated that female drug users show different patterns of resistance to drug use from those of male drug users. Although women's internal drives to deliver a healthy baby became a strong motive for them to quit using drugs (Taylor 1993; Sterk 1999), being a mother, or being concerned about children are the most compelling factors for women to quit drug use (Eldred and Washington 1976; Cuskey and Wathey 1982; Taylor 1993). With increasing indulgence in drug careers, women drug users were reported as having to face narrowing life options "primarily in the areas of family and work" (Rosenbaum 1981, 131). Their relationships with non drug-using partners were more likely to motivate them to quit drug use (Sterk 1999). However, if women married non drug-users, they had a higher likelihood of divorce and separation (Inciardi et al. 1993). Apparently, women drug-users' relationships were primarily restricted to men within the drug-use subculture (Taylor 1993). Since both job stability and quality of marriage have special consequences to help resist deviance and crime in adulthood (Sampson and Laub 1993), these variables need to be further examined among women drug users headed toward discontinuation.

Overall, in this chapter, I seek to explore and analyze factors that may consistently contribute to women's readiness for change throughout their drug-use careers. I begin with a discussion of the impact of women's social bonds (male partner, family, motherhood and work) on cessation of their drug habit. I then delineate two other themes revealed from my data, namely health related concerns, and religion. Finally, drug treatment, including compulsory treatment, voluntary treatment and self-treatment, along with their impact are fully discussed.

MALE PARTNER

Women's intimate relationships with men fell into two categories: husbands and boyfriends. Although several women were able to maintain long-term relationships with their boyfriends, generally speaking, women heroin users' relationships with their boyfriends were insecure, and lacked commitment due to frequent arrests on both sides. For these reasons, women's husbands and boyfriends had differing impacts on women's cessation of drug use.[2] In the case of women who had long lasting cohabitation relationships, the longer the time they spent together, the stronger the influence male partners had on women's drug-use behavior.[3] The study also found the drug-use status of women's male partners to be a determinant factor as far as impact on recovery is concerned: it either provided women with constructive support or enabled women's drug use.

Husband

Of the women interviewed, forty-nine (54 percent) had been married.[4] Among forty-one women who had valid marriages before or during the time they initiated heroin use, twenty women (49 percent) subsequently divorced. As shown in Table 6.1, the women who had drug-using husbands were more likely to maintain their marriage (45 percent) than those whose husbands did not use drugs (32 percent). While marriage is viewed as a "potentially transformative institution in promoting desistance from criminal behavior" (Sampson, Laub and Wimer 2006, 500), how the drug-use status of their spouses affected the women's cessation will be further examined in the following sections.

Table 6.1 Relationship between Husbands' Drug Use and Marriage (N=41)

Husbands' drug use status	Marriage status	N (%)
Drug using husband (N=22)	In Marriage	10 (45%)
	Divorced	8 (36%)
	Separated	2 (9%)
	Widowed	2 (9%)
Non drug using husband (N=19)	In Marriage	6 (32%)
	Divorced	12 (63%)
	Separated	1 (5%)

Non Drug-using Husbands

As indicated in Table 6.1, the divorce rate among women who had non drug-using husbands was significantly higher than women who had drug-using husbands (63 vs. 36).[5] Although other issues between the women and their husbands also contributed to their divorce, such as domestic violence and extramarital affairs, the data suggests that the fact that the women used heroin was a key factor. Women's readiness to change was fully encouraged and supported by their husbands before they finally divorced, in particular, during the women's initial drug-use stage. Many of these women said with gratitude that their husbands had repeatedly spent money and time on their drug treatment.

Fang used heroin prior to her marriage. Her husband tolerated her drug use, accompanying her to treatments at the beginning. Though, when Fang was unable to change herself, Fang's husband began to exercise violence against her. Fang said:

> My husband accompanied me for drug treatment at least over 20 times, including trips to other provinces, and hibernation therapy at a cost of more than 8,000 yuan. After all these attempts failed, he became very angry about my frequent relapses. He began drinking almost during every meal, and often got drunk. Eventually, he beat me for my drug use. The more he hit me, the more I wanted drugs. We divorced when my first daughter was only six months.

Women themselves were also more likely to be motivated during these initial periods because they mostly valued their relationships with their husbands. However, as shown in Fang's case, after repeated failures, neither the risk of divorce nor an actual divorce provided a sufficient impetus for the women to discontinue their drug use. As a result, the husbands finally gave up their efforts; or the women felt they were tired of their marriage because of the pressures imposed by their husbands, and therefore chose divorce.

Like Fang, before Congshan got married, her husband had known she was a heroin user. She told me she even used heroin at her wedding reception. Chongshan said, "Since I cared about my relationship with him, I was able to quit using drugs for a while." However, when Congshan felt bored staying at home (she became a housewife after she got married), she began to look for his old friends again.[6] After Congshan's husband divorced her, she was determined to quit using drugs and was able to keep clean for over a year. Shortly after Congshan remarried her husband, she became addicted again. Congshan's husband finally divorced her. When women were heavily involved in heroin use, their desire for heroin became so strong that it could make them abandon even their intimate relationships with their beloved ones.

Among six women who were able to stay in their marriage with their non drug-using husbands, none of them used heroin when they were interviewed; the duration of their rehabilitation had varied from a few months up to five years. Among them, Liang was the only woman who said she and her husband had affection for each other. Though Liang had used heroin for about two years, she had shining skin and bright eyes. Even the other respondents could not believe she was also a heroin user. Whenever I saw her at the center, she was dressed in a graceful manner. She had quit heroin three months before our interview. In the case of other women, although they were able to maintain their marriages, the quality of these marriages was greatly harmed by their long-time drug use, notwithstanding that their husbands had fully supported their drug cessation efforts in the past.[7]

Xia, who had quit heroin four years previously, had had a very good relationship with her husband who was a former classmate of hers.[8] She said her husband had been very important to her cessation, but they were not as emotionally close as they had been before. Xia said:

> One of my husband's friends frequently came to my store to use drugs; later, he died of HIV infection. My husband wanted me to be tested. Because of barriers between us, we didn't have sex very often. Due to the nature of his work, my husband often travelled to different places. He definitely had affairs with other females. Since my husband loves my daughter, and his whole family encouraged him to help me, we were able to maintain our marriage.

Regardless of the quality of women's marriages, the very existence and presence of their non drug-using husband acted as a restraint to their drug use. Their husbands' tolerance of their frequent relapses, along with the support of their families became the primary factors retaining women in their marriage and sustaining their cessation efforts. In this process, those women conscious of the fact that they were aging valued their family lives more than before, and began to appreciate their husbands' help. They made continued efforts toward cessation if their husbands were still supportive of them. However, after having used heroin for a while, women living with drug free husbands were more likely to lose common interests with their husbands—they came to favor the enlarging social network that included their drug-using peers. When their marital relationships were in crises, the women were more likely to think about going back to drugs.

Drug-using Husbands

Among the women who had valid marriage before or during their heroin use, twenty-two (54 percent) had drug-using husbands.[9] Only nine of these women used heroin prior to their marriages; all others developed drug habits during their marriage—most of the time they initiated heroin use under the influences of or together with their husbands. Compared to women with non drug-using husbands, women in this group were more likely to stay in their marriages.[10] Since nearly half of the women were able to maintain their marriages with drug-using husbands, the influence of a husband's drug use was another hurdle to a woman's cessation. Women's drug-use status showed patterns similar to those of their husbands: if a woman was an occasional drug user, her husband was likely to be the same.[11]

Xi and her husband both had a fifteen-year history of heroin use. Each had used heroin prior to their marriage. They were both reducing their doses when I interviewed Xi, who said that it was very difficult for her to quit drugs:

> My husband and I were heroin users before we married, but after we married, we decided to quit using drugs. We went to Xian, my family's hometown, and stayed for eight months without heroin. When we came back, I started to use it again. He couldn't control himself, and simply took the drug when I did. Such things always happened between us. When one of us couldn't bear the withdrawal and used it again, the other just followed.

Xi told me that she hated what she did after each relapse and wrote often in her diary to express her regrets. She admired one of her girlfriends who was able to quit and got pregnant. As a woman over thirty years of age, she was eager to have a normal family life, but she was still unable to get herself off heroin. Another woman, Bin, followed her husband's drug use during their marriage. She had been taking *guomi gels* for five days, as did her husband.[12] While in treatment, they both became volunteers in an aftercare center. Bin complained about her husband's uncontrolled drug use, and said that she could control her own drug use. But under the influence of her husband, she, too, was often out of control.

Apparently, women who were living with drug-using husbands had more opportunities to use heroin. All of them said that no one could resist such temptation. For this reason, four women were forced by their family members to go back their parents' homes. They left their husbands and children with their parents-in-law. Women themselves were also struggling between their relationships and drugs. Qiangwei said, "When we were both hooked, we wanted to separate; after we separated, once we talked to each other, we wanted to take it again."[13] While sharing a common interest in drug use bonded women to their drug-using husbands, when they manifested a different perspective on drug use, the situation normally led to divorce or separation. Among the eight women who divorced, four of these separations were directly related to conflicting attitudes toward further drug use.[14]

As discussed earlier Dan was a strong-minded person, although her addiction to heroin was attributed to the influence of her husband. Right after she was released from re-education through labor last year, she relapsed due to the influence of her husband's constant drug use. With the support of her parents, she separated from her husband. At the time of the interview she had stayed clean for fourteen months. But her husband was arrested again for his drug use. She told me how difficult her situation was:

> He has little ability to control his drug use. His family also felt incapable of helping him. I have no other solution but to divorce him. When he is released, I won't live with him. I'm very disappointed in him. If we are together, I'm not sure whether one day I'll be under his influence again. Right now in my current working and living environment, I won't even think about drugs.

Dan was strongly backed by her parents. Other women, however, were unable to completely separate from their husbands due to economic reasons. Because of narrowing social network of women heroin users, after women divorced or separated from their drug-using husbands, they were much more likely to develop new relationships with drug-using men. Among women who were separated from their husbands due to their families' pressure, Ru's relationship with her husband completely ended after their separation. However, against her family's will, Ru found another boyfriend who was also a heroin user. Women's experiences suggest that separation can only temporarily release women from the influence of drug-using partners. If they were unable to rebuild their social network, sooner or later they would come back to the drugs.

Boyfriends

Forty-one women (46 percent) in the study had never married. Except for Tong, who had been a lesbian prior to her drug use, all others had boyfriends at a certain time during their drug-use careers.[15] Even those women who were divorced, separated or widowed, had developed relationships with other men. Among women heroin users, it was also not unusual for women who remained in their marriages to have affairs with other men after their husbands were sent to compulsory rehabilitation. Although most women desired to date men who did not use drugs, the women themselves felt this was unrealistic, or they experienced communication problems with men who did not use drugs.[16] For these reasons, most of the women's boyfriends had a history of drug use. Relatively speaking, attractive women had better chances to develop relationships with men who did not use drugs. Having a boyfriend impacted women's desistance from drugs in different ways, depending on whether the boyfriend was a drug user or not.[17]

Non Drug-using Boyfriends

Once the women had become addicted to heroin, out of all the subjects in the study, only ten single women and three married women had relationships with males who did not use drugs. Compared to women with drug-using boyfriends, women with non drug-using boyfriends were more likely to be young and pretty, or come from good family backgrounds. While a few of them said that they were reluctant to tell their boyfriends about their drug habit because of people's stereotypes about drug users, some others were very honest with their boyfriends, but preferred to keep their drug-use secret from their boyfriends' families. Women's relationships with non drug-using boyfriends, and support from them, became great incentives for them to overcome their difficulties with cessation. But separation from non drug-using boyfriends was a strike against women's cessation, rendering them more likely to go back to drugs afterwards.

What happened with Zhen indicates that the positive influence of non drug-using boyfriends on women's cessation was also related to the boyfriends' families. Zhen's relationship with her ex-boyfriend sustained her abstention because she dreamed of marrying him. She told him about her previous drug use, but held it in strict secrecy from his family. However, the disclosure of her true story, two months before her planned wedding, broke up their relationship due to pressures from his family. Zhen said she then totally lost her self-confidence about returning to normal society, and picked up the drug habit again soon after separation from her ex-boyfriend. As mentioned earlier, Zhen's husband is also a heroin user, and at the time of the interview, they were both occasional users.

Compared to Zhen, Fengyi was fortunate; she has support from her non drug-using boyfriend despite strong objections from his mother. Eventually, his mother gave up and gradually accepted Fengyi. Fengyi said that her boyfriend cared about her and never asked about her previous drug use. The relationship with her boyfriend enhanced Fengyi's self-confidence about abstention. She said that she treasured the time with him, and their future together. Fengyi finished a two-year long drug-treatment program three months prior to the interview, and also got a job in a company with the help of a referral from one of her drug-using friends.

During my conversations with the women, I could tell that they all were eager to restore normal social relations. Having a boyfriend who did not use drugs was one of the important pathways of connection to conventional society. During the earlier stages of women's drug-use careers, the influence of clean boyfriends on women were less effective than in later stages. But when women had lost normal social relations due to long periods of drug use, they were appreciative of the affection and care they received from clean boyfriends. Xiaomei, over 40 years old, said that her current relationship with her clean boyfriend had been a turning point in her drug use. Xiaomei had stayed clean of drugs for nine months since her release from a compulsory drug treatment center. She said:

> The greatest motivation this time is my boyfriend. I have a girlfriend who was dating one of his friends. She then introduced me to him. My boyfriend knew that I had used drugs before and merely said, "If you can stay away from it, it's fine." He's also divorced. He has a job, and also owns two vehicles for transportation business. He's very kind to me. He pays for all my living expenses now, including rent and everyday expenses.

The women's experiences with boyfriends who did not use drugs indicates that, on the one hand, due to the stigma attached to drug users, women heroin users found it hard to develop relationships with clean men; on the other hand, their relationships with caring boyfriends was a significant factor in their drug cessation, in particular, when they were in later stages of their drug-use careers.

Drug-using Boyfriends

It is very common for women heroin users to have intimate relationships with male drug users. Before reaching a stage where the women could think about taking further action to quit using drugs, they felt more comfortable with drug-using men, who understood and shared their drug habit. Some women had long-term relationships with their boyfriends if they developed such relationships before they began using drugs. In contrast, relationships with drug-using boyfriends that developed subsequent to the women's initiation into drugs were relatively short-lived. Women's cessation is primarily influenced by their boyfriends' drug-use status. Because only few boyfriends were able to quit drug use themselves, their influence on women's cessation was usually negative.

While living on heroin, many women were unable to secure their relationships with boyfriends due to frequent arrests on both sides. If these relationships—especially their first dating experience—had developed prior to drug use, women approached the relationship more sincerely. Otherwise, as Xiaoling and several others said, drug users only made use of each other because of loneliness. For these reasons, women's relationships with drug-using boyfriends developed quickly and ended quickly. Women called this quick mating *pei tuo tuo*.[18] Shujuan explained *tuotuo* to me:

> We (drug users) like to talk about the dangers of *tuotuo*. I relapsed several times because of *tuotuo*. Drug users are very lonely, especially during their abstention. They want people to care about them. Normal romance needs at least several months to develop; we drug users develop relationships while chatting. These relationships come quickly and go quickly because people don't take them seriously. Our female friends won't share drugs with us, but our boyfriends would.

The negative impact of *tuotuo* on cessation was revealed by Shujuan's own experience. She said, "While I was in a drug treatment program, I got together with another male drug user. He relapsed three times and I always followed him." The women were well aware of the negative influence of their drug-using boyfriends. However, as drug users, women consistently told me that after several years of drug use, they had only drug-using friends in their lives. Women felt they were more accepted and better understood by drug-using males. As previously mentioned, Ru's family separated her from her drug-using husband, but she found a new boyfriend who was also a drug user. She told me how they influenced each other and how she was unable to quit heroin.

> The third boyfriend of mine is a man after my own heart. Merely a look, a word—we were induced by the other to pick up drugs again. He divorced two years ago and went back to live with his family. Sometimes we stayed at his parents' home; occasionally we went over to my parents' home. We've been in the abyss of despair: still, one drags the other. I knew I shouldn't stay with him. But once, when we separated, we both felt a great loss.

Meiru and her boyfriend were also both occasional users. Unlike many others, they had lived together for thirteen years but still had no plans to marry. Meiru's experience suggests that the longer women stayed with their boyfriends, the more deeply they influenced each other.

> My boyfriend and I influenced each other equally. Sometimes I was pulled by his forces; sometimes he restrained me. He said that my success rates were higher than his. When we first started off, we warned ourselves not to move backward. If he re-used, I would follow him. We are inseparable; we've been together thirteen years. Now we don't have any income to afford the rent. We spend time together during the day, but have to live with our own parents.

As suggested by Meiru's experience, if women did not have the courage to cut off their relationships with their boyfriends, they seemed to have little hope for successful abstention, due to their interaction with other. Wanfen, became an occasional user last year, as did her boyfriend. Having known each other for seven years, they were planning to marry. But Wanfen was not optimistic about their relationship in the future because of uncertainty about her boyfriend's future drug use. She said that, "You cannot expect that he takes drugs but she does not—nobody has such resistance."

While the majority of women and their drug-using boyfriends were still struggling with drugs, Na's boyfriend successfully quit his drug use for several years and his success had a very positive impact on her. Na had stopped using heroin for three months without relapse. She said, "We love each other wholeheartedly. To treasure our feelings and considering my age, I've decided to quit drugs and think about our marriage." The relationship between Na and her boyfriend was supported by both of their families.

Na's experience indicates that when drug-using men were able to make a firm commitment to quit drug use, they could also be positive influences on women's cessation. Having been with drug-using boyfriends in the past, many women assured me that they would not get involved with boyfriends who were still using drugs. However, even among these women, three of them, Meijun, Shan and Jun, all got involved in new relationships with boyfriends who were either current drug users, or who had recently quit drugs. This suggests that women still have lots of reality issues in their relationships with men.

FAMILY

Women's intimate relationships with male partners could strongly influence their success or failure during cessation. However, it is their families, more than any other social relations, that were the most likely to provide women with constant, strong social support. Women's families, especially the mothers, were their strongest supporters, even though family support sometimes enabled women's drug use. As revealed by the data, families generally tried vigorously to control women's drug use during the initial stages, but with repeated relapses, most families became discouraged, and sometimes their support waned. Family support was essential for all women; however, for single women who lived with their families, it was of paramount important.

Family Support

Most women heroin users come from working-class families. Drug treatment is very costly, recurring rehabilitation imposed a heavy burden for these families. But still, many women's parents exhausted their resources to help their daughters. While they could not afford financial support, due to limited financial resources, several families took their married daughters back home and supported them, while the drug-using husbands returned to their own families, along with any children involved. Although women generally reported that they were deeply touched by what their parents had done for them, their addiction to heroin superseded everything else: their behavior was still largely out of control.

Fen told me she had only used heroin a few times since her father had passed away a couple of days before our interview. She was in deep sorrow when she recalled her father's support of her despite his limited income. She said, "Whenever I wanted to stop using drugs, he gave me money, and accompanied me to treatment. But he was usually very frugal." While Fen showed gratitude toward her father's unselfish support, she also regretted her inability to quit drugs. Before I left Kunming, Fen was arrested for drug use. I had witnessed her efforts at abstinence, but they failed again.

Jingwen felt the same gratitude toward her parents as Fen. She was able to control her drug use, although over a relatively long time, thanks to the influence of her family. She said:

> My parents are my biggest support. Without them, I wouldn't have days like today. If they gave up on me, I might have wandered about the streets. My grandma loved me very much. When she passed away, I was in Changpo. My father lost some vision in one eye, and his eye surgery failed. I thought it was because he was worried about me, so I didn't take heroin for about a year.

On one hand, women's families exhausted their resources to help their daughters, and on the other hand, women were only able to quit for a while as demonstrated by Fen and Jingwen. Although the women all showed their appreciation for their families' efforts, they were still not able to restrain their drug use for a long period of time. Minghua, a girl spoiled by her family, bought drugs with her mother's money on the same day that she was released. After many frustrating attempts, most women's families had exhausted their family resources. Shujuan was heavily addicted to heroin, and on several occasions was on the verge of death. She said that her mother even knelt down and begged her to quit using drugs. Under pressure from her family, by the time of our interview, she had quit using heroin daily, but still used it sporadically. She said that she could not stop thinking about heroin.

Shunjuan's family had threatened to call the police if she used drugs again, and several parents indeed called the police and asked them to take their daughters to compulsory drug treatment. Handing in their drug-using daughters to the authorities was the families' last resort. Tingting's father is a retired senior cadre in the military. Tingting told me how her father was trying to rescue her from heroin:

> My three re-education through labor were all requested by my father. When I was arrested the first time, I didn't talk to my father for several months. I gradually understood what he did for me. If my father hadn't done so, I wouldn't be alive today. My father is over 80 years old. My home is close to the railroad; dead bodies were often found there covered by grass mats. Every time he heard that someone was found dead, he went there immediately to see whether it was me. After so many years, he still cares about me. I'm so grateful for this.

Once a wealthy business woman, Tingting spent eight years in re-education through labor because of her father. She sadly told me that all her close friends (eleven in total) who had used heroin with her were dead. She was not able to understand her father's deep love for her and the deep pain she had caused him until only recently. Tingting was full of thankfulness for what her father had done in her life.

Family's Negative Impacts and Ineffective Responses

In contrast to the families discussed above, not all families were able to provide meaningful support, either emotionally or financially, for the rehabilitation of their daughters. For women heroin users, two reality issues were of prime concern during cessation: except for financial support for daily expenses, another concern was housing. Very few women owned their own apartments, and when they had no income at all, they could not afford to rent apartments on their own. They had to rely completely on their family for a place to stay. Thus, some women were driven into family relations they did not want to be involved in.

Both Xi and her husband had no income from legitimate jobs. They had to share a two-bedroom apartment with her in-laws and the family of her brother-in-law. Xi and her husband were both using heroin in reduced doses. She said her relapse was often due to problems in her family. She said:

> My husband's elder brother (a non heroin user) often fought with his father. The couple had double the income of his parents, but never paid for food. His sister-in-law often verbally abused his parents. For this reason, one time my husband kicked her. The police were called in. I also fought with her because she always looked down upon us. My husband also occasionally fought with his brother. Aside from the pain in my body during abstention, these family tensions often drew me back to heroin.

A drug-prone family environment also vastly increased women's chances of continuing their addiction rather than abstaining from drugs. Qiaoling, the only woman in the study whose mother, Jiahui, was also a drug user, complained that her mother had never shown affection to her during her childhood. But heroin connected them together. After Qiaoling initiated heroin use with her friends, she began to use heroin together with her mother.[19] Like Qiaoling, Lin, too, did not need to hide her drug use at home. She said:

> After I and my husband divorced, we two still lived together. We sold our apartment and all our furniture, and then we went back to his mother's home. His mother's second husband also took heroin. His mother is the person who could look on the bright side of things no matter what happens. She wasn't bothered by our drug use, and left us alone. We three then used drugs together.

It is worth noting that the families of those women, who spoiled their daughters during childhood, generally lost the ability to exercise a strong impact in their adulthood, due to long-standing overindulgence. Fang said, "When we were caught, my mother would take us breakfast, and ask what we wanted for dinner. Perhaps if I had had a stern mother, it would have made things different."[20] There is no doubt that Fang's mother's weakness fostered the continued drug use of her children, and hardly made them think of quitting. Furthermore, in extreme cases, women told me that their parents, out of despair, even aided or purchased drugs for them.

Most of women were eager to quit heroin, but failed repeatedly. Compared to other social resources, they viewed their families as the most reliable source of support. After years of heroin use, and repeated failures, most of these families had lost hope of rescuing their addicted daughters. These parents felt mentally and physically exhausted.[21] Thus, the impact of women's families on their daughters' cessation was closely related to the duration of women's drug-use careers. As the women's addiction deepened, the families' expectations and ability to restrain their daughters' drug use gradually weakened. While these women wanted to regain their families' trust, they also recognized that this would not occur overnight, after their parents' heart-breaking experiences.

WORK

Prior to using heroin, and during the early stages of their addiction, the majority of women in the study maintained a legitimate job. Women who had no employment comprised 23 percent of the total. In contrast, when the interviews were conducted, only nineteen women had a job, which comprised 21 percent of the samples.[22] While analyzing women's current drug-use status in relation to their work status, an apparent connection between employment and drug cessation emerged. Unlike women who were unemployed, out of the working women, only three women used heroin on a few occasions.[23]

After many years of drug use, women heroin users used to draw a distinguishing line between themselves and non drug-using people, whom they always called *zheng chang ren*—"normal people." By defining themselves as separate from normal people, they implied they were the abnormal people in society. Many of them had lost relations with their families, male partners, relatives, or friends. What is more, they did not have financial resources to support their everyday lives. For these reasons, employment became symbolic in their lives: they believed that this was the only way by which they could reenter society.[24] Many women felt worthless and rejected by society due to their unemployed status. In contrast, women who were employed, regardless of the type of work they did, regained much self-confidence about their abstention and future prospects.

Based on my interviews, among many other things, women believed that employment would be the key to their eventual success. Women viewed work as a chance to restore their ruined social relations, and to show the success of their rehabilitation. Nevertheless, when confronted with difficulties in their lives, work alone was sometimes not strong enough to keep them away from drugs. Yuzhen had been working as a staff member in a drug treatment program. She had been free of heroin for three years. But when she and her boyfriend separated five months before the interview, she had a relapse. She said:

> I thought my work was an important factor in my abstention. If I leave here, there's a big chance I'll use heroin again. Separation from my boyfriend was a hard blow. Before I had my relapse several months ago, I had seen my boyfriend using heroin. I didn't want to touch it. After I lost him, I began to take heroin on a daily basis for about twenty days. I was almost addicted again before it was recognized by my colleagues and reported to the director.

Still, these working women told me that they were very fragile during the times they faced life difficulties. When they could not handle their problems, they would revert to drugs. Having a satisfying job provided by one of her relatives, Xia had successfully abstained from heroin for four years. Still, she said that the temptation to use drugs was always there, especially when she was in a dark mood.

> Our family has moved, so I don't meet those drug-using folks very often. But I still run into them on the street on my way home from work. To those who are close to me, I still say "Hi". When they invited me to go for *liao liao xin yua*, I still hesitated, especially during the days I was in low spirits.[25] Last year, I met my friends again on the street, and they told me that they just bought heroin. I was so tempted that I followed them. Since I hadn't used heroin for several years, after merely a few tokes, I lost consciousness. After half an hour, they were able to revive me. But I almost died.

Although the women I interviewed were different in many ways, they had one desire in common: all were eager to have a job. However, as stated by several women, the reality was disheartening. Women who did have jobs got them thanks to their families' social relations, or referrals through their networks of friends. Dan, for example, was very fortunate to have a family who helped her get a job even before she was released from incarceration. Otherwise, women had to be very sociable persons with excellent verbal skills to gain employment.

Song, Tingting's current female partner, had served four times in compulsory rehabilitation and three in re-education through labor.[26] Both women were released this year, but had no jobs and no income. Song told me she had not used heroin for four months, the longest record in her heroin career. But she was frustrated with her current economic situation: having no income at all. She said:

> Getting a job would be the best thing for me. After all, a person needs money to eat. When I was first released, I went out every day. But nothing turned up. If I get a job, I might have a chance to abstain. My parents passed away. One of my brothers also died of heroin. Another brother doesn't have the ability to help me. All my friends are those with a similar background to mine. What I can do now is to take one step at a time and see what will happen next. Live for today, I don't know what's waiting for me tomorrow. If I was severely frustrated, I might get heroin to comfort me.

After my interviews with Song and Tingting, they both chose to stay in the drop-in center as volunteers. They visited the center almost every day and were actively involved in it. In this way, they occasionally earned a little money. Although they still worried about their income, I did not see much sadness in their faces. During my interviews, I witnessed many women who were eager to quit heroin. Ultimately, however, their efforts need to be recognized and supported by society. Xinyi believed that the government should show real concern for drug users rather than just dispersing slogans. She expressed her thoughtful opinion about the issue:

> Once, a group of government officials from a northern province came to Kunming for a project. They asked a question: What should government do to control drug use? I said, "Place a table in front of a compulsory drug rehab and provide jobs to those who are released. The government has merely said, 'Reject drugs, and treasure your life.' But if people don't care about their lives, what do you really do with them?" I told them to go to the compulsory drug rehab to find answers. I mean, only when people show their love and concern for us, they can truly help us.

As suggested by Xinyi, women heroin users, as a disadvantaged social group in Chinese society, are confronted with many life issues after their long-term drug-use careers. For reentry into society, employment and necessary social welfare will give them meaningful assistance. Compared to women whose families were still able to support them, several women were living in extremely difficult situations because they could not get any support from their families. The data suggests that support from women's families and from society will be beneficial for their rehabilitation. However, the help available to most women was far below what they needed.

In general, women heroin users had very limited access to the job market due to factors such as age, limited education and a history of drug use. Still, drop-in centers and after-care treatment programs have provided opportunities for them to work as volunteers, with the possibility of being promoted to the ranks of paid staff members. During my contacts with these women, I found that those who worked in drug treatment programs, either as volunteers or staff, were more positive about their rehabilitation and future. This was especially the case with women who had worked there for several years. Among six women who had quit heroin for more than three years, three worked in drug treatment programs as staff members. While helping others with their drug problems, these women also built up their own self-determination. In comparison, women who had just started work as volunteers were still in transition. The above discussion suggests that opportunities to work were critical to the success of women's rehabilitation. In spite of all this, for complete cessation of drug use, employment alone might not be sufficient.

MOTERHHOOD

Previous research conducted in the Western countries has indicated that women's roles as mothers had a profound impact on their cessation of drug use.[27] Because women's relations with their children begin with pregnancy and continue throughout their lives, their responsibilities as mothers experience significant shifts along with their children's growth. The data suggests that whether women's concerns about their children eventually becomes sufficient reason for women to discontinue drugs varied with the stage of parenting the women happen to be in.

Pregnancy

According to China's birth control policy, each Chinese couple can have only one child, although exceptions are made for certain minority nationalities. Among forty-nine women with marital history, forty-one women had at least one child. Among them, twenty-one women delivered their child/children prior to their heroin use; twenty women delivered their babies during their drug-use careers. Only a small portion of women gave up their privilege of bearing a child. The reasons stated for not having a child were either that the woman was too preoccupied due to the heroin, or that she was concerned for the child's future.

Of the twenty women who had babies after their heroin use began, twelve women told me that they had used heroin during pregnancy, some before they knew of their pregnancies, and some even after they knew; eight of them had drug-using male partners. Among these women who became pregnant while on heroin, eight who claimed that they did not use heroin during pregnancy were already in rehabilitation by that time. Because women heroin users often experience a pause in menstruation during drug use, it is likely that the pregnancies were not identified during the early months of gestation, but only became evident when the symptoms became apparent. Ni was not prepared to have a child when she learned she was pregnant. At that time, she was living with her boyfriend. Ni and her boyfriend desired to have a child, but despite the pregnancy, they were both, nevertheless, unable to quit drugs. She said:

> Each time I hit the aorta. I didn't have a menstruation cycle. I wasn't aware of my pregnancy until the fetus was three or four months old. I discussed the pregnancy with my boyfriend (current husband) and decided to have the baby. We thought, if one day we died of heroin, we wouldn't have a life to continue for us. I never stopped using heroin during my pregnancy; abstention during that time would have been too painful. My son was never breast-fed.

Among the twelve women who used heroin during pregnancy, seven women used it all throughout; two women quit heroin after they realized they were pregnant; three others picked up heroin after they learned they were pregnant. It suggests that pregnancy was rarely a reason for women in the study to stop using drugs. Women with drug-using male partners faced double challenges—their own drug habit and the influence of their partners. While abortion is a common practice in China, women heroin users were reluctant to visit a doctor—they did not want to be bothered. Therefore, they had a high likelihood of giving birth to an addicted baby if they were on drugs during the pregnancy. Even if women were fully aware of the potential harm heroin could cause a fetus, they ignored these factual possibilities and instead relied on luck and chance.

Although all women who used heroin during pregnancy claimed that their children were healthy and normal, some of them admitted that their children had bad tempers and were easily irritated. The local government in Yunnan has in recent years begun to collect data and report the annual birth rate of heroin babies. However, most of these children were not identified by the officials. In my follow-up study, a few more women told me that they thought their child might be heroin baby due to certain abnormal behaviors. When I conducted an interview with a woman drug dealer, she nursed her three-year-old son right in front of me. She had no idea about when she could wean the baby.

Being a Mother

As discussed in Chapter 1, Chinese women's roles as mother and wife are magnified by traditional Chinese culture. For most women, being a mother means bearing responsibility for her children. I was curious as to whether the existence of children—the added family responsibilities—would facilitate women's desistance from heroin use. Among Chinese families, it is a common practice that grandparents take care of the grandchildren.[28] Similarly, in the case of the women heroin users in this study, it was the children's grandparents who removed the children from their drug-using parents.[29] If women's husbands were not drug users, their children might remain with them. But if both women and their husbands were drug users, in most cases, their parents took charge of their grandchildren for the benefit of these children. Indeed, many of these women, their responsibilities as a parent were virtually taken over by their own parents or by their parents-in-law.

The women's parents may have lost hope as far as their drug-using daughters were concerned; they rarely gave up support of their grandchildren. Ni said that she had never looked after her son, a 4-year-old boy, from the day he was born. Jia had twins, a daughter and a son, who were 14 years old at the time of the interview. Her biological mother and foster mother each took a twin and did not allow her to meet the children for a period of time. Women drug users had no choice but to accept such an arrangement. However, since the children were not around, women did not need to hide their drug use at home, which gave them more freedom to use drugs. Kaili told me about her separation from her daughter:

> My daughter was taken care of by my parents-in-law. We only visited her on the weekend. We couldn't take any responsibility; and we shouldn't do any harm to her either. When she was with us, we hardly gave her three meals a day. When we were incarcerated, she began to stay with her grandparents. She wasn't close to us. We tried to get her back several times, but finally my parents-in-law took her away again. I don't feel bad now because I enjoy my leisure.

Although the levels of concern each of the women felt about her children were different, they all felt guilty about their lack of responsibility toward their children. Both Jie and her husband were drug users. Jie's husband died of withdrawal in police custody while awaiting a transfer. The only thing that really made Jie sad was the negative influence on her daughter. Another woman, Dan, felt self-reproach about her influence on her son. This sentiment, along with other factors, led to her current cessation. She told me:

> My son is 5 years old this year. When I was sent to compulsory rehabilitation, he was just over two. His grandparents often took him to visit

> me. He asked me, "Mom, why can't you come back home?" I told him that I was working there. He then asked, "Why is the front gate locked when you're working?" Recently, when we passed there by chance, he was still able to recognize the place. He told me, "Mom, here is the place where you were working." It was a big surprise to me.

Although women worried about their influence on their young children, quite often their sense of responsibility was replaced by the momentary enjoyment of drugs. In contrast, women with young adolescents took their children's opinions more seriously. This was particularly true in the case of those who had daughters. Ping's daughter was twenty years old and worked as a professional dancer. Three months ago, Ping quit heroin use solely because of her daughter. When she shared her feelings with me, she was very emotional.

> This time I quit for my daughter. She cried every day. She begged me, "Mom, don't take it." If I pick up heroin again, I'll shoot myself. When I abstain, I might hit the wall, or attempt suicide. I must be handcuffed; no one would be able to control me. During my first three months of abstention, I didn't go out of my home. I got drunk every day. I drank alcohol like drinking water.

Although Ping had firmly decided to quit heroin for the sake of her daughter, and although she held firm to this decision, she told me that occasionally, she still could not stop thinking about drugs.[30] As their daughters grew older, the women took into more sincere consideration, their daughters' future, such as marriage. They were also tired and exhausted by their daily lives on heroin. Although women's responsibilities as mothers provided an inner impetus for them to desist from drug use, their increasing concerns about their children should be understood in conjunction with other changes in their drug-use careers—their maturation in their lives as well as their maturation in their addiction.[31]

HEALTH-RELATED CONCERNS

The decision to explore health-related concerns emerged from my data during the initial interviews. In the course of these, I witnessed that heroin use caused many health-related problems for the women heroin users, especially for those who had used heroin for a long period of time.[32] The study found that chronic diseases alone seldom constituted a real reason for the women to terminate their drug use. The women might temporarily desist from using drugs because of health problems, but these reasons for cessation would not sustain them very long. Their explanations were mainly "Too busy" or "Don't care."

Yi, a cancer survivor, told me she did not care about herself too much while on heroin. Yi said that surgery only caused a pause in her heroin use; it did not stop her from using drugs. For such a young girl, Yi's story was sorrowful. She said:

> I had ovarian cancer: my ovaries were taken out along with my uterus. My intestines were also infected. I've had five chemotherapy treatments. If I hadn't been using drugs, I probably would have visited a doctor earlier. When I found bumps in my abdomen, I thought, "I've stepped onto this route to heroin. Death is nothing big to me." Because I was taking drugs, I didn't have the time or the mood to take care of my own body.

Heroin's effects on women's health can be devastating. Except for chronic diseases, women heroin users also suffered from other health related problems. Ping was still an attractive, middle-aged woman, but when she showed me her decayed teeth, I was shocked. Since Ping never injected heroin and insisted on snorting it, her front teeth had decayed and had been reduced to black roots. She was ashamed to open her mouth and never sought to visit a dentist because of the cost. Ping was not the only woman whose teeth had decayed due to snorting. Because these women often saw that the same type of health-related problems frequently occurred in the everyday lives of others, they rarely said that they were motivated to quit using drugs because of certain chronic or non –chronic-illness related to heroin use.

Due to the increasing HIV infection among heroin users, this study concerned whether widespread HIV infection among drug users would restrain women from using drugs. Sadly, the findings indicate that women heroin users generally were not concerned much about HIV. However, there were significant group differences. Women who used heroin only with their boyfriends or husbands maintained some degree of precaution. But women who had frequently changed sexual partners, or had engaged in the sex trade, did not consider the risk of HIV infection to be a serious factor.

Xinyi was an outspoken person. She had thin, curved eyebrows and bright red lipstick. Her nails were decorated with her own special design. She explained, "When we decided to take up the life of the needle, we weren't afraid of anything—not even death. Who cares about HIV?" Yuan was the only woman who initiated talk about her HIV infection even before I proposed the topic to her. She had just started a methadone treatment program; people with HIV could participate in the program with reduced fees. She tried to hold back her tears, but they still coursed down her cheeks. She said:

> The end of last year, I was sent to the emergency room; I knew I was infected. I was two months pregnant and bleeding heavily. The fetus died in my belly, and due to an excessive loss of blood, I needed a

> transfusion. The blood tests showed that I was positive. Afterwards I went to the epidemic-prevention station and had a reexamination. The doctors told me that I was only at the early stage of HIV. There were no significant symptoms until now.

Yuan guessed that her HIV infection was caused by needle sharing. Although Yuan did not quit using heroin right after she learned of her HIV infection, she felt that she treasured every minute now, and would not take action to revenge herself against society. Unlike Yuan, Xiaoling said that if she was infected with HIV, she would act differently. After she tested for HIV and received a negative result, she decided to quit using heroin. This happened several weeks prior to the interview. She said:

> When I worked at a nightclub, I always used a condom. Even if you didn't want to, your clients want you to. But if it's with my boyfriend, I don't think about it too much. I lived with an HIV carrier for several years, a female user. I knew she was a HIV carrier, but I still shared syringes with her. Several days ago, I gave myself the courage to take this test. I learned that I'm fine. Now, I'll take the opportunity given by God—to be a good person.

Since most women were not willing to talk about their HIV tests during face-to-face interviews, the exact number of women who were infected by heroin use was unknown. Based on my conversations with Fang, who worked at the drop-in center, it seems that the actual infection rate among women drug users was very high. She commented, "I've never taken an HIV test. At this center, it's very common. This one is HIV infected, another one also is. They're all living well, though, like nothing happened."

During my conversations with the women, it was very disturbing to hear about so much physical and emotional damage caused by heroin. However, these unfortunate events alone rarely drove women to cessation. I was also struck by the women's recklessness; their own health and safety meant little to them. As the women repeatedly said, "Aside from heroin, nothing else is in my mind." However, a few women, such as Xiaoling, did benefit from positive messages about their health, and these gave them hope to begin a new life, and to try and refrain from using drugs to some degree.

RELIGION

As briefly discussed in Chapter 1, China is a country with a long tradition of Buddhism. During the Cultural Revolution, people's religious freedom was completely repressed. With economic reform, more and more people began to pursue religious freedom and become involved in religious activities. Besides the religions typically attached to China's traditional culture, such as Buddhism and Islam (in the case of ethnic minorities), Christianity regained popularity in China. During my fieldtrip in 2005, I had the opportunity to meet missionaries from Hongkong and Thailand who voluntarily organized Bible study and Gospel detoxification (referred to as *fu yin jie du)* in Kunming.[33]

Among the women in the study, five believed in Buddhism; three women identified themselves as Christians; six women who belonged to an ethnic minority were Muslims. The religious tendencies of the women were primarily influenced by family members. Due to the small sample of women affiliated with religion in the study, it is hard to arrive at any firm conclusions. But religion did indeed give women much hope for their future, as compared to many others in the study who felt hopeless.

Xinyi, who had joined local Bible study activities, came in for our interview. She had been married for two months in 2005. While she was struggling with her marriage, she began to use alcohol, which almost took her life. She said, "After I drank a bottle of white liquor, I lost consciousness. The next day, my friends at the gospel meeting came to my home. I truly felt that God was concerned about me." After Xinyi survived alcohol poisoning, both Xinyi and her mother became Christians. She had not touched heroin for three months. She continued:

> When I have difficult times, I pray, and then I feel it is easier than before. When I was using drugs, I felt like I carried a big mountain on my back; now, because of my faith, the mountain was taken away. Indeed, nothing is difficult in this world. A song we sang at the gospel meeting touched my heart and made me cry. When I came out of the gathering, looking up in the sky; the sky is still the same sky; but look at me–the person has changed. I remind myself, don't think so much about what you've done; think about joyful moments.

I could see the happiness in her face. She was quite confident about herself. She told me that she had learned to trim fingernails, and went shopping to distract her thoughts from drugs. She also became involved in an Internet cafe. Another woman, Suzhen who is also a Christian, came from a Christian family. She was strongly supported by her three sisters who were also strong believers, even though her parents had passed away. She said:

> I'm from a Christian family; I was baptized when I was eight. Because of our faith, our family members care very much about each other. My parents and sisters were all church goers. My sisters were in the choir. I go to church on Sunday. Now, I like to read the Bible and pray before I go to work. I read the Bible when I have time to do so. When you have problems you think of Jesus—he's not pleased about them.

Suzhen said nobody in her church knew she had ever used heroin. She felt she had committed blasphemy against the name of God.[34] Unlike other women in the study, after Suzhen separated from her husband many years ago, she did not get involved with any other men. Despite her drug use, Suzhen passed on the Gospel to other non-believers. When Suzhen was released from the compulsory drug treatment center, she was referred to a job by her friend Xia, and she has not touched heroin at all once she began working.

When women were affiliated with religion, no matter what religion they believed in, it provided them with reasons to explain why certain things had happened in their lives, and the encouragement to face these issues by relying on their faith. Unlike women who were Christian, the women who were Buddhist were more likely to believe that each life was destined for a certain path. Buo said that many drug users were Buddhist, because Buddhism provided an explanation of the pain they had suffered in previous lives. She also told me that Buddhist principles gave her the wisdom of reason: to determine what to do and what not to do. These women generally did not exhibit the hopelessness I witnessed among many other women.

TREATMENT

China's national drug control policy on illicit drug use was first addressed in the Decisions on the *Prohibition of Drugs by the Standing Committee of the National People's Congress* (NPC) (1990), and delineated in the *State Council on Compulsory Treatment* (1995) issued by the State Council, which provided guidelines for provincial and municipal governments to enact corresponding statutes and regulations. According to these decisions, drug use itself is not a criminal offense, but a violation of public administrative regulations. Those who smoke and inject drugs are subject to an administrative penalty by law enforcement agencies, consisting of fifteen days in detention, and/or a fine of 2,000 yuan. In addition, drug users are subject to a compulsory rehabilitation program (three to six months, and not more than one year) operated by the local law enforcement agencies. If a drug user has gone through a compulsory rehabilitation program, the second arrest will require him/her to serve one to three years in a re-education through labor operated by local judicial authorities.

According to the national narcotics control policy, three modalities for drug treatment became available in China: voluntary drug treatment, compulsory rehabilitation and re-education through labor. Voluntary drug treatment services emerged in the early 1990s, and have gradually increased in number since then. Compulsory drug rehabilitation programs were created in early 1990 specifically for drug users. In the beginning, these programs were operated by the Civil Affairs Department (such as in Kunming), and then were transferred to local law enforcement. Re-education through labor was also compulsory in nature, and was primarily used to confine those who committed misdemeanor crimes, without posting criminal charges against them. It was used to incarcerate and educate drug users, though the drug users were usually put into a separate unit, away from people who committed other crimes.

After several years of debates, the *Anti-Drug Law of the People's Republic of China* (2007) was finally enacted on June 1, 2008. There are two dramatic changes in sanctions on illicit drug use: the new law repeals detention for re-education through labor, as well as monetary penalty for drug users. Compulsory drug rehabilitation becomes the only administrative sanction for drug users, with one year as the minimum term, and three years as the upper limit. Instead of long term re-education through labor, the new law also emphasizes community based treatment programs; and law enforcement can order up to three years of community rehabilitation before releasing the drug users.

Compulsory Rehabilitation

Among the women in the study, the majority had had at least one contact with compulsory drug treatment programs. Seventy-five women (83 percent) had gone through compulsory rehabilitation programs a total of 175 times (mean =2.3). Among them, forty-four women (57 percent) had also served time in re-education through labor (mean =1.5) programs, ranging from one year to eight years.[35] Only fifteen women (17 percent) had never been to any compulsory drug treatment program, but had only undergone voluntary treatment programs.

The majority of women went to compulsory treatment programs upon arrest. Only on few occasions were women handed in by their family members. To escape compulsory treatment, women knew how to take advantage of their families' social relations. Ping, who in the past had worked for law enforcement herself, told me that almost all her family members were policemen. Every time she was arrested, she mentioned her family members' names, and each time, she was released. Although she used heroin for thirteen years, Ping only went to Changpo once—sent there by her outraged family, and not by the police.

However, most women were not as lucky as Ping. They repeatedly served time in compulsory treatment programs. In order to end this vicious cycle, some drug users made up fake stories, about HIV infections, but although this excuse worked for a while, it eventually failed to prevent incarceration. Some women who had nobody to rely on and learned to use self-mutilation from other drug-using peers. Women referred to this practice as *zican*. For instance, Yuan escaped a three-year incarceration by patting a needle into her chest, but there was a price to pay: pain in her chest. During my interviews with Ling, she showed me a scar more than five inches long on her stomach. She said it was a result of her *zican*—she inserted 18 cm long steel plate from her mouth. Although she succeeded that time—escaping re-education through labor, she was sent to the program on another occasion.

Inside the Compulsory Program

Before re-education through labor was repealed by the new anti-drug law, the compulsory drug treatment program in China was supervised by different agencies: the compulsory drug rehabilitation center was under the control of city law enforcement;[36] re-education through labor was managed by correctional officers under the municipal or provincial judiciary branch. In both programs, drug users were required to perform manual work, or work in the fields during the day. Although these two types of programs were both compulsory, drug users serving times in the compulsory drug rehabilitation center have to pay their own living expenses—about 3,000 yuan for six months. If a drug user cannot pay the fee, they usually have to spend another six months working in the program instead.[37]

Only a few women believed that the compulsory drug treatment program was an effective approach for drug users; most women showed strong objection to it. They complained about the strict discipline, long working hours, poor living conditions within these facilities, and in particular, the low respect accorded them. Xiaoling was sent to the compulsory program only once. She said:

> Compulsory rehabilitation means you must obey the orders. If you want to drink water, even if it's right there, you can't take it without permission. If the group leader dislikes you, he might withhold water for the entire day. Like releasing feces and urine, thirst is out of people's control. But you must wait for the scheduled times. In the bathroom, there are only three stalls. Within half an hour, over three hundred people had to line up to use them. For those taking medicine for the initial treatment, diarrhea was frequent; an urge to void might occur every five or ten minutes. Sometimes people couldn't wait until their turn, and voided in their clothes.

According to the accounts by women, the physical environment inside the compulsory rehabilitation programs was worse than that in re-education through labor, especially during the strike-hard operations. As pointed out by Xiaoling and other women, because of limited number of police personnel, the drug users who were chosen by officers to act as team leaders might actually supervise hundreds of confined women. Lina was sent, twice, to both compulsory drug rehabilitation programs as well as to re-education through labor programs. She had been released from compulsory rehabilitation about twenty-days prior to our interview. She said her experience in those places made her determined to quit; she would never want to go back.[38] She complained about the poor management of the facility:

> The work load was so high that I couldn't even write a letter to my family. The mental pressure was high, too. You have to squat down even to talk to the group leader. A group leader, who used to be also a

> drug user, manages several hundred other drug users. Our group leader had spent six years inside and didn't want to come out. Sometimes even the officers solicited her opinions. She usually had seven or eight attendants who followed her orders.

Lina also felt frustrated with the poor living conditions in the compulsory drug rehabilitation program:

> During strike-hard operations, two single beds were used by six individuals; sometimes people even slept on the floor. If you went to the bathroom at night, you lost your space when you returned. I fear to think about taking a shower and going to the bathroom. Too many people were living and working together, and had all kinds of diseases, such as sexually transmitted diseases, tuberculosis, pneumonia and hepatitis.

As also indicated by other women, they were more concerned about the living conditions inside the compulsory drug rehabilitation center, than with the initial physical pain they experienced while in rehabilitation. Those who were from wealthy families especially felt emotionally depressed because of the way they were treated. In addition, those who had stayed in district centers also reported violence and drug use. Qing said:

> Once, I was caught right after I'd stolen more than 2,000 Yuan worth of things from the store. I was sent to a district compulsory drug rehabilitation center. People in my cell saw I had new clothes in a big bag and asked for them. I'd heard about violence there before. I gave all my things to them. At night, I heard someone being beaten by others in the next cell. It lasted until the next morning. When the officer came around, the attendants just said, "She's craving". There were big group leaders and small group leaders. They also had two goons. Every newcomer was beaten by them. The others all admired me for not being beaten by them.

In addition to reports of such violence, the women also gave me information about drug use inside the district compulsory program facilities. Li once spent six months in one of the district compulsory centers several years ago. She not only confirmed violence among drug users, but also told me about secret drug dealing inside. She said:

> When I had my third arrest, I was sent to the district center. My family paid fines so they didn't transfer me to Changpo. People even took drugs into the facility by hiding substances inside pears, shoes, and clothes (under the zipper or shoulder pad) that their family or friends gave to them during visitation. If you've got money, you are still able to use drugs inside. When my father came to pick me up after several

> months, he was surprised at how thin I was. He didn't know I was still using drugs.

Women said that drug users inside these facilities were very realistic. Women who had money—given to them by their families during visitation—were treated better than those whom no one cared about. Women from Kunming were treated better than those from other cities or other nearby provinces, such as Sichuan and Guizhou. Compared to short-term compulsory rehabilitation, women generally felt more comfortable with re-education through labor programs. They said that at least they had the chance to talk to correctional officers. When they had problems, officers met with them for face-to-face conversations, something that almost never happened in the rehabilitation center.

Another increasing concern raised by women was the rise in homosexual practices inside compulsory drug treatment centers. Qing and several others said that homosexuality is very common inside both compulsory drug rehabilitation and re-education through labor facilities. She told me what she had observed as an insider in one of these places:

> People were so bored, and some of them were very curious. If they paid money to the group leaders, they could sleep next to each other. The officers were all aware of it, but were unable to control it. Too many people had such relationships. Some females had no family support. They were pitiful. Those "men" took care of them, and they satisfied their physical needs. People would fight against their rivals, and even commit suicide for their lovers.[39]

Impacts on Discontinuation

Although both the central and local governments have invested huge amounts of money in compulsory drug treatment programs, women reported that the way the program was operated had increased their resentment toward the authorities and society in general. In particular, women became very emotional when they shared their experiences in the compulsory rehabilitation programs with me. In contrast, according to women's statements, re-education through labor programs provide drug users with better treatment, living conditions and counseling services, but women complained that these programs were too long, and they subsequently experienced problems in adjusting themselves to a changing society.

Tingting gave me in-depth accounts about re-education through labor programs. She was sent to compulsory rehabilitation and re-education through labor three times each. Not including her time in compulsory rehabilitation, she spent eight years in re-education through labor, and had been released within two weeks before our interview. She seemed very sad about her current situation. She felt totally lost after her release. She said:

> The most terrible thing for drug users is *xiangyin* (psychological dependency). When people were locked up, they thoroughly despaired. Re-education through labor is good. But according to my experience, something was wrong with this model. Our labors, including manual work, and picking beans, disconnected us from the changing society. I'm ten years behind in my knowledge and skills. When I was released, I didn't know how to use a cell phone. My soul is still empty. I can only relate to my drug-use companions again.

Tingting said that she was not even ready to come out when she was released a month ago. She continued:

> Though I have bodily strength, my mind is very empty. I thought, if I went out blindly, I've wasted my three years inside. What a pity! My family members saw me coming in and out every day and didn't know how to comfort me. I went to several places for a job, but, for all kinds of reasons, nothing worked out. I thought, the purpose of legal controls is to make people good, but I've lost my ability to adapt to this changing society.

As Tingting revealed, she was not sure how long she could maintain her current situation—staying away from drugs—because she lacked money to support her daily expenses. Women told me that when they were on drugs, they always had money with them because of illegal activities. But after they quit using drugs, they also stopped all income-generating activities. They were barely able to secure their living expenses. It is partially for this reason that the women had high recidivism rates after their release.

Although physical dependency could be eliminated within a short time, psychological dependency would be a life-long struggle for women drug users. Especially after long-term incarceration, women said they wanted to soothe themselves right after their release. It was quite common that women used heroin on the very day that they were released. According to Min, who was released on the same day of my interview with her, if someone was sent back to the facility after ten days, it was not a surprise.

As stated by Tingting, Minghua and other women, women heroin users had not only lost the trust of their family members after many years of repeated relapses, they had also lost their social relations with non drug-using friends. After they were released, and if society failed to provide them with further opportunities, they only had drug-using friends available. Another unintended downside of the compulsory treatment program was that women had a chance to meet more drug-using friends while incarcerated. Jun said, "I recognized only a few drug users on the street before my first arrest. After I came out, I knew more people than before. The compulsory program is a big dye vat." Lei said that due to peer influences, and failure in finding a job, her abstention never lasted more than half a year, unless she went to other places for treatment.

> The friendships developed inside are quite special. We helped each other while incarcerated. I took our friendships sincerely. After we were out, I might invite you to go out playing today, and you might treat me for dinner tomorrow. I always warned myself, taking (heroin) once or twice is all right; but I can't be hooked. However, many things are out of your control. After one or two months, the next compulsory treatment will be waiting for you.

Based on the previous discussions, it appears that while the quality of compulsory treatment programs is important, it is very crucial to provide after-care programs that can satisfy the urgent needs of women heroin users after release. The fact is that the majority of women had nothing to do after they were released. Aside from their drug-using friends, many women did not have other friends who would continue relationships with them, and so they were more likely to accept various offers from their drug-using friends.

Voluntary Drug Treatment Programs

With increasing drug use in Kunming, voluntary drug treatment programs emerged in the early 1990s and have increased in numbers since then. Until recent years, the most prevalent voluntary drug-treatment program in Kunming was operated by Daytop. The annual cost of the Daytop program is about 7,000 to 9,000 yuan ($980–$1,260), a sum still beyond the reach of many drug-users' families. Other voluntary drug treatment programs include medical treatment programs at hospitals or clinics, and community-based programs (such as drop-in centers) providing after-care services free of charge. So far, no comprehensive studies have been conducted to evaluate the effectiveness of these programs, nor have comparisons been made between these programs and compulsory drug rehabilitation programs.

Overall, women who participated in paid voluntary drug treatment programs, typically Daytop, gave very good ratings to these programs' effectiveness with respect to their behavioral changes. In particular, classes provided by the programs have improved their self-confidence in rehabilitation, and have strengthened their ability to resist temptation from other peers. However, most women in the study were not able to participate in Daytop programs due to the higher cost. Still, for them, several after-care programs were available. As presented in Chapter 2, after-care programs provide entertainment, work-related or learning-based activities to help drug users obtain the skills necessary for jobs, or merely a place to spend leisure time in.

Ni decided to quit drugs after her husband was arrested and sentenced to two years of incarceration. She was participating in an after-care program at the time of my interview with her. She wanted to keep herself busy and forgot about drugs. She described her experience to me:

> Right now I'm participating in an after-care treatment program from 9:00 AM to 5:00 PM every day. Unless you have things you must do, attendance is mandatory. I learned how to knit red ribbons there. Everyone has her *lian mian* (self-esteem). If other people can do, I can do it, too. I've been working for half a month. They provide lunch and also pay 4 yuan ($0.5) as transportation subsidies per day. After a month, participants can make money based on the products that they produce. A quick person could possibly make 200 yuan ($25) per month.

Most importantly, these after-care programs have given women drug users opportunities to be involved in the operation of such programs, by employing them as volunteers, staff members or project managers. Women gained much self-confidence in the course of working with team members and helping other drug users. Jie had quit heroin for two months after she joined the same program that Ni participated in. Since then, she has not used heroin even occasionally. She was actively involved in the program rather than being only a participant, like Ni. She told me how voluntary treatment programs differ from compulsory treatment programs. She regained her self-esteem as a volunteer there. She said:

> Every time I was released from compulsory treatment, I used drugs right away. If you don't have strong faith to quit, no matter how many times you are arrested, you'll still find a way to take drugs again. My experience in the voluntary program helped me to make my own commitment. As a volunteer, I go to compulsory rehabilitation centers to give lectures to other users; they all call me "teacher." I feel very much respected.

When I was working on my interviews with women, the government had just initiated a methadone program for heroin users. Drug users over 20 years of age, who were residents of Kunming, with two compulsory rehabilitation confinements, and at least one time in re-education through labor, were qualified to apply for the program. Participants only needed to pay 10 yuan ($1.2) per day. However, applicants were required to show records proving their participation in compulsory rehabilitation and re-education through labor. If drug users did not keep their records, they had to go to their local police station to get documentation, and since many drug users would not keep records, and did not dare to take themselves to the police station (many of them were using heroin), these documentation requirements actually kept out some potential applicants.

Nine women in my study enrolled in the methadone program. Qiangwei, who recently participated in the program with her husband, told me about her initial experience with the program. She said:

> Each person takes methadone once day. No matter how much you take, you only pay 10 yuan ($1.2) each time. The total cost is 300 yuan

> ($37) per month. Both my husband and I are taking methadone now. Many persons still take heroin during the initial period. We did the same thing. Among those in the program, someone usually suggests that we get some (heroin). We are all so tempted. Of the initial fifty participants, about half were still using heroin secretly. But after you use methadone for a short period, you'll lose your sensitivity to heroin. You don't have interest in using heroin again.

As Qiangwei and other women have stated, the methadone treatment was very effective in overcoming initial difficulties of withdrawal. Moreover, the biggest challenge for women quitting heroin often was their psychological dependency on drugs; methadone worked well on this part, too. Women told me they could not enjoy the pleasure of heroine while on methadone, which was very helpful for their cessation. If the women on methadone treatment had male partners, the latter were generally involved in the program, too. Han was in the program with her boyfriend. She felt a big relief while not on heroin.

> My boyfriend affects me a lot when I'm taking methadone, I'm feeling so good. I began to use methadone first. He was still injecting at that time. Under his influence, I injected several times, too, but I didn't feel the effects of heroin that much because of the methadone treatment. When he joined me in the program, he lost his interest in heroin. Many people in our neighborhood were arrested recently (for drug use). He began to change his mind. Now, while I go out on the streets, I'm not flustered.

The women on methadone were all feeling good about their progress, and showed much confidence in their future treatment. Unlike many other women, they were more likely to tell me their plans for the future, for example, looking for a non drug-using boyfriend, or finding a job. Nonetheless, women showed their concerns about potential addiction to methadone after they had used it for a long time. When I talked to women who were not on the methadone program, they generally felt it was too costly to enroll in it, even though reduced fees were available to some individuals.

Self-treatment

During women's drug-use careers, almost all had attempted to quit using drugs either voluntarily or under pressure from their families. Due to the high cost of residential voluntary drug treatment, women and their families often chose self-treatment. Before the Chinese central government began to impose greater control over its retail drug market in recent years, people could virtually purchase almost all prescription drugs from drugstores, and consequently, people self-treated minor or even serious symptoms as a common practice. Almost all women heroin users in the study had experience in purchasing medicine by themselves, often relying on remedies that were recommended by their drug-using acquaintances.

However, with more small drugstores opening, it is hard to control illegal sales completely. Many women regularly took drugs recommended by their peers as a substitute for heroin. After many people became addicted to them the government prohibited the substitute drugs. Drugs used as a substitute for heroin are types of tranquilizers, some of which are even more addictive than heroin, including dihydroetorphine, tramadol hydrochloride, triazolam and compound diphenoxylate. These drugs emerged on the drug market one after another: after one was banned, another soon became available. However, when these drugs were used by drug users, they had no knowledge of their potential dangers. For example, dihydroetorphine emerged on the market in early 1990s. Women who had used heroin during that time were all familiar with it. Ni told me her experience with it. She said:

> In 1992, an outpatient detoxification clinic affiliated with a major hospital in Kunming sold *kou han pian* (dihydroetorphine) as a drug for heroin addiciton. Since I really wanted to quit drugs, my family bought it for me. I used it for two years. I didn't know that it would lead to more severe addiction. It was also more expensive than heroin—for you had to use it about every hour. Many people died from an injection of *kou han pian*. After a few years, the government banned drugstores from selling it.

Some women in the study also used triazolam together with heroin, or as a substitute for heroin. Xiaoling told me triazolam addiction made her crazy when she was sent to the compulsory drug rehabilitation program. She described her severe withdrawal to me:

> I once became addicted on *san zuo lun* (Triazolam). When I had a craving, I behaved like a person with epileptic seizures. When I was sent to the compulsory drug rehab, their drugs for treatment didn't work on me. I had to put a comb in my mouth to prevent biting my tongue. I didn't drink, eat or smoke for almost two weeks. Two big girls (also drug users) were arranged to watch me all the time. I forgot who I was, and where I slept. My memory was gone. Even the officers were scared by my reactions.

Even though earlier drugs were prohibited by the government, again new drug compounds such as diphenoxylate (named "*small white pill*" by women) were pursued by heroin users as a treatment for heroin addiction. During my interviews, Hua, Yan and several others were using it because they heard stories from others of its effectiveness. Hua was expecting to get rid of heroin by using this new drug. What she knew was that this drug was used to treat a stomach disorder. She told me that in previous years, drugstores had sold this drug mainly to those believed to be drug users. She took out a small bottle from her pocket and showed me the name of the drug on it. Hua told me:

> Both my boyfriend and I were reducing our doses of heroin. I heard about a small white pill (the compound diphenoxylate) from those who had quit.[40] They all said the drug is very effective. I think the drug is used to treat digestive disorders, but I didn't ask any doctor about it. I began to use it yesterday. Normally, people take three pills a day, but we have to use twenty pills a day.

Lacking knowledge about the medical functions of these drugs used for treatment, women's enthusiasm for treatment eventually led to even more serious addictions to other types of drugs. Many women in the study suffered from these new drugs that were highly recommended by their peers. I heard a number of sad stories from women, who took these drugs without being aware of the potential harm to their health.

In addition to the drugs mentioned above, women often used alcohol during their rehabilitation. Women commonly said that they could not even smell alcohol during their drug use. But after they quit, many of them became heavily dependent on it. According to women heroin users, alcohol conflicts with heroin. Women totally ignored the addictive nature of alcohol, and felt there was nothing wrong with using it; moreover, alcohol consumption was cheaper than heroin, and there was no prohibition against it. Hua said:

> When my boyfriend served his two years in re-education through labor, I began to *chi hua yao* (use drugs occasionally). On the days I didn't take heroin, I started drinking. I could drink liquor by the half cup. If I had *tou zui* (occasional drug use) one day, I drank the next day to control it. To help me, my mother infused a big bottle of liquor with some medicinal herbs. So long as I drank, my mother felt really happy. She always said, "Drink it and go to bed early." She knew that if I drank, I wouldn't take heroin.

In addition to searching for substitute drugs and drinking alcohol, women's families who had relatives in other places often sent them to those places for rehabilitation—usually remote areas in Yunnan or other provinces. Families expected that the change in social environment would isolate the women from their drug resources and fellow drug users. Indeed, these women all said that they were able to quit drug use during their say in those places.[41] However, no matter how long the women stayed in these places, half a year or a year, once they came back to Kunming, they picked up heroin again. Several women also told me that they played mahjong to switch their focus away from heroin. At the drop-in center, the most popular pastime for both women and men was playing mahjong.

CONCLUSION

A series of social and individual-related factors concerning women's desistance of their drug-use careers have been examined in this chapter. Due to the complexity of the issue of cessation of drug use, it is hard to conclude that any single factor, or combination of factors, could be generally applicable to all women subjects in the study. Rather, the influences of these factors on women's drug-use careers have individual variations, and are also dynamically related to the changing Chinese society.

Among women's social bonds, their relationships with their male partners were found to play the most critical role in women's cessation due to intimate involvement with a partner. Male partners impacted women's discontinuation from two opposing directions: positive or negative. Whether the impact was positive or negative was primarily determined by the drug-use status of the male partners, as well as by the women's marital status. Non drug-using male partners were evidently more likely to have an encouraging effect on women's cessation; in contrast, drug-using male partners often pulled the women back into the drug-use culture. Women's husbands and boyfriends also had varying impacts on women's cessation: drug free husbands had more positive influences on women's cessation, but husbands who used drugs exercised more negative impacts. Long-term cohabitation with boyfriends followed the same pattern as that of husbands.

Women's relationships with their families were the most reliable social resources that they could count on during their cessation. For women who had lost their intimate relationships, jobs, and housing, family became the only shelter they could possibly depend on. The emotional and financial support from families then sustained women's lives and enhanced their self-confidence about cessation. In terms of women's motherhood, the study noted that while women were motivated to desist drug use when they became pregnant, they rarely achieved this goal. However, as their children grew up, women had increasing inner drives to terminate their drug use. Because most children were being raised by women's families, the mothers experienced a sense of failing their motherhood responsibilities; however, this did not necessarily lead to a loss of self-identity.[42] The impact of motherhood on women's cessation showed both similarities and differences with respect to gendered theories in the Western literature.

Interviews with the women revealed that those who were in their late 30s and 40s showed great concerns for their families and children. They felt they no longer fit into their drug-use careers—losing the ability to secure drug money due to aging, becoming tired of lives on heroin and feeling burnt out. This was especially an issue among those women who had a long history of heroin use. These findings suggest that Winck's (1962) "maturing out" theory may have great potential in explaining women's cessation of drug use.

With respect to treatment, the impact on women's cessation differed according to the modalities of treatment. The compulsory drug rehabilitation programs in Kunming have significant Chinese characteristics. Local law enforcement has both the authority to arrest a drug user and issue an administrative order for compulsory treatment. The effectiveness of these programs is very limited, due to the poor physical environment and the way the programs are operated. Women's needs are often ignored, and this results in the negative effect of increasing their resentment of the programs. According to the women's testimonies, incarceration failed to prevent their continued drug use. It merely served to physically isolate them from drug resources. Upon release, the women went for drugs to release their longstanding depression.

The effectiveness of these programs is also impeded by a lack of sufficient social services for drug users after they reenter society. Women believed that employment would be the most important factor in sustaining their return to normal society. It is evident that women who have stable jobs were more likely to discontinue heroin use, and abstain from drugs for a longer time. In reality, however, after women heroin users were released from incarceration, they could barely find work opportunities. It is exceedingly hard for the women whose families do not have the capacity to support them.

Another serious concern is related to women's voluntary treatment. Within the changing social climate of recent years, the current culture is no longer favorable for heroin use, and therefore more women heroin users experience social pressures to quit drug use. The cost of voluntary treatment, however, blocks many women's opportunities to go for it. On the other hand, community-based aftercare programs are promising. Lacking knowledge about the potential harm certain drugs can cause, many women have become addicted to substitute drugs. This suggests that urgent and immediate action is necessary to remove dangerous drugs from the retail market. The experiences of these women also suggest that "natural recovery" (Robin 1974)—which involves removing women from drug sources—was very successful in helping women discontinue their drug use, but the desistance only lasted for a very limited time.

Finally, as suggested by Waldorf (1983, 237), women drug users who were eager to quit drugs, must be able to break ties with other drug users and develop new social networks and a new identity. If women cannot receive sufficient social support, their drug-using peers will continue to influence their drug-use careers. Cessation of drug use is a complicated process that results from the interaction of a variety of social factors and factors related to the individual. Although a single factor might strengthen women's incentives to quit using drugs, it rarely leads them to make a firm commitment to cessation.

7 Conclusions and Policy Implications

The preceding chapters of this study have examined the drug-use careers of women heroin users through a series of in-depth interviews, accompanied by observations from the field. Beginning in the late 1980s, which saw the first generation of heroin use in China, the experiences of these women offer a unique opportunity for the exploration of women's drug-use careers. These preceding chapters have studied the initiation of women into heroin use, explored the factors that facilitated their addiction and continued heroin use, and examined those that provided the impetus for discontinuation. As Johnson, Dunlap and Tourigny (2000) have described, each phase of drug use has its period of expansion, of plateau, decline and persistence. It can be observed that in its experience with heroin, China, as a country, too, has gone through the same phases in the past two decades. Although in present day China, heroin is not pursued by urban youth in the same way as it was in the past, the population of heroin users still remains consistently high today.

According to the women's own testimony, as recorded in previous chapters, the research findings suggest that women's heroin use careers, from initiation to discontinuation, were characterized by both social and individual factors, and in particular, the influence of China's changing social and economic context in the reform era. At the societal level, China's economic reform and open-door policies greatly motivated a portion of people in China to work hard and succeed. Unlike women drug users in inner-city neighborhoods of New York City, who lacked social resources and were surrounded by a breakdown of physical conditions (Dunlap and Johnson 1996), many women in this study, in fact, had been small business owners who had achieved a fair measure of economic success in the reform era. Their improved economic status, in fact, enabled the women to become more involved in commercial and recreational activities. These changes in their status provided them with opportunities to pursue hedonistic lifestyles similar to those of some women in developed countries. In the changing social context, many women in this study enjoyed going out, and were immersed in the pursuit of popular culture even before they initiated heroin.

The growth of heroin trafficking from the Golden Triangle into China created enormous drug-use opportunities for women in Kunming. The tradition of opium use in Kunming, along with a lack of knowledge about heroin, caused women users to underestimate the potential harm this newly available drug could inflict. What this study reveals is that heroin use among women was the inevitable product of social, economic, cultural and political changes in China at the end of the 1980s. Even if the Chinese government had responded swiftly to this emerging social issue, say, for example, by preventing illicit drug use through far-ranging drug education programs in the early stages of the epidemic, and providing effective treatment modalities, it might have succeeded only in minimizing the scope of heroin abuse rather than in eliminating it. It is recognized that resolving a social issue is a complicated process, one that involves a series of actions by politicians and government agencies (Gerber and Jensen 2001).[1,2]

Overall, cutting off the drug supply in the local communities should become a priority of policy makers and local government. As the interviews reveal, while law enforcement agencies did indeed enhance their arsenal in the fight against drug trafficking, they could not effectively target big drug traffickers, and eliminate the large numbers of heroin retailers on the street. Minority ethnic nationalities from remote areas are heavily involved in both wholesale and retail drug networks. Apparently, the mobility of this population has increased the difficulties that law enforcement agencies face in apprehending them. A variety of settlements in the Northern Train Station area with both social and physical disorders have certainly made the area a nest of criminal activity. These are all issues that Kunming, a city in its transition toward modernization, must face. Meanwhile, there is no doubt that widespread police corruption is also an obstacle in enforcing the country's anti-drug laws. Thus, if drug supplies continue to flourish, it will be hard to detach drug users from these resources, and wean them away from their addiction.

The interviews conducted in the study indicated that two sets of factors closely affect the initiation of individual women into heroin: factors related to the women's social relation, and situational factors. Factors in women's social relation, including family, peer and intimate relationships, predisposed them to fall victim to the drug-prone social culture, while situational factors—chances of being exposed to heroin use—were also related to the women's social relation. As discussed in previous chapters, in the case of the women in this study, family relationships as well as performance in school both contributed to early delinquent behavior such as smoking and drinking, and early dating, as well as to deviant behavior during adolescence. Women who exhibited early delinquency or deviant behavior were more likely to associate with friends who were like themselves, for mutual support, rendering themselves vulnerable to the drug-prone subculture. In contrast, women not attached to street culture were more likely to be influenced by their male partners or by female friends with whom they had close relationships.

The changes in Chinese culture following the reform have deeply altered family structures, child-rearing practices, and the world of children, as described by Elder (1998) in her *Children of the Great Depression*. With increasing divorce rates and single parenthood, the family, one of the most important social control agents in Chinese society, began to lose its function. The findings of this study underline the importance of the influence of family and school, and suggest early intervention if problems at home or in school encourage delinquent behavior and illicit drug use by girls. Parents need to maintain good communication with their children, rather than leaving all child-raising responsibilities to the grandparents. Too much strictness as well as too much indulgence both negatively affect the development of young girls; and it would be wise for those parents who divorce and live separately from their daughters, to maintain close emotional ties with them. As this study demonstrates, women who lack support from their families are more likely to seek emotional support from their peers, sometimes those delinquents. The study, therefore, suggests providing counseling services in school for students who have problems at home, and creating social service agencies within communities, to administer the same kind of counseling services.

A shared characteristic among participants in the interviews was that most women were not motivated to study and were uncompetitive in schools (some of them were from poorly run schools). The schools, and teachers in these schools, either failed to pay special attention to the young girls with poor academic performance, or completely ignored them. Lacking the necessary concern and caring from either family or school, young females often sought out peers for support and sharing. They associated mostly with similar trouble-makers at school, and in society, they hung out with others like themselves. The study suggests that early prevention focusing on those at-risk young girls would be beneficial and increased communication between families and schools is both urgent and essential. Also, school officials ought to give all students equal attention and opportunities for growth, regardless of academic performance.

While factors related to family and school remain relatively stable, and it is reasonable to expect that they have long-term impacts on women's lives, women's relationships with their peers and with men were important social networks that provided them with easy access to heroin. These relationships, too, were often a result of both family and school factors. When using heroin became a fashion among youngsters in Kunming in the early years, its use was not always linked to delinquency. Some women began to use heroin out of curiosity, or due to an inability to refuse someone's invitation to try it; other women initiated heroin because of their relationships with male partners, either husbands or boyfriends. How young females choose their friends and dating partners is a critical issue and can influence their motivation (or lack thereof) to experiment with drugs. Whether these young girls' families could provide immediate and effective advice to their young daughters becomes a very crucial question.

Although the majority of women in the study had no delinquent history, they were generally involved in illegal, or in some cases, criminal activities, while in the stage of continued heroin use. This indicates the important link between heroin use and deviant/criminal acts. Except for a small portion of women committing crimes (primarily dealing drugs), all other women were primarily engaged in prostitution or property-related illegal activities. Rarely did the women in the study engage in violent crime. These findings are quite consistent with research on women's illicit drug use in Western literature.

Another issue during the stage of continued drug use is related to the risks of heroin injection. The majority of women in the study injected their drugs, and most of them shared needles or syringes with others. Many women also changed sex partners frequently. Even women who were married, or had long-term relationships with their boyfriends, had brief sexual encounters with other males because their long-term male partners were frequently incarcerated. Women who engaged in sex services said, in general, that whether they insisted on the use of condoms or not was mainly determined by the attitude of their clients. Some women were simply careless as regards to sexual conduct with all their male partners, whether long-term or short-term. Increased reports of HIV infection among women in the follow-up study, and the fact that a few of the women still continued to engage in sex services after they were aware of their HIV infection, suggest an urgent need for both HIV control and prevention, as well as HIV education. Although the government has begun to provide free treatment to those who tested positive for HIV in recent years, the government should also take a more active role in supervising and following these cases, so as to minimize the risk to the general population, and to contain mother-to-child-transmission.

Women's cessation of drug use was also closely related to the government's drug control policies. Since the first legislation on the prohibition of drugs was passed by the Standing Committee of the National People's Congress in 1990, the Chinese government began to initiate numerous anti-drug campaigns both at the national and local levels. Strike-hard operations were more frequent in Kunming than elsewhere in China, on account of Kunming's severe drug abuse problems. From 1999 to 2007, the total number of drug users who served time in compulsory treatment programs in the country ranged from 300,000 to 368,000 per year. In 2005, 84,000 drug users were detained in compulsory drug treatment programs in Yunnan. This figure constitutes 13 percent of all drug users incarcerated in the country (NNCC 1990–2008), and suggests that law enforcement has strongly relied on sanctions to control drug use in recent years. Nevertheless, the number of drug users in the country was still soaring.

Women's experiences indicate that ongoing drug control policies exercise a profound influence on their drug use- careers. The majority of women in the study had been arrested and detained in compulsory drug treatment programs solely because of their drug use. Many of them were repeatedly sent to compulsory drug treatment programs even after the new anti-drug law was enacted. However, these compulsory programs generally failed to prevent women's continued drug use due to high recidivism rates—none of the women who had quit heroin for more than six months credited incarceration with being a major factor in their cessation.

The newly enacted anti-drug law (2007), which emphasizes developing community-based drug treatment programs, is certainly a big step forward in the country's anti-drug policies since the early 1990s, reflecting the urgent need for the rehabilitation of drug users. In a related initiative, at the end of 2010, the administrative power of the Kunming Compulsory Drug Rehabilitation Center, the first compulsory drug treatment facility to be established by law enforcement authorities in China, was handed over to the Kunming Municipal Justice Bureau, and the new compulsory drug isolation facility also went into service. It is expected to see more changes in the near future due to the changes of administration of compulsory drug rehabilitation programs.

Indeed, to respond to the increasing numbers of drug users, more compulsory drug treatment facilities have been built nationwide. In 2003, 583 compulsory rehabilitation centers and 151 re-education through labor centers were used to confine drug users in China (NNCC 2003). Still, even the increasing construction of compulsory facilities in the country cannot catch up and keep pace with the needs of the fast-growing drug-use population. A shortage of police personnel and professional drug counselors has turned treatment programs away from their intended purpose. Locking up drug users and enforcing labor or manual work can only suffice to occupy their time and satisfy the financial needs of the programs. According to the women, the poor management of the compulsory drug rehabilitation also hinders the effectiveness of the program. Some of the issues in this respect included crowded facilities, the indifferent attitude of the officers, few counseling services and lack of educational programs.

The current study suggests that the failure of compulsory programs lies in the nature of the programs themselves. Based on lessons learned in the past several decades from the United States—a country recognized as having rigorous drug control policies and advanced research on drug-related issues—mandatory sentencing and incarceration have failed to solve illicit drug-use problems. The newly enacted anti-drug law in China repealed re-education through labor as a compulsory alternative, and has switched its focus to community-based treatment programs. This is certainly a good sign in the development of China's anti-drug policies. The government must focus on the quality of the newly established compulsory drug isolation programs to make them more effective. Mandated manual work should not be used as a primary method to manage women drug users inside the facilities. Rather, improving living conditions, and providing educational and vocational programs for women drug users will be meaningful. If women are well prepared while within the facilities, once released, their transition into regular society will be smoother. Counseling services should also be provided at such facilities to help women deal with stress and resolve their problems.

At the same time, police strategies should also be reexamined. Law enforcement agencies have absolute authority to arrest drug users and send them off to be incarcerated. Because no social service agencies were in place to address women drug-users' performance in the community, police made their decisions solely based on women's previous arrest records, rather than taking women's current efforts as a reference. As witnessed by the study, some women in a transitional period were rearrested and sent back to compulsory drug rehabilitation. The special needs of those women who were mothers were also largely ignored. Taking these observations into consideration, this study suggests that deciding whether a female drug user should be sent to a compulsory drug isolation program, or be allowed to stay in a community-based treatment program, should be based on the overall performance of women drug users instead of merely on the evidence of a relapse. Meanwhile, social service agencies and counselors in the local communities should all be invited to provide an assessment of the women's performance in the communities.

In recent years, the central government has advocated developing voluntary treatment programs in local communities. Methadone clinics, part of state-operated, voluntary drug treatment programs, began to increase in considerable numbers across the country. However, the effectiveness of the programs has been hindered due to the lack of adequate and systematic services provided by these programs. Women heroin users merely made their daily trip to the clinic, and walked away once they had taken the drugs. Women heroin users have many misgivings about participating in these programs. Many of them merely took the methadone treatment to avoid legal sanctions during police hard strikes. The study also indicates that community-based after-care programs are highly praised by women heroin users, and that such programs show promising results.

Meanwhile, in order to help women drug users stabilize their lives after reentry into society, the government should grant former drug-users equal opportunities for school, employment and social welfare. During my interviews with women heroin users in 2005, several women complained that on account of their history of drug use, they were not able to receive the minimum living allowance guaranteed to urban citizens. My follow-up interviews with women heroin users in 2008 suggest significant changes have been made recently: qualified women heroin users receive not only the minimum living allowance, but also low-rent housing and an access to medical insurance provided for low-income citizens by the government. While educational and vocational training within compulsory drug treatment programs should be provided, continued training programs within communities need to be encouraged and fully funded.[3] Most importantly, women's lives after release should be overseen by a series of social service agencies rather than being supervised only by the police.

Having used heroin for many years, all the women without exception were not leading the lives they had expected to lead, and were living in enormous pain. Women in the later stages of their heroin use careers admitted that they were no longer using the drug for pleasure, but because they were psychologically dependent on it, especially in the absence of other things to do or to look forward to, in their daily routines. At the end of each interview, almost all the women expressed regret about their life on heroin. I can deeply empathize with these women's struggles in their lives with heroin: they are exhausted and to be pitiful. While they struggled to change themselves, one failure after another brought them extreme disappointment and frustration. Xiaoling told me of her struggles:

> After I used heroin for a while, I reached a point where I couldn't sustain myself physically anymore. I dreamed about quitting heroin, changing my life; and regaining normal life and health. But after I abstained, I was still unable to have a normal life. I always went back. My body's pains from withdrawal drove me to bang my head against the wall. I wished I could commit suicide, but I didn't have the courage to do it. When addiction came back, I forgot all my dreams; but after a while, I felt deep regret.

When women could not get out of this vicious cycle, they became extremely depressed. Many women exhibited suicidal tendencies. The risk of death was quite real to women heroin users; death was closely related to their everyday life. Women called themselves survivors of heroin because of frequent deaths among their drug-using friends. The suicide rate in China has increased rapidly since the economic reform, particularly among Chinese women. Although there are very few studies of suicide rates among drug users, we can expect the suicide rate among women heroin users to be much higher than among the general population. Of the women in the study, five told me they had attempted suicide (as did two more in the follow-up study), while many others said that they thought about it. Of those who had attempted suicide, only one gave up after just one attempt; all the others tried repeatedly. All of the women reported that their suicide attempts occurred at the burn out stage; they all tried to commit suicide by overdosing on heroin. Heroin itself eventually became a deadly weapon against the women.

Not all of the women who attempted suicide were living in economic hardship. Their desire to return to society, and restore their social relations with families and friends were so acute that they were very frustrated when their efforts failed. Women heroin users always liked to say that no one could understand the pain and struggle in a drug-user's life. In the words of Fan, who grew up in a wealthy family: "I felt exhausted about my life on heroin. I wanted to be a normal woman: I dream of a family and a child of my own." This is the sentiment that emerges from deep within the hearts of many of these women.

After over twenty years of prevalence of heroin use in China, more and more people, including women heroin users, have come to realize the consequences of heroin use. Many of these women are at a cross-road with respect to their drug-using careers, and are looking for opportunities to make changes. In response to their demands, society should step up and put forth solid efforts to assist these disadvantaged women in weaving new self-identities and normal social relations.

Epilogue

After I returned from my first fieldtrip to China in 2005, I have been working diligently on making transcripts, translating and analyzing the data. For three years, the women whom I had interviewed continued to live vividly in my mind. I could not stop thinking about how much I felt the need to go back again to Kunming to visit these women who had put their trust in me and shared their life experiences with me. My research had connected me profoundly with this group of women, who had the same dreams as many other women in China. I knew they were all struggling with their heroin use and that they also faced great challenges in other aspects of their lives, including family, intimate relationships, parenting, work and money for survival. I wished them the best of luck in dealing with whatever issues they had to confront.

Support from my current institution enabled my dream to come true. During my follow-up study, I was able to locate twenty-five of the original ninety women (28 percent) and interview them once again. These interviews and field observations allowed me to further examine changes in women's drug use careers over the three-year span. The interviews focused on changes in women's heroin use and in their significant life events, including family and spousal relationships, parenting, work and health, treatment and imprisonment. Compared to the time of my original data collection, women were more open and friendly, without concern for any precautions, as they had been at the time of the previous interviews. They not only shared their own life experiences with me, but also provided me with information about other women respondents. Sadly, two of the original respondents had passed away—one of liver disease and the second from a fire that she herself had set. The women's lives had undergone great changes since the original interviews.

FAMILY, INTIMATE RELATIONSHIPS AND PARENTING

Since the original interviews, two women, Jing and Lan, who had been struggling with their marriages at that time finally got divorces. They had both found new boyfriends, who also had a history of drug use. They seemed very happy in their new relationships. Jing was once a daily drug user and now was a volunteer in an after-care program; Lan continued her work in an after-care program where her boyfriend was a staff member. She was promoted to the position of peer trainer. While Jing still used heroin occasionally, Lan firmly stated that she had never done so.

Five women had gotten married, but only Bing married a man who did not use drugs. Two of them, Tingting and Wanfen, had become mothers. Bing was a big surprise to me. When I interviewed her in 2005, she had just begun a relationship with her drug-using boyfriend. They were both daily drug users at that time. In contrast to her previous heavy make-up and strange, tacky outfit, she now had barely visible make-up, which showed up her healthy, smooth skin. Her close-fitting T-shirt and pink jeans revealed her nice shape. She said that since she did not use heroin any more after she got married, the heavy make-up that was used to cover her bad skin color was no longer necessary. She had a very close relationship with her non drug-using husband and they lived in an apartment of their own. She was working in a game parlor making 600 yuan monthly, with free lunch and dinner. She had also adopted a homeless dog. While several other women also tried working at the kind of job Bing had, they all quit due to boredom and the low income.

Jia's husband was working with her in an after-care program. In contrast, three other women, Wanfen, Wei and Tingting, were still struggling with their husbands' continued heroin use. Wanfen, a very stylish woman, who had always had her hair set in large waves, no longer dressed the way she had before, and simply had a pony tail. She was now the mother of a two-year old boy. During the original interview, she had told me that she was hesitating to marry her boyfriend (current husband) because of his uncontrollable use of drugs. However, she finally changed her mind due to her pregnancy. She felt very frustrated with her husband's constant drug use, which also led her to several relapses. In the meantime, the couple's financial situation was also not in good shape—they had no reliable income except for the support from families on both sides. She belittled her husband for being incapable of making money either legally or illegally. For this reason, she was planning to leave Kunming to work in a new business with one of her close friends. But she had two worries: how to get rid of the methadone addiction and who would take care of the baby?

Another woman, Wei, also married the man she was previously dating, who had a long history of drug-use. Wei looked very healthy with a smooth forehead and long dyed hair. Though she was in love with her husband, some reality issues persisted. She and her husband were both on methadone treatment, but her husband still frequently used drugs and could not find a job. Wei had to continue work in a nightclub. As a newly married woman, she simply said that she was selling beer there (so called "Miss Beer"). But for people understood the culture of nightclub, all knew what this could mean to her. Tingting's husband had been re-arrested and was serving a two-year term in compulsory drug treatment. Tingting was very excited about the fact that her husband would be released within a month. Tingting, once a lesbian, was living with Song at the time of my original interview. She told me she had decided to separate from Song because Song's drug use was out of control, and she was always asking for money from Tingting. Before their separation, Tingting spent 20,000 yuan obtained from her father to open a new business on drugs with Song. Song was arrested twice within a period of three years. She was serving her second term—three years in re-education through labor. Tingting, once a successful businesswoman, now assisted her mother-in-law, staffing the entrance to a gated community. In this way, she shared half of a monthly salary of 600 yuan with her mother-in-law. Tingting was still unable to completely control her own drug use. Her little boy, who was almost 2 years old, was the great gratification of her life.

Regardless of their previous marital status, most of the women who had remained single broke up with their boyfriends. Caiyun was the only one who was able to maintain her relationship with her boyfriend, even though he was more than ten years younger than her. Ciayun was very satisfied with her relationship and told me that she had never touched heroin again after my interview with her. While most women generally did not report significant trauma upon separating from their boyfriends, two of them, Meijuan and Fang, had experienced very difficult times in their lives because of their commitment to their relationships.

Meijuan was a 43-year-old woman. When I interviewed her in 2005, she had just begun a relationship with a man who was in his thirties. On one occasion, I saw them kissing each other in public in front of a few other drug-using peers—which was not quite usual among Chinese women, in particular at her age. The man was still using heroin on a daily basis at that time, whereas Meijuan had abstained from heroin for five years. Meijuan told me that, shortly after our original interview, she followed her boyfriend's example, and used heroin again. She was arrested and sent to Changpo for a year. A few months before my follow-up study, the man had an affair with another wealthy businesswoman. This was very difficult for Meijuan, who had supported him for three years. To prove her love, Meijuan cut herself many times with a fruit knife right in front of her boyfriend. She showed me the new scars on her wrists. Earlier in her life, before Meijuan divorced her husband, she had also attempted suicide after she witnessed her husband using heroin with another woman. Meijuan firmly said that she was determined to leave her boyfriend, and develop a new relationship. However, when she answered phone calls from the boyfriend during my conversation with her, her voice became very gentle, belying her words.

Fang, who worked wholeheartedly as a peer trainer when I first met her, was very energetic with respect to her work and new relationship—her boyfriend was also a peer trainer. She continued to be a staffer in the same aftercare program, but she and her boyfriend had separated. He had found a new lover, also a drug user, and had moved out of the apartment where Fang and he had lived together. Fang was a little overweight when I interviewed her in 2005, but now she looked unusually thin and pale. She told me that the separation led her to attempt suicide by taking four bottles of sleeping pills. Her eyes were full of tears. A mother of two girls, she sadly told me that she was pregnant again at the time of their separation. Although her boyfriend, too, still worked in the same program, they were like strangers to each other.

After these separations, most of the women developed new relationships with men having histories of drug use. Ning, a 40-year-old woman, was a little upset as she told me that her new boyfriend was Rong's former boyfriend, a handsome man who was over ten years younger than she was. The man was working in her brother's business, while she stayed at home as a housewife. Though Ning's relationship with her boyfriend was steady, she was unsure about the future because of the age difference between them. On another occasion, Jia's former boyfriend became Yan's new one, even though Yan did not want to admit it. In contrast to all these women, Jinwen was the only one who had a non drug-using boyfriend. Jingwen still had her long glossy black hair and spoke slowly. She said that her boyfriend knew she had used drugs in the past, but still treated her well. They were planning to get married within the year.

The women who had children liked to share information about their children with me, in particular, when their children got married or found jobs. For example, Chao's son got his first job as a driver and was able to support himself. Chao was very proud of him. Caiyun's son got married and was planning to have a baby. Though Caiyun was financially dependent on her boyfriend, she said that she would not ask her son for money, now that he had his own family. Although these women felt very joyful about their children's growth and successes, as mothers, they sometimes had other worries. Ning's daughter, for example, got married to a farmer in a remote village in Yunnan and had a baby. Ning was very anxious about her daughter's future but she could do nothing about it.

WORK AND HEALTH

The follow-up study revealed that among the twenty-five women, eleven were jobless (44 percent); eight (32 percent) worked in after-care programs (including one as a staffer, three as peer trainers and four as volunteers); three (12 percent) had temporary jobs (a gate-keeper, a cashier in a game parlor and a salesperson at a supermarket). Among three others (12 percent), one worked in a nightclub as "Miss Beer"; two were active drug dealers (both had drug selling history). Overall, and consistent with previous findings, women who were working in the after-care programs as staffers or peer trainers were more successful than others in controlling their drug habit, though they, too, experienced relapses.

Fang, Jia, Yuzhen and Chao were women who were in the best position—staff members in the after-care program. Except for Fang, however, the other three all had relapses in the period following the original interviews. Jia and Yuzhen were demoted to a lower position—peer trainer and volunteer respectively. Chao was arrested and served one year in Changpo. Upon her return, Chao came back to the after-care program and began once more as a volunteer, then was promoted to peer trainer. Though working as a volunteer carries no monthly salary, some women still liked to do so for various reasons: passing time, associating with peers, or hoping for promotion to a higher position, such as that of peer trainer (with a monthly salary of 300 yuan) or staffer (500 yuan monthly). Besides Yuzhen, Jing, Yuan and Lei were also volunteers in an after-care program.

Among the three women who had temporary jobs, as previously mentioned, Bing working as a cashier in a game parlor, and Tingting assisting her mother-in-law a gate-keeper, Jingwen was the only one who made hard efforts to go back to conventional society. She was once arrested for purchasing drugs, together with her former boyfriend who was also a drug user. After serving six months in Changpo, she was released. Now Jinwen looked very energetic and full of self-confidence. She told me that she could not believe that her first job had been that of a janitor in a supermarket. Her dedication to the job opened new avenues for her—she was then promoted to a salesperson in the same supermarket, advertising new products to customers. She could earn about 1,500 yuan each month and was very happy with her new relations, both with co-workers as well as with customers. She was living with her new boyfriend, who had no drug experience, in a village within the city, where their rental property earned them a very good profit (at least 20,000 yuan a year).

Among three other women, except for Wei working in the nightclub, Congshan and Xia, were active drug dealers. When I first met Congsha, in 2005, she had just finished her second term in re-education through labor. After the original interview, she was sent back for another two years in re-education through labor for her drug dealing. Without her family's social connections, she would have served two years in labor camp—a much harsher sanction than re-education through labor. Compared to two years ago, Congshan's appearance had not changed a lot. Though her skin color appeared darker than before, but she was still very attractive. She said that shortly after her recent release, she began to use heroin, and that until recently she had been using drugs on a daily basis (three injections a day). Selling drugs helped her to secure the drug money and also make some extra gains. She had at least six people who asked her for heroin each day and she could earn 200–300 yuan by selling one gram. She was very delighted about her sales on the day of the interview—one person had asked her for three grams of heroin. She had no idea what would happen in her life, but could only hope for good fortune. Among all the women, the change in Xia was a big shock to me. Like Congshan, Xia was also selling drugs. I had been very impressed by her long abstention from heroin (according to the 2005 interview, she had had only one relapse since 2001). She was living with her husband, who did not use drugs, and she was very lucky to hold a position as a clerk in a company whose director was a relative. One of her best friends had died of an HIV infection, and I still remembered Xia telling me that her husband suspected she may be infected, too. Sadly, and unfortunately, five months earlier, Xia had been identified as being HIV positive. She was extremely depressed by this grim fact. She said that her husband showed similar symptoms, but was still unaware about the situation. Since then, she quit her job and began to use heroin again. She had sold heroin many years ago when she had been heavily addicted to drugs. She said her intention was not to earn big money, it was merely to sustain her drug use and pay for the family expenses since her husband, too, had no job, and had nothing to do but stay at home. Xia's case illustrated a very typical situation described by many women—selling drugs with license. The fact that she was HIV positive may provide her immunity from further legal sanction.

The risk of HIV infection was a big threat to the women's lives. While only two women from among the original sample (Yuzhen and Yuan) were known to be HIV positive, my follow-up study indicates that the number could potentially be very high among women drug users (five women drug dealers and two sex workers were also HIV positive). Of the eight HIV infections I knew of during the follow-up study (N=25), six had been identified after my original interview—Xia, Fang, Jia, Lan, Tingting and Yan. I could tell that Yuan, Fang and Lan were in very poor health—they had visibly lost their normal body shape and looked very pale and skinny. The changes in these women's appearance were astonishing. Yuan, who was identified as HIV positive in 2005, had once been a beautiful young woman. Now, she had a very dull skin color and was in a very low mood. Her mouth was full of decayed teeth, and only black roots were left. She said she had frequently had high fevers that lasted about ten days each time. During my interview with her in 2005, she had been worrying about examination fees for the HIV test. At present, free HIV testing programs are available in certain after-care programs. The women told me that the government provided free anti-virus medication to individuals who were infected and needed medical attention. Yuan, Fang, Lan, were all on these medications by the time of the follow-up study. Sadly, Tingting, mother of a newborn baby, was also found to be HIV positive, five months before she delivered the baby. She was unsure about the condition of the baby's health.

My conversations with women indicate that an HIV infection received better support among their drug-using peers. For example, Jia married her husband after she had already been identified as HIV positive, even though he was infection-free. In contrast, public reaction to HIV infection could be extreme. Yan told me that whenever she went to the subdistrict office to get her monthly minimum living allowance, she had to put on a face-mask and gloves before she entered the office at the request of the lady in charge.

MODALITIES OF TREATMENT

When I conducted the original interviews, methadone treatment programs in Kunming had been started less than three months earlier. By the time of my follow-up study, methadone treatment had become the major modality for women drug users, spurred on by more frequent crackdowns on drug use. However, the potential harm of methadone treatment was widespread among the women; rumors in the drug user community seemed to play a very influential role on women's perceptions. Eight women in all had participated in methadone treatment, but only five of them were still on the treatment at the time of the follow-up interviews.

Wei received the methadone treatment right after the program was first available in Kunming. When I initially met her in 2005, she had been enrolled in the program for only two months. After she had married her boyfriend after the original interview, her husband joined her in methadone treatment. Wei complained of frequent stomach pain and severe constipation. Her husband had lost his sexual ability while on treatment. While constipation seemed quite a common problem among all the women, some other concerns were also raised. Ning told me that she often experienced headaches, sweating and had no strength in her body. Yuan said that methadone reduced the effectiveness of the anti-HIV medication. The most serious concern among the women was the addictive nature of the drug. In general, women felt it was far more difficult to quit methadone than heroin. Almost all women who were on methadone wanted to abandon the program sooner or later.

Besides the methadone treatment, self-treatment by abusing prescription drugs was still a common practice. Diphenoxylate (referred to by the women as the "small white pill") was still quite popular. Six women within the past three years had used it. Among them, Yan had the longest history of abusing it. Yan started to try it during the original interview, and was still using it interchangeably with heroin at the time of the follow-up interview. When she couldn't find heroin, she used the small white pill instead. She never used the two at the same time. By the time of the follow-up interview, she was taking fifteen pills at a time (0.25 gram), twice a day. At the beginning, however, she had been taking less than five pills each time. Yan said that this medication was still available over-the-counter, and could be easily bought from the local pharmacy, but the price had increased to 7 yuan from the previous 1.7 yuan per bottle. She normally purchased a whole pack of twenty-four bottles. Compared to methadone (10 yuan each time), Yan felt that this self-treatment cost less and was more convenient for her.

Due to lack of confidence in methadone treatment, its cost and inconvenience (the daily trip for treatment), women were much more likely to undergo it merely as a safe way to escape being arrested for heroin use. Based on my conversations with women in the follow-up study and my field observations, many women still occasionally used heroin while on methadone treatment. The relapses affected almost all the women in the follow-up study, with two exceptions: Caiyun and Ming. For this reason, within three years, fourteen women had been arrested for drug use and nine of them were incarcerated for periods ranging from six months to two years.

Chao looked like a completely different person. In place of her previously short hair, she now had long hair with amazing curves. Unlike her earlier mannish way of dressing, she wore a tight blouse and straight slim jeans. She was working as a peer trainer at the time of the follow-up interview. She had become addicted again in 2006, due to a break-up with her boyfriend and was arrested and sent to Changpo. After she was released in 2007, she reunited with her boyfriend. Lingling who was naturally disabled, and as previously mentioned, she did not show any obvious change. Within a few seconds after she sat down, however, she began to sob over her mother's death. She regretted how she had behaved, and had kept the secret to herself. She felt it was a big release to share it with me. When Lingling had been taking care of her, Lingling's mother had to be hospitalized. When her mother complained about chest pains at night, Lingling, who was on drugs, did not take it very seriously. After she fell asleep beside her mother for a while, she was woken up by the nurse and was informed that her mother was gone. Though Linling was arrested several times, she was released each time, mostly because of her health condition.

WHAT WE CAN LEARN

My follow-up interviews with twenty-five women in Kunming revealed that, although the majority of women could control their drug use for a while, the journey from controlled use to sustained abstinence was an almost impossible endeavor for most of them. Only four women affirmed that they had not used heroin since the original interviews. They had also never enrolled in methadone treatment. These women told me that they grew tired of heroin use and also of the lifestyle it involved. One of them, Ming, in fact said that even though her husband often used heroin right in front of her, she was never tempted to use it again.

My interviews and field observations suggest that the number of daily heavy drug users was diminishing significantly. Most women heroin users, regardless of their treatment status, were only occasional drug users, due to the frequent crackdowns on drug use and heroin's increased price on the illegal market. Changes in anti-drug legislation have fostered changes in the careers of women drug users. Though the re-education through labor program had been repealed, compulsory drug treatment programs can still keep drug users confined for a maximum of three years. Juan was once a heavy user who spent another two years in re-education through labor after my original interview. Now, she only used heroin sporadically. Her husband was still in Changpo when the follow-up study was conducted. She believed that it would be very silly for anyone to be heavily addicted at the present time. It was simply not worth doing it.

While the community drug treatment model is still making its way across the country, access to social welfare provided by the government has given the women great incentives to control their drug use or to aim for abstention. When I conducted interviews in 2005, none of the women subjects received a minimum living allowance from the local government. In contrast, at the present time, nine of the women heroin users enjoy the same rights as other low-income people in the city, receiving 255 yuan each month from the local government (the standard was made based on the local social economic development level). Several of them also applied for a medical care program that required a small payment every year, and low cost housing provided by the government. To secure these social benefits, the women told me that they had to undergo urine tests on a regular basis and participate in community service each week. If there were any violations, the sub-district office would take away their social benefits right away. Yan, who eventually got her application approved after a year, told me that people have to wait for at least six months to reapply for these benefits. Both Yan and her little boy received money from the government, which was a big help for her, a single mother.

Notes

NOTES TO CHAPTER 1

1. The designation "China" will be used to denote the People's Republic of China throughout this work.
2. Based on publications by Chinese scholars, the resurgence of illicit drug use in China began in the mid-1980s (Cui Min 1999).
3. Ensuring the communist ideology and socialist system were the priority of the Party-State.
4. The average annual disposable per capita income in China in 1978 was only 134 yuan ($85) (5153 yuan [$721] in 2009) in rural areas, and 315 yuan ($199) (17,175 yuan [$2,404] in 2009) in urban areas (NBSC 1978–2009).
5. The exchange rates adopted by the study are based on information from two web sources: (1970–1989) from http://intl.econ.cuhk.edu.hk/ (The Chinese University of Hong Kong); (1990–2010) from http://www.x-rates.com/.
6. To implement the open-door policy in order to attract foreign investments, China's new culture of ownership featured three types of foreign enterprises (contractual joint ventures, cooperative ventures and solely foreign-funded ventures) that were set up with a series of preferential policies.
7. This is a Chinese proverb. In 1962, Deng Xiaoping first used it as a metaphor in his public statement regarding the development of the rural economy: to be practical and realistic. It became an important guideline in the reform era.
8. These cities are located in the southeastern part of China along the coastline. Shenzhen, Shantou and Zhuhai belong to Guangdong Province. Shenzhen is contiguous to Hong Kong and Zhuhai is adjacent to Macao. Xiamen is in Fujian province.
9. The Chinese Gross Domestic Product (GDP) has seen a rapid growth in the past three decades, climbing from less than $ 1 trillion in 1980 to nearly $5 trillion in 2009. World Bank National Accounts Data. http://data.worldbank.org/indicator/NY.GDP.MKTP.CD?page=5. Accessed January 10, 2010.
10. Based on his observations of nineteenth-century France in rapid social transition, Durkheim proposed the concept of anomie in *The Division of Labor in Society* (1893/1965) and further developed this concept in his work *Suicide* (1897/1951).
11. There are five autonomous regions in China (Guangxi Zhuang Autonomous Region, Xinjiang Uygur Autonomous Region, Ningxia Hui Autonomous Region, Tibet Zang Autonomous Region and Inner Mongolia Autonomous Region). They are all located in the western region.
12. NNCC is the abbreviation for National Narcotics Control Commission.

13. Opium poppy cultivation in Myanmar and Laos (PDR) gradually decreased in the 1990s. Opium production in Afghanistan has significantly increased in the past decade. In spite of a decline in supply, heroin trafficked to China still comes primarily from the Golden Triangle. The National Narcotics Control Committee of China predicted that the flow of illicit drugs from Afghanistan would continue increasing in the future (NNCC 2006).
14. Unfortunately, precise official statistics of drug trafficking were not generally available.
15. Drug-related crime includes the manufacture, transport, sale, and trafficking of drugs.
16. Such a sharp increase was primarily due to increased production by underground factories in Guangdong and Fujian in the late 1990s (NNCC 1999).
17. A female must obey her father before marriage, obey her husband after marriage and obey her son after her husband's death.
18. Foot binding was eventually stopped in the 1920s (Gallagher 2001).
19. The first Constitution was enacted in 1954. In 1975, 1978 and 1982, new Constitutions were written. In 1999, the Constitution was revised based on the 1982 Constitution.
20. The College Entrance Exam was revoked in 1966 during the Cultural Revolution.
21. As of 2010, the proportion of women entrepreneurs in China was between 20–25 percent (Shi 2010).
22. These figures are far above the biologically normal level of gender ratio at birth: 100 (girls) to 105–106 (boys) (Greenhalgh and Li 1995).
23. These cities are the capital cities of Liaoning Province, Hubei Province and Yunnan Province respectively.
24. Multiple sex partners among female drug users: 70.3 percent for needle sharers, 56.3 percent for non-needle sharers, and 10.5 percent for non-IDUs (Lau et al. 2005).
25. The importance of the career approach is also reflected in publications by the National Research Council's Panel on Research on Criminal Careers: *Criminal Careers and Career Criminals* (Blumstein et al.1986).
26. Maxwell (2005) states that experience, prior theory and research, pilot studies and thought experience are the four major sources of the conceptual context.

NOTES TO CHAPTER 2

1. A hidden population has been defined as "a subset of the general population whose membership is not readily distinguished or enumerated based on existing knowledge and/or sampling capabilities" (Wiebel 1990, 6).
2. The distinct features indicated by Strauss include "theoretical sampling and certain methodological guidelines, such as the making of constant comparisons and the use of a coding paradigm, to ensure conceptual development and density" (Strauss 1987, 5).
3. The Han are the dominant nationality in China (94 percent of the total population in the country) together with fifty-five minority nationalities.
4. *Beidu* village is a village in which almost all villagers participate in carrying drugs for others. *Mazai* is a person who helps other people buy and (or) carry drugs from the Golden Triangle, or who leads the way for others to cross the border.
5. Kunming was established by the Yuan Dynasty in 1275. Since then it has been the province's political, economic and cultural center.

6. The distance from Dongchuan District to Kunming is about 157 kilometers.
7. Until the Tongzhi Era (1862–1875) of the Qing Dynasty only a few provinces in China cultivated opium (Xian 2005).
8. As indicated in the previous chapter, the total number of registered drug users in the country was only 148,000 (based upon data in 1991). Yunnan Province accounted for more than one third of registered drug users in the country by that time.
9. The funding for my fieldtrip in 2005 amounted to $2,500, a Dean's Research Grant from the School of Criminal Justice, Rutgers University.
10. Women who had interview experience were more likely to be those working for the voluntary drug treatment centers or drop-in centers.
11. Staff working for the center often took turns cooking lunch and sometimes dinner on their own and solicited a very small amount of money for it.
12. During my follow-up study, I interviewed the girl's mother. She was released from the compulsory drug rehabilitation center. She had tears in her eyes when she mentioned that donation organized by her drug-using peers.
13. We encountered a female drug user on the street who was in great fear of being arrested. She was carrying her friend's baby to distract people's attention. She did not show up for my formal interview in 2005, but I was able to locate her for the follow-up study in 2008.
14. All women who were of the Hui minority nationality were Muslim.
15. Please see the next chapter for detailed explanations.
16. This figure excludes one woman whose two sons died in a car accident.
17. In China, a graduate from a technical secondary school receives a diploma equivalent to a high school diploma.
18. This figure includes three dropouts from elementary school, two from middle school, three from high school, one from the technical secondary school and one from college.
19. Based on the 2006 official report from the Kunming Bureau of Statistics (KBS 2006), elementary school graduates, and middle school graduates in Kunming accounted for 32.8 percent and 30.3 percent accordingly.
20. However, the unemployment rate in the city was only 4.2 percent in 2009, based on the official government report (NBSC 2009).
21. I received support from both RSCA (Research, Scholarship and Creative Activity) Grants and Global Initiative Grants from the Dean's Office (College of Humanities and Social Science) at California State University, Stanislaus, totaling $4,500.
22. The first legislation against illicit drug use in China—*The Anti-Drug Law of the People's Republic of China* (2007) was enacted on June 1, 2008.
23. Several women told me that they heard about my return from other drug-using folks and expected to meet me again.
24. As mentioned earlier in this chapter, during the follow-up study, only the re-interviews were conducted in the community drop-in center.
25. She was released from the compulsory rehabilitation center only a couple of days prior to the interview.

NOTES TO CHAPTER 3

1. Lian and Ru's parents were alcoholics; Jun's father (also a drug dealer) and Qiaoling's mother were heroin users; Yun's father was a drug dealer; Yun's mother stole steel from her factory.
2. Although these women had siblings using heroin, none of them initiated heroin use with them.

3. The relationships between women heroin users and their families showed a pattern similar to that identified in an earlier study—demonstrating two extremes: they were either denied gratification or were spoiled (overindulged) (Chein et al. 1964, 313).
4. None of these women used heroin before their parents divorced.
5. Among the women in the study, several women had disabled parent(s). Both Qing and Wei's parents were deaf and mute; Qing's mother and Lingling's father were mentally ill.
6. Jia's marriage was arranged by her foster parents and she did not get along with her husband. She separated from him after her twins were born and eventually obtained a divorce.
7. Re-education through labor, or *laojiao,* was used to detain and rehabilitate persons for petty crimes, such as illicit drug use, drug possession or trafficking in small amounts.
8. Based on a review of studies in the 1990s, Robers, Nishimoto and Kirk (2003), indicate that among substance abusing women, those who had a history of sexual abuse ranged widely from a low of 9 percent to a high of 75 percent.
9. She hid from her mother and did not take the high school entrance exam. She then began to work at temporary jobs to earn money for the family.
10. Qing's parents were barely able to read and write; her mother was afflicted with mental illness.
11. Qing graduated from middle school at age 15 and then began a small business after two years. In the same year she got to know her boyfriend (ex-husband), and soon lived with him. Due to excessive violence against her, Qing divorced her husband after her son was born.
12. Yun's elder brother was sentenced to imprisonment for robbery before he reached age 18, and became a street hustler after his release; her younger brother followed the path of her elder brothers. Yun and her two brothers were involved in selling drugs after their father was released from the prison and soon after they were addicted on heroin.
13. In 2005, 22.33 million of the urban population (excluding 3.62 million unemployment insurance recipients) received minimum wage security welfare from the government (NBSC 2005). As a result of economic reform, two distinct social groups have emerged in urban China: the extreme rich and the extreme poor.
14. Grades, academic ability and negative attitudes about school and teachers are consistently strong predictors of dropping out of high school (Mensch and Kandel 1988, 96).
15. Women who had problems in their families (neglect or abuse) were more likely than others to show delinquent behavior in school (Kaufman and Widom 1999).
16. Mahjong: A game originating in China, with a history of several hundred years. Young people often play mahjong as a means of gambling, while seniors play for entertainment.
17. Both her ovaries and her uterus were removed due to oophoroma (a rare ovarian tumor).
18. According to Sullivan (1989, 29), school achievement, particularly for younger people, constitutes the largest component of their human capital when they enter the labor market.
19. By the time of women's heroin initiation, two women held positions as clergy in law enforcement; one woman served in the military for three years and then worked for her family's enterprise; three who graduated from secondary professional school worked in technical positions.

20. Both smoking and drinking are viewed as predictors for future drug use (Kandel 1980).
21. Leaving parents or guardians prematurely increases adolescents' risk of using drugs (Krohn, Lizotte and Perez 1997).
22. Young women's romantic relationships with men are significantly affected by their history of adolescent deviant behavior; they have a high likelihood of having an antisocial partner when they enter adulthood (Simons et al. 2002).
23. The "three-good" student honor system emphasizes the virtues of good morals, studying hard and excellence in sports. It has been revamped in recent years after being practiced for five decades.
24. Yun's father was a drug trafficker; Lian's parents were alcoholics.
25. Among these women, Shan was the only woman who maintained a good relationship with her parents.
26. "Miss three-accompanies" is a designation used to refer to young girls working in entertainment venues who provide accompaniment services that typically include singing, dancing and drinking.
27. According to the Criminal Law of P. R. China (Article 347): whoever smuggles, traffics in, transports or manufactures heroin of not less than 50 grams, shall be sentenced to fixed-term imprisonment of fifteen years, life imprisonment or death; of not less than 10 grams but less than 50 grams, shall be sentenced to fixed-term imprisonment of not less than seven years and shall also be fined; of less than 10 grams shall be sentenced to fixed-term imprisonment of not more than three years, criminal detention or public surveillance and shall be fined.
28. According to the Criminal Law of P. R. China (Article 349): whoever shields offenders engaged in smuggling, trafficking in, transporting or manufacturing of narcotic drugs or whoever harbors, transfers or covers up, for such offenders, narcotic drugs or their pecuniary and other gains from such criminal activities shall be sentenced to fixed-term imprisonment of not more than three years, criminal detention or public surveillance.
29. He was never caught by the police, but was stabbed to death in a fight on a bus.
30. Job waiting team: Young people who just graduated from middle or high school were usually assigned temporary work in their parents' work units (if their parents worked for large factories).
31. The Regulations of the PRC on Administrative Penalties for Public Security was enacted on March 1, 2006.

NOTES TO CHAPTER 4

1. Among eight women who had a history of opium use, only one was addicted to it; three others had tried K powder, cannabis or dihydroetorphine (called *ko han pian*) before they used heroin, but none of them became addicted to these drugs.
2. According to Kandel and Yamaguchi (2002), smoking, drinking, and marijuana use are prerequisites for hard drug use. Based on a national sample of heroin users (N=38,561) Inciardi, McBride and Surratt (1998) indicate that none of these heroin users began their drug use careers with heroin.
3. Other women's employment status at heroin initiation: 23 percent were jobless, 8 percent were in school, and 2 percent were clerks (also 9 percent worked in nightclubs).
4. Ning ran a jewelry business (jade) and Xia had a tobacco business. Both businesses brought them very good fortune.

5. A woman drug dealer interviewed in the follow-up study also initiated heroin use in Ruili in 1986. She confirmed that heroin was available in a few upscale hotels in Kunming by that time.
6. In the planned economy era, the succession system was used to solve the employment problems of workers' children. With the development of the market economy, the system has been abolished in China.
7. According to Zinberg (1984, 184), social change has a great impact on the development of the individual's personality on both a short term (consciousness) and long term basis (personality modification).
8. Married women include those women who were in marriages (living with their husbands) and those who became widows, or were divorced or separated from their husbands. The category of women who initiated heroin with their husbands also includes Ping and Weihua who used heroin with their ex-husbands (due to long-term impacts prior to their divorces).
9. Yingyu was the only woman with a marriage history, but used heroin with her boyfriend (after her second divorce).
10. The minimum marriage age in China is 20 for women and 22 for men.
11. Using a national sample of heroin users in 1987, a study indicates that most heroin users initiated heroin by age 21 (Inciardi, McBride and Surratt 1998); The National survey by SAMHSA (2006) indicates that in that year, the average age at the first use of heroin was 20.7 years (in a range of 12 to 49 years); based on data from the 1998 National Drug Strategy Household Survey about people aged 14 years and over in Australia, the mean age at first use of heroin was 22 (1955–1969 birth cohort), 20 (1970–1974 birth cohort) and 18 (1975–1979 cohort) (Degenhardt, Lynskey and Hall 2000).
12. Kandel (1980) suggests that being single, divorced or separated are high risk factors for illicit drug use.
13. Please also see studies by Hser, Anglin and McGlothlin 1987; Stephens 1991; Klein, Elifson and Sterk 2003.
14. Rosenbaum (1984) found that women heroin users who were introduced to heroin exclusively by their men were likely to be older than women who used heroin on account of other social relationships.
15. Only three women said that their male partners lured them into heroin to continue maintaining relationships with them or for money.
16. Meiru dated her husband while in school, and lived with him since the age of 19.
17. Three women in this group, including Meiru and Weili, were not smokers when they began using heroin.
18. In the study, fifteen women had heroin-using siblings, and two women had a heroin-using parent. The women used heroin either before, or at the same time, as their siblings; the two parents, Qiaoling's mother and Jun's father were both using heroin prior to their daughter's initiation.
19. Fei's uncle and aunt had both died. Their home was sold to pay debts and their children sent to an orphanage.
20. As witnessed in the United States, heroin epidemics occurred when the drugs were easily available and easily accessible on the street (Chitwood, Comerford and Weatherby 1998).
21. A similar pattern was identified in a study conducted among women crack users in New York (Maher 1995), but there were also significant differences.
22. In Rosenbaum's study (1981), young women were often led to heroin by their female friends or friends in a mixed-sex group.
23. As suggested by Golub and Johnson (1994), the individual drug user's pathway is also determined by the broader social context, including the current stage of the drug epidemic.

NOTES TO CHAPTER 5

1. According to Becker (1967, 168), drug users learn "definition of the drug-induced experience" from other experienced users in certain drug-using cultures before they obtain enough experience by themselves."
2. Women who had drug-using male partners experienced a quick escalation of drug use after their initial trial of heroin.
3. Many women had the same experience as Juan. They told me that if the purity of heroin was high, they could smell the pleasant smell of a delicious apple.
4. Only a few women in the study gave themselves their first shot of heroin.
5. Rosenbaum (1981) suggests that injection is a symbolic act in the careers of heroin users, because it changes drug users' perceptions about themselves; they go from being a mere drug user to becoming a street junkie. However, Taylor's study (1993) did not confirm a significant change in women's perception in this regard.
6. For example, although Congshan injected heroin for only half a year, the backs of her hands became infected. She had to undergo surgery, and then went back to snorting. After that, she never injected again.
7. International Day against Drugs is on June 26. Women subjects referred to it as "6/26."
8. The Yi nationality constitutes one of the major heroin selling groups in Kunming. The women often called them *lao Yizu*. Previously known as being poor, and coming from the remote countryside, many of them have made big money from the underground drug selling business and settled down in Kunming.
9. My informant had quit using drugs for about two weeks, so she felt secure about herself. Still, when we walked out of that street, an undercover agent riding on a motorcycle followed us and briefly questioned her.
10. The price of heroin varies with its purity. As the purity increases, so does the price.
11. People can easily purchase syringes and needles from local drug stores without a doctor's prescription.
12. Individuals who sold out drug dealers, or other drug users' names to the police, could become victims of acts of revenge carried out by unidentified parties. One woman told me that she knew that a person who betrayed others was hamstrung once he was released from the compulsory drug rehabilitation center.
13. Changpo refers to the Compulsory Drug Rehabilitation Center of Kunming, which is located at Changpo, Kunming.
14. In a few cases, women who were capable of making good money from illegal activities supported their male partners' drug use.
15. Most women drug users were found participating in deviant street networks before they took drugs (Rosenbaum, 1981; Taylor 1993; Maher 1997; Sterk 1999; Sommers et al. 2000).
16. *Momo dance hall*: "Momo" means intimate touching. Similar dance halls are also found in other cities in China.
17. Though the living conditions and incomes of the rural people in China have been greatly improved after the economic reform, they are still stereotyped (by people living in the urban areas) as being rural.
18. Women also made profits from selling wine, alcohol and beer to their clients.
19. As suggested by Boyle and Anglin (1993), even for prostitution, the most convenient income-generating activity for women drug users, experience is required in order to be successful.

20. Based on accounts from women in the study, women working in nightclubs in Kunming must perform a striptease before their clients, for tips of 200 yuan or higher.
21. Women performed oral sex for men right in the middle of the dance stage in the darkness, or had sexual intercourse with men on the benches on the sides. Once the lights came back on, they quickly separated from each other, and the girls had money in their hands. During one of my fieldtrips to these dance halls, I saw a man on the bench with a girl on his lap, shamelessly rubbing her breasts even when the lights were on.
22. Rosenbaum's study (1981, 70) briefly states that women's involvement in criminal activity was through a "come-with-me" type of informal training in a mixed-sex group in which both male and female drug users were involved.
23. In Maher's study (1997), women drug users who engaged in shoplifting were always aided by men because men had connections with an underground market to cash proceeds.
24. Four women were sentenced to one or two years in re-education through labor or to labor camps for drug dealing.
25. Unfortunately, she passed away several months after the interview.
26. A Tier 3 drug dealer indicated that if she had to do so in order to protect herself, she only sold out those people she hated to the police—normally people who owed her drug money.
27. Tier 1 and Tier 2 women drug dealers normally maintained several different residences, or frequently changed the places where they lived.
28. Na engaged in blackmail in1993. According to the Judicial Interpretation by the Supreme Court of the People's Republic of China in 2005, her case will be classified as robbery.
29. *Ge zhu*: Ge means "slice off". Zhu means "pig". The term implies extortion of money from rich people.
30. Two other women in the follow-up study told me they put LSD (known as *mi huan yao,* a strong semi-artificial hallucinogen) into their clients drinks in order to rob them once they had lost clarity of mind: one of the women did this in a dance hall, the other, in a nightclub.
31. When I interviewed her, her husband was serving a two-year term for heroin use. Ni lived with her new boyfriend. Before I left Kunming, Ni was arrested again for relapse.
32. Ling has three sisters and one brother: her brother and one sister were also heroin users; two other sisters cut off contact with them.
33. Rong told me that she did not intend to come back to Kunming. However, she spent all her money and had to borrow some from her friend in Kunming for a return ticket. Sadly, she left her little boy in the hotel room during the daytime all by himself, but found a babysitter for him when she went out gambling at night.
34. Based on studies of male drug users, Kandel and Davies (1991) concluded that illicit drug use is positively associated with intimacy among members of male friendship networks.

NOTES TO CHAPTER 6

1. In Mann, Charuvastra and Murthy (1984)'s study, it is indicated that drug users' motivation for change has three different levels: uninternalized motivation, ordinary internalized motivation and very profound motivation.
2. Yamaguchi and Kandel (1985) indicate that the rate of women stopping the use of marijuana increased after their marriages.

3. Sampson, Laub and Wimer (2006) indicate that desistance from crime may not be limited to marital relationships alone. Cohabitation is growing and more normative among young cohorts. They suggest that future research look at the role of cohabitation in desistance from crime.
4. Among them, eight women either divorced or became widows before their drug initiation.
5. Two more women (Jing and Lan) divorced after the initial interviews in 2005.
6. Congshan's ex-husband was a manager in a hotel and always came home very late.
7. Among these women, Lan was released from re-education through labor three months ago. Her husband discussed divorce with her after she returned. Yuwei and Zhenli separated from their husbands for a while and then reunited with them. Except for Liang, only two women (Xia and Yuan) were able to keep their marriage intact, but Yun's husband did not even know she was a heroin user.
8. Xia only took heroin on one occasion in the past four years.
9. Based on my follow-up interviews, five women got married with drug-using men after my initial interviews.
10. At the time these women were interviewed, only two women's husbands were able to quit heroin use —those of Lei and Kaili. Lei's husband divorced her and Kaili was still in her marriage.
11. Lenard and Homish's study (2005) concludes that women marijuana users were less likely to be influenced by their drug-using spouses during their cessation. However, women exerted much more positive impacts on their husbands' cessation.
12. The medicine invented by Yunnan Medical College is used for heroin treatment in Kunming.
13. Qiangwei attempted suicide several times after she failed to persuade her husband to quit heroin prior to their marriage.
14. Three others divorced because of a third party; one woman divorced on account of discordant relationships with her husband.
15. Sampson, Laub and Wimer (2006) indicate that desistance from crime may not be limited to marital relationships alone. They suggest future research look at the role played by cohabitation in desistance from crime.
16. Rosenbaum (1981) suggests that women have reduced options where selecting husbands is concerned, because men who don't use drugs have no interest in addicted women. The current study indicates that women themselves have a mental block about developing such relationships.
17. Yamaguchi and Kandel's (1985, 1315–1316) study of marijuana users indicates that men and women who had never married nor became parents, and those who married but divorced or separated have a consistently strong propensity to resume marijuana use.
18. In the folk language of Yunnan.
19. Only after Qiaoling and her mother both enrolled in a voluntary drug treatment program, Qiaoling was able to develop a truly close relationship with her mother. At the time of the interview, Qiaoling and Jiahui had both abstained from drugs for a year.
20. Fang has two brothers in the family. Both of her brothers were heroin users. Her younger brother died of heroin abuse.
21. When I sat in at a community meeting to which the heroin users' parents had been invited, I could truly feel the dilemma these parents were facing: hoping to help but so terrified by all that had happened in the past.
22. The findings of the current study are consistent with Rosenbaum (1981): women's occupational options are significantly reduced because they either could not secure their original jobs or felt reluctant to pick up low-paying jobs.

23. Several women had just started their rehabilitation a couple of months prior to the interviews.
24. As revealed in Sampson and Laub's (1993) life-course perspectives, work stability is one of the key variables that help individuals desist from criminal behavior.
25. Liao liao xin yuan: in folk language, it means "fulfill your dream" or "satisfy yourself."
26. Song spent seven years in re-education through labor. Adding the time she served in compulsory rehabilitation brought the total to ten years.
27. Previous research suggests that being a parent, or increasing parental roles, were more likely to motivate drug users to discontinue their drug use (Rosenbaum 1981; Esbensen and Elliott 1994).
28. Studies in the United States also reveal that drug-using women are not expected to raise their children; the responsibility is taken over by other relatives (Johnson, Dunlap and Maher 1998).
29. Since the mid-1980s, maternal drug use is subject to legal sanction in many states in the United States. Children were removed from drug-using women (Boyd 1999).
30. I was repeatedly told by the women that getting rid of physical dependence is relatively easy, but getting rid of psychological dependence is difficult.
31. Winick (1962) attributed termination of drug use to maturation in the life-cycle, maturation in addiction itself, or a reflection of these two processes.
32. Women heroin users had experienced significant physical breakdowns, including severe heart and lung problems, high blood pressure, cancers, HIV infection and nervous breakdowns.
33. I also attended their gatherings a few times. Several women told me they were finally through with heroin, but they refused to accept my invitation to be interviewed, for reasons that were unclear.
34. Suzhen was lured to use heroin by her drug-using boyfriend, who later became her husband; however, he separated from her many years ago.
35. The accumulated time spent in re-education through labor programs.
36. In Kunming, the compulsory rehabilitation center operates at the city and district levels: drug users might be transferred to the city rehabilitation center or stay at the district center at the discretion of the district police department.
37. Several women in the study had to stay for an extra six months to pay off their expenses, since their families had refused to pay on their behalf.
38. Despite Lina's determination, it was surprising that she was re-arrested about one week after my interview with her.
39. Tingting committed suicide when she was in re-education through labor on account of her relationship with Song.
40. After the interviews were done in the summer of 2005, on December 1, 2005, the State Food and Drug Administration Department prohibited pharmaceutical retailers selling drugs on a published list, which included diphenoxylate.
41. Women's experiences suggest that—changes in women heroin users' social environment could lead to very successful abstinence (Robin 1974; 1976). Unlike veterans in Robin's studies, who ultimately left their drug-using environment, in this study, the women all went back to Kunming because of their ties with their hometown.
42. Murphy (1992, 211) suggests that "failure at mothering, loss of their children's custody, meant failure at being a woman" because of a loss of their self-identity.

NOTES TO CHAPTER 7

1. The Chinese central government has been criticized for not taking firm action against heroin use during its initial stage (Zhou 2000).
2. Gerber and Jensen (2001) indicate that many social problems go through a series of four stages: incipiency, coalescence, creation and policy formation, and legitimization.
3. Evaluations of vocational intervention programs indicate that programs engaged in developing drug users' personal competency, work skills, job opportunities, and placement possibilities are beneficial to drug users (Platt 1995, 64).

References

IN ENGLISH

Akers, Ronald L. 1991. *Drugs, Alcohol and Society: Social Structure, Process and Policy*. Belmont, CA: Wadsworth.

Anderson, Tammy L. 1998. "A Cultural–identity Theory of Drug Abuse." *Sociology of Crime, Law, and Deviance* 1: 233–262.

Anglin, M. Douglas, and Yih–ing Hser. 1987. "Addicted Women and Crime." *Criminology* 25 (2): 359–397.

Auerbach, Carl F., and Louise B. Silverstein. 2003. *Qualitative Data: An Introduction to Coding and Analysis*. New York: New York University Press.

Bakken, Borge. 1993. "Crime, Juvenile Delinquency and Deterrence Policy in China." *The Australia Journal of Chinese Affairs* 30: 29–58.

Bailey, Paul. 2001. "Active Citizen or Efficient Housewife: the Debate over Women's Education in Early Twentieth Century China." In *Education, Culture and Identity in Twentieth–Century China,* edited by Glen Peterson, Ruth Hayhoe and Yongling Lu, 318–347. Ann Arbor, MI: The University of Michigan Press.

Ball, John C., and Richard W. Snarr. 1969. "A Test of the Maturation Hypothesis with Respect to Opiate Addiction." *Bulletin on Narcotics* 21: 9–13.

Baumler, Alan, ed. 2002. *Modern China and Opium: A Reader*. Ann Arbor, MI: The University of Michigan Press.

Becker, Howard S. 1953. "Becoming a Marijuana User." *The American Journal of Sociology* 59(3): 235–242.

Becker, Howard S. 1963. *Outsiders: Studies in the Sociology of Deviance*. New York: The Free Press.

Becker, Howard S. 1967. "History, Culture and Subjective Experience: An Exploration of the Social Bases of Drug–Induced Experiences." *Journal of Health and Social Behavior* 8(3): 163–176.

Belknap, Joanne. 2001. *The Invisible Woman: Gender, Crime, and Justice*. Belmont, CA: Wadsworth/Thomas Learning.

Bloom, Barbara, Barbara Owen, and Stephanie Covington. 2003. *Gender–Responsive Strategies: Research, Practice and Guiding Principles for Women Offenders*. Washington, DC: National Institute of Corrections.

Blumstein, Alfred, Jacqueline Cohen, Jeffrey A. Roth, and Christy A Visher, eds. 1986. *Criminal Careers and "Career Criminals."* (Volume I and II). Washington, DC: National Academy Press.

Bourgois, Philippw, and Eloise Dunlap. 1993."Exorcising Sex–for–Crack: An Ethnographic Perspective from Harlem." In *Crack Pipe as Pimp: An Ethnographic Investigation of Sex for Crack Exchange*, edited by Mitchell S. Ratner, 97–132. New York: Lexington Books.

Boyd, Susan C. 1999. *Mothers and Illicit Drugs: Transcending the Myths*. Toronto: University of Toronto Press.

Brown, Richard H. 2002. "The Opium Trade and Opium Policies in India, China, Britain and the United Sates: Historical comparisons and Theoretical Interpretations." *American Journal of Social Science* 30(3): 623–656.

Brook, Timothy, and Bob T. Wakabayashi. 2000. "Introduction: Opium's History in China." In *Opium Regimes: China, Britain, and Japan,* edited by Timothy Brook and Bob T. Wakabayashi, 1839–1952. Berkeley: University of California Press.

Chein, Isidor, Donald L. Gerard, Robert S. Lee, and Eva Rosenfeld. 1964. *The Road to H: Narcotics, Delinquency and Social Policy*. New York: Basic Books.

Chen, Xiaojin, Kimberly A. Tyler, Les B Whitbeck, and Dan R. Hoyt. 2004. "Early Sexual Abuse, Street Adversity, and Drug Use among Female Homeless and Runaway Adolescents in the Midwest." *Journal of Drug Issues* 34(1): 1–22.

Chesney–Lind, Meda, and Karen J. Laidler. 1997. "Drugs, Violence, and Women's Crime." In *The Female Offender: Girls, Women and Crime*, edited by Meda Chesney–Lind, 120–142. Thousand Oaks, CA: Sage.

Chitwood, Dale D., Mary Comerford, and Norman L. Weatherby. 1998. "The Initaiton of the Use of Heorin in the Age of Crack." In *Heorin in the Age of Crack–Cocaine*, edited by Inciardi, James A.,and Harrison Lana D., 51–76. Thousan Oaks, CA: Sage.

Chu, Godwin C., and Yan'an Ju. 1993. *The Great Wall in Ruins: Communication and Cultural Change in China*. Albany: State University of New York Press.

Coleman, James S. 1988. "Social Capital in the Creation of Human Capital." *The American Journal of sociology* 94 (Supplement.): S95–120.

Coombs, Robert H. 1981. "Drug Abuse as Career." *Journal of Drug Issues* 11(4): 369–387.

Cuskey, Walter R., and Richard B. Wathey. 1982. *Female Addiction: A Longitudinal Study*. Lexington, MA: Lexington Books.

Dai, Bingham. 1937. *Opium Addiction in Chicago*. Shanghai: Commercial Press. Reprint in 1970. Montclair, NJ: Patterson Smith.

Denton, Barbara, and Pat O'Malley. 2001. "Property Crime and Women Drug Dealers in Australia." *Journal of Drug Issues* 31(2): 465–486.

Day, Carolyn, Linette Collins, Louisa Degenhardt, Clare Thetford, and Lisa Maher. 2004. "Reliability of Heroin Users' Reports of Drug Use Behavior Using a 24-Month Timeline Follow–Back Technique to Assess the Impact of the Australian Heroin Shortage." *Addiction Research and Theory* 12(5): 433–443.

Degenhardt, Louisa., Michael Lynskey, and Wayne Hall. 2000. *Cohort Trends in the Age of Initiation of Drug Use in Australia*. Technical Report 83. Sydney, Australia: National Drug and Alcohol Research Center.

De Quincey, Thomas. 1821. *Confessions of an English Opium Eater.* New York: Oxford University Press. Reprint in 1985.

Deng, Xiaogang, and Ann Cordilia. 1999. "To Get Rich is Glorious: Rising Expectations, Declining Control, and Escalating Crime in Contemporary China." *International Journal of Offender Therapy and Comparative Criminology* 423: 211–229.

Dikőtter, Frank, Laris Laamann, and Xun Zhou. 2002. "Narcotic Culture: A Social History of Drug Consumption in China." *British Journal of Criminology* 42: 317–336.

Dunlap, Eloise, Andrew Golub, Bruce D. Johnson, and Damaris Wesley. 2002. "Intergenerational Transmission of Conduct Norms for Drugs, Sexual Exploration and Violation: A Case Study." *British Journal of Criminology* 42: 1–20.

Dunlap, Eloise, and Bruce D. Johnson. 1999. "Gaining Access to Hidden Populations: Strategies for Gaining Cooperation of Sellers/Dealers in Ethnographic Research." *Drugs and Society* 14(1/2): 127–149.

Dunlap, Eloise, and Bruce D. Johnson. 1996. "Family and Human Resources in the Development of a Female Crack Seller Career: Case Study of a Hidden Population." *Journal of Drug Issues* 26(1): 175–198.

Durkheim, Emile. 1893. *The Division of Labor in Society,* translated by Simpson, George. New York: The Free Press. Reprint in 1965.

Durkheim, Emile. 1897/1951. *Suicide: A study in Sociology*, edited by George Simpson (with an Introduction), translated by Spaulding, John A., and George Simpson. New York: The Free Press.

Ebrey, Patricia B. 2002. *Women and the Family in Chinese History.* New York: Routledge.

Elder, Glen H., Jr. 1994. "Time, Human Agency, and Social Change: Perspectives on the Life Course." *Social Psychology Quarterly* 57(1): 4–15.

Elder, Glen H., Jr. 1998. *Children of the Great Depression.* (25th Anniversary Edition). New York: Westview Press.

Eldred, Carolyn A., and Mabel N. Washington. 1976. "Interpersonal Relationships in Heroin Use by Men and Women and Their Role in Treatment Outcome." *The International Journal of the Addiction* 11(1): 117–130.

Esbensen, Finn–Aage, and Elliot, Delbert S. 1994. "Continuity and Discontinuity in Illicit Drug Use: Patterns and Antecedents." *Journal of Drug Issues* 24(1/2): 75–98.

Evans, Harriet. 1997. *Women and Sexuality in China: Female Sexuality and Gender since 1949.* New York: Continuum.

Fagan, Jeffrey, and Ko–lin Chin. 1991. "Social Processes of Initiation into Crack." *Journal of Drug Issues* 21(2): 313–344.

Faupel, Charles E. 1991. *Shooting Dope: Career Patterns of Hard–Core Heroin Users.* Gainesville, FL: University of Florida.

Feldman, Harvey W., and Michael R. Aldrich. 1990. "The Role of Ethnography in Substance abuse Research and Public Policy: Historical Precedent and Future Prospects." In *The Collection and Interpretation of Data from Hidden Populations,* edited by Elizabeth Y. Lambert, 19–37. NIDA Research Monograph 98. U. S. Department of Health and Human Services. Washington, DC: U. S. Government Printing Office.

Feng, Shuliang. 2001. "Crime and Crime Control in a Changing China." In *Crime and Social Control in a Changing China,* edited by Jianhong Liu, Lening Zhang, and Steven F. Messner, 124–130. Westport, CT: Greenwood Press.

Fetterman, David M. 1998. (2nd ed). *Ethnography: Step by Step.* Thousand Oaks, CA: Sage.

Fisac, Taciana. 2003. "Social Anomie and Political Discourse in Contemporary China." In *China Today: Economic Reforms, Social Cohesion and Collective Identities*, edited by Yaciana Fisac, and Leila Fernández–Stembridge, 149–172. London: RoutledgeCurzon.

Gallagher, Mary. 2001. "Women and Gender." In *An Introduction to Chinese Culture through the Family*, edited by Howard Giskin, and Bettye S. Walsh, 89–106, Albany, NY: State University of New York Press.

Gerber, Jurg, and Eric L. Jensen. 2001. "The Internationalization of U.S. Policy on Illicit Drug Control." In *Drug War American Style: The Internationalization of Failed Policy and its Alternatives*, edited by Jurg Gerber and Eric L. Jensen, 1–18 . New York: Garland Publishing.

Glaser, Barney C., and Anselm Strauss. 1967. *Discovery of Grounded Theory.* Chicago: Aldine.

Goffman, Erving. 1959. "The Moral Career of the Mental Patient." *Journal for the Study of Interpersonal Processes* 22(2): 123–142.

Goffman, Erving. 1961. *Asylums.* Garden City, NY: Doubleday.

Goldstein, Paul J., Barry J. Spuny, Thomas Miller, and Patracia Bellucci. 1990. "Ethnographic Field Stations." In *The Collection and Interpretation of Data from Hidden Populations*, edited by *Elizabeth Y. Lambert*, 87–102. NIDA Research Monograph 98. U. S. Department of Health and Human Services. Washington, DC: U. S. Government Printing Office.

Golub, Andrew, and Bruce D. Johnson. 1994. "Cohort Differences in Drug–Use Pathways to Crack among Current Crack Abuses in New York City." *Criminal Justice and Behavior* 21(4): 403–422.

Gorbach, Pamina M., Caroline Ryan, Vonthanak Saphonn, and Roger Detels. 2002. "The Impacts of Social, Economic and Political Forces on Emerging HIV Epidemics." *AIDS* 6 *(Suppl.4)*: 35–43.

Gottfredson, Michael R., and Travis Hirschi. 1990. *A General Theory of Crime*. Stanford, CA: Stanford University Press.

Greenhalgh, Susan, and Jiali Li. 1995. "Engendering Reproduction Policy and Practice in Peasant China: for a Feminist Demography of Reproduction." *Signs* 20(3): 601–641.

Greenleaf, Vicki D. 1989. *Women and Cocaine: Personal Stories of Addiction and Recovery*. Los Angeles: Jack Artenstein.

Hamid, Ashley. 1998. *Drugs in America: Sociology, Economics, and Politics*. Gaithersburg, MA: Aspen.

Hammersley, Martyn, and Paul Atkinson. 1995. (2nd ed). *Ethnography: Principle in Practice*. New York: Routledge.

Hao, Wei, Shuiyuan Xiao, Teiqiao Liu, Derson Young, Shanmei Chen, and Diran Zhang, et al. 2002. "The Second National Epidemiological Survey on Illicit Drug Use at Six High–Prevalence Areas in China: Prevalence Rates and Use Patterns." *Addiction* 97(10): 1305–1315.

Heckathorn, Doughlas D. 2002. "Respondent–Driven Sampling II: Deriving Valid Population Estimates from Chain–referral Samples of Hidden Populations." *Social Problems*, 49(1): 11–34.

Hirschi, Travis. 1969. *Causes of Delinquency*. Berkeley, CA: University of California Press.

Hser, Yih–ing, M. Douglas Anglin, and William McGlothlin. 1987. "Gender Differences in Addict Careers: Initiation of Use." *American Journal of Drug and Alcohol Abuse* 13: 33–57.

Hser, Y–I, M. D. Anglin, and K. Power. 1993. "A 24–Year Follow–Up of California Narcotics Addicts." *Achieves of General Psychiatry* 50: 577–584.

Hser, Yih–ing, Chih–ping Chou, and M. Doughlas Anglin. 1990. "The Criminality of Female Narcotics Addicts: A Causal Modeling Approach."*Journal of Quantitative Criminology* 6(2): 207–228.

Inciardi, James A., Dorothy Lockwood, and Anne E Pottieger. 1993. *Women and Crack–Cocaine*. New York: Macmillan Publishing Company.

Inciardi, James A., and Anne E Pottieger. 1998. "Drug Use and Street Crime in Miami: An (almost) Twenty–Year Retrospective." *Substance Use and Misuse* 33(9): 1839–1870.

Inciardi, James A., Duane C. McBride, and Hilary L. Surratt. 1998. "The Heroin Street Addict: Profiling a National Population." In *Heroin in the Age of Crack–Cocaine*, edited by James A. Inciardi, and Lana D. Harrison, 31–50. Thousand Oaks, CA: Sage.

Inglehart, Ronald. 1997. *Modernization and Postmodernization: Cultural, Economic*, and *Political Change in 43 Societies*. Princeton, NJ: Princeton University Press.

Jacka, Tamara. 2005. *Rural Women in Urban China: Gender, Migration and Social Change*. Armonk, NY: M.E. Sharpe.

Jeffreys, Elaine. 2004. *China, Sex and Prostitution*. New York: Routledge Curzon.

Johnson, Bruce D., Eloise Dunlap, and Sylvie C. Tourigny. 2000. "Crack Distribution and Abuse in New York." In *Illegal Drug Markets: From Research to Pre-*

vention policy, edited by Mangai Natarajan, and Michael Hough, 19–58. Crime Prevention Studies Volume II. Monsey, New York: Criminal Justice Press.

Johnson, Bruce D., Eloise Dunlap, and Lisa Maher. 1998. "Nurturing for Careers in Drug Use and Crime: Conduct Norms for Children and Juveniles in Crack–Using Households." *Substance Use and Misuse* 33(7): 1511–1546.

Kandel, Denise B. 1980. "Drug and Drinking Behavior among Youth." *Annual Review of Sociology* 6: 235–285.

Kandel, Denise B., and Kazuo Yamaguchi. 2002. "Stages of Drug Involvement in the U. S. Population." In *Stages and Pathways of Drug Involvement,* edited by Denise B. Kandel, 65–90. Cambridge: Cambridge University Press.

Kassebaum, Patricia A. 1999. *Substance Abuse Treatment for Women Offenders: Guide to Promising Practices.* Rockville, MD: U.S. Department of Health and Human Services.

Kaplan, Howard B., and Joseph H. Meyerowitz. 1970. "Social and Psychological Correlates of Drug Abuse: A Comparison of Addict and Non–Zddict Populations from the Perspective of Self-Theory." *Social Science and Medicine* 40: 203–225.

Kaufman, Jeanne G., and Cathy S. Widom. 1999. "Childhood Victimization, Running Away, and Delinquency." *Crime and Delinquency* 36(4): 347–370.

Klein, Hugh, Kirk W. Elifson, and Claire E. Sterk. 2003. "Perceived Temptation to Use Drugs and Actual Drug Use among Women." *Journal of Drug Issues* 33(1): 161–191.

Krohn, Marvin D., Alan J. Lizotte, and Cynthia M. Perez. 1997. "The Interrelationship between Substance Use and Precious Transitions to Adult Statues." *Journal of Health and Social Behavior* 38(1): 87–103.

Lambert, Elizabeth Y., and W. Wayne Wiebel. 1990. Introduction. In *The Collection and Interpretation of Data from Hidden Populations.* NIDA Research, edited by Elizabeth Y. Lambert, 8–10. Monograph 98. U.S. Department of Health and Human Services. Washington, DC: U.S. Government Printing Office.

Lau, Joseph T. F., T Feng, X. Lin, Q. Wang, and H. Y. Tsui. 2005. "Needle Sharing and Sex–Related Risk Behaviors among Drug Users in Shenzhen, a City in Guangdong, Southern China." *AIDS Care* 17(2): 166–181.

Lindesmith, Alfred R. 1938. "A Sociological Theory of Drug Addiction." *American Journal of Sociology* 43: 593–613.

Lindesmith, Alfred R. 1947. *Opiate Addiction.* Bloomington, IN: Principia Press.

Liu, Jianhong, and Steven F. Messner. 2001. "Modernization and Crime Trends in China's Reform Era." In *Crime and Social Control in a Changing China,* edited by Jianhong Liu, Lening Zhang, and Steven F. Messner, 3–22. Westport, CT: Greenwood Press.

Lenard, Kenneth E., and Gregory G. Homish. 2005. "Changes in Marijuana Use over the Transition into Marriage." *Journal of Drug Issues* 5(2): 409–430.

Maher, Lisa. 1995. "In the Name of Love: Women and Initiation to Illicit Drugs." In *Gender and Crime*, edited by R. E. Dobash, R. P. Dobash and L. Noaks, 132–166. Cardiff, Australia: University of Wales Press.

Maher, Lisa, and Kathleen Daly. 1996. "Women in the Street Level Drug Economy: Continuity or Change?" *Criminology* 34: 465–491.

Maher, Lisa. 1997. *Sexed Work: Gender, Race, and Resistance in a Brooklyn Drug Market.* New York: Oxford University Press.

Mann, N.R., V.C. Charuvastra, and V.K. Murchy. 1984. "A Diagnostic Tool with Important Implications for Treatment of Addiction: Identification of Factors Underlying Relapse and Remission Time Distributions." *International Journal of the Addictions* 19(1): 25–44

Maxwell, Joseph A. 2005. (2nd ed). *Qualitative Research Design: An Interactive Approach.* Applied Social Research Method Series, Volume 41. Thousand Oaks, CA: Sage.

Mears, Daniel P., Matthew Ploeger, and Mark Warr. 1998. "Explaining the Gender Gap in Delinquency: Peer influence and Moral Evaluations of Behavior." *Journal of Research in Crime and Delinquency* 35: 251–266.

Meter, Karl. M. V. 1990. "Methodological and Design Issues: Techniques for Assessing the Representatives of Snowball Samples." In *The Collection and Interpretation of Data from Hidden Populations*, edited by Elizabeth Y. Lambert, 38–50. NIDA Research Monograph 98. U.S. Department of Health and Human Services. Washington, DC: U.S. Government Printing Office.

Mensch, Barbara S., and Denise B. Kandel. 1988. "Dropping Out of High School and Drug Involvement." *Sociology of Education* 61(2): 95–113.

Miller, Jean B. 1976. *Toward a New Psychology of Women.* Boston: Beacon Press.

Miller, Eleanor M. 1986. *Street Women.* Philadelphia: Temple University Press.

Murphy, Sheigla. 1992. *"It Takes Your Womanhood": Depersonilfication, Resistance and the Persisting Self.* PhD diss, University of California, San Fransisco.

Nagin, Daniel S., and Raymond Paternoster. 1994. "Personal Capital and Social Control: The Deterrence Implications of a Theory of Individual Differences in Criminal Offending." *Criminology* 32(4): 581–606.

Neuman, W Lawrence. 2003. *Social Research Methods: Qualitative and Quantitative Approaches.* New York: Allyn & Bacon.

Neuman, W. Lawrence., and R. J. Berger 1988. "Competing Perspectives on Cross–national Crime: An evaluation of Theory and Evidence." *The Sociological Quarterly* 29: 281–313.

Ogden, Suzanne. 2002. "Chinese Nationalism: the Precedence of Community and Identity over Individual Rights." In *China's Developmental Miracle: Origins, Transformations and Challenge,* edited by Alvin Y. So, 224–245. Armonk, NY: M.E. Sharpe.

Padmohoedojo, Paulina G. 2004. *Review and Assessment of the Current Organizational Structure of the NNCC, China, and its Capacity to Understand and Respond to the Emergent Issues of Drug Abuse related HIV.* The National Narcotics Control Commission of China. Accessed March 30, 2006. www.unodc.un.or.th/drugsandhiv/Projectfindings/NDBA/NNCC%20China%20Assessment–09–01–04.ppt

Patton, Michael Q. 2001. (3rd edition). *Qualitative Evaluation and Research Methods.* Newbury Park, CA: Sage.

Platt, Jerome J. 1988. (2nd edition). *Heroin Addiction: Theory, Research and Treatment* (Volume 1). Malabar, FL: Robert E. Krieger Publishing Company.

Platt, Jerome J. 1995. *Heroin Addiction: Theory, Research and Treatment* (Volume 2): *The addict, the Treatment Process, and Social Control.* Malabar, FL: Robert E. Krieger Publishing Company.

Pohl, Joanne, and Carol Boyd. 1991. "Female Addiction: A Concept Analysis." In *Drugs, Crime, and Social Policy: Research, Issues, and Concerns*, edited by Thomas Mieczkowski, 138–152. Boston: Allyn and Bacon.

Prochaska, J. O., J. C. Norcross, and J. C. Norcross. 1992. "In Search of How People Change: Applications to Addictive Behaviors." *American Psychologist* 47(9): 1102–1114.

Ren, Xin. 1999. "Prostitution and Economic Modernization in China." *Violence against Women* 5(12): 1411–1436.

Rhodes, Tim, and David Moore. 2001. "On the Qualitative in Drugs Research (Editorial Review)." *Addiction Research & Theory* 9(4): 279–297.

Richie, Beth E. 1995. *Compelled to Crime: The Gender Entrapment of Battered Black Women.* New York: Routledge.

Roberts, Amelia C., Robert H. Nishimoto, and Raymond S. Kirk. 2003. "Cocaine Abusing Women who Report Sexual Abuse: Implications for Treatment." *Journal of Social Work Practice in the Addiction* 3(1): 5–24.

Rosenbaum, Marsha. 1981. *Women on Heroin*. New Brunswick, NJ: Rutgers University.

Rubin, Herbet J., and Irene S. Rubin. (1995). *Qualitative Interviewing: The Art of Hearing Data*. Thousand Oaks, CA: Sage.

Sampson, Robert J., and John H. Laub. 1993. *Crime in the Making: Pathways and Turning Points through Life*. Cambridge, MA: Harvard University Press.

Sampson, Robert J., John H. Laub, and Christopher Wimer. 2006. "Does Marriage Reduce Crime? A Counterfractual Approach to Within–Individual Causal Effects." *Criminology* 44(3): 465–508.

Schroeder Ryan D., Peggy C. Giordano and Stephen A. Cernkovich. 2007. "Drug Use and Desistance Processes." *Criminology* 45(1): 191–222.

Shelley, Louise I. 1981. *Crime and Modernization*. Carbondale, IL: Southern Illinois University Press.

Sifaneck, Stephen J., and Alan Neaigus. 2001. "The Ethnographic Accessing, Sampling and Screening of Hidden Populations: Heroin Sniffers in New York City." *Addiction Research & Theory* 9(6): 519–543.

Simons, Ronald L., Eric Stewart, Leslie C. Gordon, Rand D. Conger, and Glen H. Elder, Jr. 2002. "A Test of Life–Course Explanations for Stability and Change in Antisocial Behavior from Adolescent to Young Adulthood". *Criminology* 40(2): 401–434.

State Council AIDS Working Committee Office/UN Theme Group on AIDS in China. 2007. *A Joint Assessment of HIV/AIDS Prevention, Treatment and Cure in China*. Accessed January 10, 2011 at http://www.chinaids.org.cn/n435777/n443716/6399.html

Substance Abuse and Mental Health Services Administration (SAMHSA). 2006. *The 2006 National Survey on Drug Use and Health: National findings*. Washington D. C. Department of Health and Human Services. Accessed October 17, 2007 at http://www.oas.samhsa.gov/nsduh/2k6nsduh/2k6Results.cfm

Sommers, Ira, Deborah Basin, and Jeffery Fagan. 1994. "Getting out of the Life: Crime Desistance by Female Street Offenders." *Deviant Behavior* 15: 125–149.

Sommers, Ira, Deborah Basin, and Jeffery Fagan. 2000. *Workin' Hard for the Money: The Social and Economic Lives of Women Drug Sellers*. New York: Nova Science Publishers.

Spradley, James. 1979. *The Ethnographic Interview*. New York: Harcourt Brace Jovanovich College Publishers.

Sterk, Claire E. 1999. *Fast Lives: Women Who Use Crack Cocaine*. Philadelphia: Temple University Press.

Stephens, Richard C. 1991. *The Street Addict Role: A Theory of Heroin Addiction*. Albany, NY: State University of New York Press.

Strauss, Anselm L. (1987). *Qualitative Analysis for Social Scientists*. New York: Cambridge University Press.

Strauss, Anselm, and Juliet Corbin. 1998. (2nd edition). *Basics of Qualitative Research: Techniques and Procedures for Developing Grounded Theory*. Thousand Oaks, CA: Sage.

Strauss, Shiela M., and Gregory P. Falklin. 2001. "Social Support Systems of Women Offenders Who Use Drugs: A Focus on the Mother–Daughter Relationship." *American Journal of Alcohol Abuse* 27(1): 65–89.

Sullivan, Mercer L. 1989. *"Getting Paid": Youth Crime and Work in the Inner City*. Ithaca, NY: Cornell University Press.

Taylor, Avril. 1993. *Women Drug Users: An Ethnography of a Female Injecting Community*. Oxford: Clarendon Press.

Travis, Jeremy. 1995. *Childhood Victimization and Risk for Alcohol and Drug Arrests.* (Research Preview). Washington, DC: U.S. Department of Justice. National Institute of Justice.

United Nations Office on Drugs and Crime (UNODC). 2004. *Drugs and HIV/AIDS in South East Asia. A Review of Critical Geographic Areas of HIV/AIDS Infection among Injecting Drug Users and of National Program Responses in Cambodia, China, LaoPDR, Thailand and Vietnam. Bangkok, Thailand.* Accessed May 12, 2006 at http://www.unodc.un.or.th/g22/publications/HIV–AIDS.pdf

United Nations Office on Drugs and Crime (UNODC). 2006. *World Drug Report.* Accessed January 10, 2011 at http://www.unodc.org/unodc/en/data-and-analysis/WDR-2006.html

Vold, George B., Thomas J. Bernard, and Jeffrey B. Snipes. 1998. (4th edition). *Theoretical criminology.* New York: Oxford University Press.

Waldorf, Dan. 1983. "Natural Recovery from Opiate Addiction: Some Social–psychological Processes of Untreated Recovery." *Journal of Drug Issues* 13(2): 237–280.

Waldorf, Dan, Craig Reinarman, and Sheigla Murphy. 1991. *Cocaine Changes: The Experience of Using and Quitting.* Philadelphia: Temple University Press.

Wang, Yaping. 2004. *Urban Poverty, Housing and Social Change in China.* New York: Routledge.

Warr, Mark. 1996. "Organization and Instigation in Delinquent Groups." *Criminology* 34(1): 11–37.

Warr, Mark. 2002. *Companions in Crime: the Social Aspects of Criminal Conduct.* New York: Cambridge University Press.

Wiebel, W. Wayne. 1990. Identifying and Gaining Access to Hidden Populations. In *The Collection and Interpretation of Data from Hidden Populations*, edited by Elizabeth Y. Lambert, 11–18. NIDA Research Monograph 98. U.S. Department of Health and Human Services. Washington, DC: U.S. Government Printing Office.

Willis, Katie, and Catherine Rushforth. 2003. *The Female Criminal: An Overview of Women's Drug Use and Offending Behavior.* Trends and Issues in Crime and Criminal Justice (No. 264). Canberra, Australia: Australian Institute of Criminology.

Winick, Charles. 1962. "Maturing out of Narcotic Addiction." *Bulletin on Narcotics* 14: 1–7.

Wright, John Paul, and Francis T. Cullen. (2001). "Parental Efficacy and Delinquent Behavior: Do Control and Support Matter?" *Criminology* 39(3): 677–706.

Zhang, Chiyu, Rongge Yang, Xueshan Xia, Shaoying Qin, Jianping Dai, and Zunbin Zhang et al. 2002. "High Prevalence of HIV–1 and Hepatitis C Virus Co–Infection among Injection Drug Users in the Southeastern Region of Yunnan, China." *AIDS Journal of Acquired Immune Deficiency Syndromes* 29(2): 191–196.

Zheng, Wang. 2003. (2nd Edition). "Gender, Employment and Women's Resistance." In *Chinese Society: Change, Conflict and Resistance,* edited by Elizabeth J. Perry and Mark Selden, 162–186. New York: RoutledgeCurzon.

Zhou, Yongming. 2000. *China's Anti–Drug Campaign in the Reform Era.* Singapore: World Science Publishing.

Zinberg, Norman E. 1984. *Drug, Set, and Setting: the Basis for Controlled Intoxicant Use.* New Haven, CT: Yale University Press.

IN CHINESE

Cha, Haomin, Xiaolin Li, Shirong Wang, and Chengzheng Zhao. 2003. "Surveys on Drug Use Behaviors, Knowledge and Attitudes towards HIV/AIDS among 100 Female Heroin Users." *Chinese Journal of Drug Dependence* 12(2): 135–138.

Chen, Fang. 2003. *The Lost and Chasing: Changes of Chinese Women's Social Values during the Turn of the Centuries*. Beijing: Chinese Social Sciences Press.

Chen, Yongmei, Zengzheng Wang, Hongmei Yang, and Ligong Chen. 1999a. "An Overview of Women's Drug Use in Wuhan." *Chinese Journal of Drug Dependence* 6(23): 16–20.

Chen, Yongmei, Zengzheng Wang, Ligong Chen, and Hongmei Yang. 1999b. "The Family Background of 310 Female Drug Users in Wuhan." *Chinese Journal of Drug Dependence* 8(4): 300–303.

Chinese Academy of Social Sciences. 2010. *Blue Book of 2010, the Rule of Law*. Beijing: Social Science Academic Press.

State Council of the People's Republic of China (SCPRC). 2005. White Paper on Gender Equality and Women's Development. Accessed November 10, 2010 at http://www.china.org.cn/e-white/20050824/index.htm

Chu, Huanke. 2001. "The Developing Patterns of Drug-Related Crime in Shaanxi." *Journal of Fujian Public Safety College* 15(4): 59–95.

Cui, Min. 1998. "The Trend of Drug-Related Crime within 13 Years." *Journal of Chinese People's Public Security University* 1(1): 35–39.

Cui, Min. 1999. "The Developing Patterns of Drug-related Crime." In *The Trend of Drug-Related Crime and Controlling Strategies*, edited by Min Cui, Qiuguan Duan, Binsen Luo, Ruolei Tang, Quansheng He and Minai Ma. Beijing: Police Education Publisher.

Fang Cai, Zheng Zhenzhen, and Yang Du, eds. 2005. Chinese Academy of Social Sciences. *China's Population and the Labor Report (No.7)*. Beijing: Social Sciences Literature Press.

Guo, Xiang. 1997. "Drug-related Problems in China and Controlling Strategies." *Journal of Political Science and Law* 4: 19–28.

He, Bingsong. 2001. "Patterns of Criminal Gangs in Mainland China." *Tribune of Political Science and Law* 1: 61–73.

He, Xuesong. 2002. *Chinese Society Observed from a Sociological Perspective*. Shanghai: China Eastern University of Science and Technology.

Huang, Minghua. 1995. "A Study of Drug-related Problems from a Geographical Perspective." *Journal of Suzhou Railway Teachers College* 12: 1–10.

Kunming Bureau of Statistics (KBS). 2006. Population Survey Data based on 1percent of Random Selected Samples in Kunming in 2005. Accessed January 10, 2011 at http://www.china.com.cn/chinese/renkou/1199140.htm

Kunming Bureau of Statistics (KBS). 2009. *2008 Kunming Economic and Social Development Statistical Bulletin*. Accessed January 10, 2011 at http://cxyr.xxgk.yn.gov.cn/canton-model26/newslist.aspx?classid=121844

Law Yearbook of China. 1978–2008. Law Yearbook of China Editorial Board. Beijing: China Law Press.

Li, Shuangqi. 2004. "The Reasons for Illicit Drug Use among 240 Drug Users in Fujian." *Chinese Criminal Science* 4(13): 101–110.

Liang, Jinyun, and Gang Lu. 2000." Illicit Drug Use and Its Controls in Xishuang Banna." *Journal of Yunnan Police Officer Academy* 2: 59–65.

Liao, Huailing, Dewen Yu, and Guangtai Chen. 2004. "Increasing Threats of AIDS."*Yang Cheng Evening News,* March 24. Accessed August 23, 2006 at http://www.cnki.net

Liao, Quanming, and Hui Li. 2003. "A Review of Studies on Illicit Drug Use in China." *Journal of Yunnan Police Officer Academy* 3: 17–20, 76.

Li, Xiaoqin. 2004. "AIDS around Us." *Lanzhou Daily*, November 30. Accessed May 21, 2006 at http://www.cnki.net

Liu, Jun, Xiaoming Si, and Hongyun Li. 2004. "Illicit Drug Users in Dalian." *Chinese Journal of Drug Abuse Prevention and Treatment* 10(1): 24–25, 42.

Liu, Zheng. 2006. "The Public is Much Concerned about Social Convention, Social Security and Education." *Xinhua News Agency*, January 10. Accessed January 10, 2011 at http://news. xinhuanet. com/society/2006–01/10/content–4035036. htm

Liu, Zong, Boyang Li, and Enlin Shi. 2003. "Illicit Drug Use and its Prevention." *Journal of Northwest Minorities University* 2: 125–129.

Ma, Hongbo. 1999. "Changes in Narcotics Control Policies among the Countries Neighboring Yunnan." *Journal of Yunnan Police Officer Academy* 2: 16–20.

Ma Minai. 1999. "The New Characteristics of Drug–Related Crime in Yunnan." In *Studies on Narcotic Controls in Yunnan*, edited by Luo Bingsong and Liang Jinyun. Beijing: The Mass Press.

Ministry of Civil Affairs of the People's Republic of China (MCAPRC). 2005. *China Civil Affairs' Statistical Yearbook*. Beijing: China Statistics Press.

Ministry of Civil Affairs of the People's Republic of China (MCAPRC). 2009. *Development of Civil Affairs Report*. Accessed January 2, 2011 at http://cws.mca.gov.cn/article/tjkb/

Ministry of Public Security of China (MPSC). 2006. *An Overview of Criminal Cases in China*. Accessed July14, 2006 at http://www. mps. gov. cn/cenweb/brjlCenweb/jsp/common/three–jsgl. jsp?category=700710&category–pic=700710099

National Bureau of Statistic of China (NBSC). 1978–2005. *National Economic and Social Development Statistical Bulletin*. Accessed December 12, 2010 at http://www.stats.gov.cn/tjgb/

National Bureau of Statistic of China (NBSC). 2009. *Provincial Statistical Report (Yunnan)*. Accessed December 20, 2010 at http://www.stats.gov.cn/tjgb/

National Narcotics Control Commission (NNCC). 1998–2010. Annual Report on Drug Control in China. Accessed March 25, 2011 at http://www.jhak.com/jdzy/zgjdzy/20100402/1779.html

Qin, Heping. 1998. *Opium Problems and Opium Suppression Movement*. Chengdu, Sichuan Province: Sichuan National Publishing House.

Shao, Qin. 2002. "An Investigation: HIV Infection Rates Increasing among Female Drug Users." *Law & Life* 12: 19–20.

Shi Qingqi. 2010. "Status of Chinese Women Entrepreneurs and Sustainable Development." Accessed November 10, 2010 at http://money.163.com/10/0111/19/5SP7PNOM0025439H.html

State Council of the People's Republic of China (SCPRC) 2005. *White Paper on Gender Equality and Women's Development*. Accessed November 10, 2010 at http://www.china.org.cn/e–white/20050824/index.htm

Su, Junyi, and Yu Guo. 2004. "Illicit Drug Use in Hangzhou during 1997–2002." *Chinese Journal of Drug Abuse Prevention and Treatment* 10(4): 199–202.

Su, Zhonghua, Wei Hao, Shuiyuan Xiao, Changhe Fan, Hongxian Chen, Tieqiao Liu, and Desen Yang. 2005. "A Longitudinal Survey of Patterns and Prevalence of Addictive Drug Use among General Population in Five (or Six) Areas with High–Prevalence in China from 1993 to 2000." *Chinese Journal Drug Dependence* 14(1): 47–53.

Sun, Dahong. 2005. Study "Narcotic Control Regulations and Launch a People's War against Illicit Drugs."*Yunnan Daily*, June 24. Accessed August 30, 2006 at http://ynjd. gov. cn/

Tang, Ruolei. 1999. "Narcotics Controls in the Republic of China." In *The Trend of Drug-Related Crime and Controlling Strategies*, edited by Min Cui, Qiuguan Duan, Binsen Luo, Ruolei Tang, Quansheng He, and Minai Ma. Beijing: The Police Education Press.

Tian, Yu, and Wenhan Yang. 2004. "The Ministry of Public Security Takes Crackdown on Drug Trafficking." *Xinhua News Agency*, July 28. Accessed on December 24, 2010. http://www.people.com.cn/GB/shizheng/1027/2672708.html

Wang, Lin, and Na Gan. 2005. "HIV Infection from High Risk Group to the General Public in Yuannan." *China News Agency,* November 27. Accessed August 31, 2006 at http://cn.news.yahoo.com/05-11-/1063/2g9i0.htm

Wang, Xi. 2004. "The Demographic Characteristics of Drug Users in Fujian." *Journal of Fujian Public Safety College* 6: 9–11.

Wang, Zengzheng, Yongmei Chen, Hongmei Yang, and Ligong Chen. 2001. "Relationships between Female Drug Abuse and Socio-Psychological Health." *Chinese Journal of Drug Dependence* 10(1): 61–63.

Wang, Yongzhi. 2005. "Over 90 Percent of Chinese People More Concerned about Social Convention." *China News Net,* February 3. Accessed July 12, 2010 at http://www.chinanews.com/news/2005/2005-02-03/26/536715.shtml

Xia, Tilei. 2005. "Female College Students are Busy on Dating Rather Than Job Hunting." *Chuncheng Evening News*, October 19. Accessed August 26, 2006 at http://www.xinhuanet.com

Xian, Bo. 2005. *The History of Opium*. Beijing: Chinese Art and History Publisher.

Xu, Jingyue, and Fei Chen. 2006. "Criminal Cases Reported by Law Enforcement." Xinhua Daily Telegraph, January 19. Accessed July 12, 2006 at http:// news. xinhuanet. com

Yang, Fengrui. 2005. "Launching a People's War against Narcotics." A Speech in a News Conference held by the State Council of China, May 26. Accessed September 25, 2005 at http://www.ynjd.gov.cn

Yang Lijun. 2003. *Causes of Contemporary Drug Problems and Prevention in China*. Beijing: The Mass Press.

Yang, Ling, Ji Liu, and Tinghu Kang. 2004. "Self-Esteem and Family Background of 242 Female Drug Users." *Studies of Psychology and Behavior* 2(2): 430–433.

Yang, Ling, Lianrong Sun, and Xiongying Li. 2002. "Connections between Women's Drug-Taking Behaviors and Social Contexts." *Journal of Northwest Normal University (Social Science)* 39(6): 129–132.

Yang, Shuhua, Xiaoyan Shi, Hongbin He, Yan Li, Liqiang Wang, and Shanshan Li. 2005. "Harsh Crackdowns on Drugs in Kunming." *Yunnan Daily*, June 22. Accessed March 28, 2011 at http://www.cnki.net

Yang, Zhongmin, and Min Cui. 1999. "The New Drug Epidemic." In *The Trend of Drug-Related Crime and Controlling Strategies,* edited by Min Cui, Qiuguan Duan, Binsen Luo, Ruolei Tang, Quansheng He and Minai Ma. Police Education Publisher: Beijing: Police Education Publisher.

Yu, Haibin. 2002. "A Report from Compulsory Drug Rehabilitation Center in Shanxi." *Journal of ShanXi Police Academy* 1: 24–29.

Yun, Gong. 1993. "Narcotics in Yunnan." In *Narcotic Controls by Law Enforcement,* edited by Weigang Ma. Beijing: Police Education Publisher.

Yunnan Narcotics Control Bureau (YNCB). 2003. "The New Solutions for Narcotics Controls in Yunnan." *Journal of Yunnan Public Security College* 2(2): 12–14.

Yunnan Police Officer Academy Research Team (YPOART). 1999. "Current Drug Problems, Developing Trend and Responding Strategies." In *The Collection of Studies on Narcotic Control in Yunnan*, edited by Luo Bingsong and Liang Jinyun. Beijing: The Mass Press.

Yunnan Yearbook. 2005. Kunming, Yunnan: Yunnan Yearbook Press.

Zhang, Na. 2008. "More than 90 Percent New HIV Infection Cases Were Related to Illicit Drugs or Sexual Transmission." Yunnan Information News, February 6. Accessed July 21, 2010 at http://www.chinanews.com.cn/jk/ysbb/news/2009/02-06/1553332.shtml

Zhang, Xiaohu. 2002. "Crime Rates in China's Social Transition." *Chinese Criminal Science* 8: 71–75.

Zhang Yi. 2006. "The Embarrassments of Female College Students for Their Marriages." *Asian Times (Chinese)*, June 21. Accessed August 26, 2006 at http://chinanews.co.com.cn/jk/ysbb/

Zhao, Zihui. 2004. "Women Drug Use and Determinants Used in Drug Dependence Treatment." *Journal of Chinese Women Institute* 3: 15–18.

Zhao Zihui, Xiaodan Wang, Yong Da, and Long Zhang. 2005. "Attributes and Socialization of Female Drug Abuse and Countermeasure to Responses." *Chinese Journal Drug Dependence* 14(1): 127–129.

Zhou, Mi, Baoseng Zhou, and Qihai Gai. 2001. "A Logistic Analysis of Female Drug Use in Shenyang." *Journal of Chinese Psycho Health* 15(6): 405–406.

Zhu, Binling. 2001. "Illicit Drug Use and Its Controls in Fujian." *Journal of Fujian Public Safety College* 15(4): 81–83.

Zhu, Duanqiang. 1999. "Narcotics in Yunnan." *Journal of Yunnan Normal University* 31(1): 64–67.

Index

For Product Safety Concerns and Information please contact our EU representative GPSR@taylorandfrancis.com
Taylor & Francis Verlag GmbH, Kaufingerstraße 24, 80331 München, Germany

www.ingramcontent.com/pod-product-compliance
Ingram Content Group UK Ltd.
Pitfield, Milton Keynes, MK11 3LW, UK
UKHW022000180926
475701UK00003B/113
9780415852142